FIGHTERS
AND
LOVERS

Theme in the Novels
of John Updike

FIGHTERS
AND
LOVERS

Theme in the Novels
of John Updike

JOYCE B. MARKLE

English Department
Loyola University of Chicago

New York: NEW YORK UNIVERSITY PRESS   1973

Copyright © 1973 by New York University

Library of Congress Catalog Card No.: 72-96469
ISBN: 0-8147-5361-2

Second Printing, 1974

The excerpts from the works of John Updike, *Assorted Prose, Beck: A Book, Couples, The Music School, Of the Farm, Pigeon Feathers, Rabbit, Run, Rabbit Redux, The Same Door, The Centaur,* and *Poorhouse Fair* are reprinted by permission of the publisher, Alfred A. Knopf.

Manufactured in the United States of America

Contents

Introduction   1

1. *The Poorhouse Fair:* Essential Thematic Principles   13

   1. Death and Dehumanization   13
   2. The Christian Mythos   23
   3. The Love of Craft and History   27
   4. "Yes but": Thematic Qualifications   34

2. *Rabbit Run:* The Self-Centered Lover   37

   1. The Earth-Bound Humanitarian: Eccles   37
   2. Circles and Nets: The Basketball Imagery   42
   3. The Lover as Star Player   47
   4. Existential Aspects   55

3. *The Centaur:* The Altruistic Lover   61

   1. The Use of Mythology   61
   2. The Character of George   70
   3. The Volvox: Altruism, Death, and Time   72
   4. The Vision of Love   77
   5. Peter: Rabbit and His Search, Continued   81

4. *Of the Farm:* Psychological Considerations   84

   1. The Character of the Mother   84
   2. The Lover as Myth-Maker   87
   3. Oedipal Conflicts   93
   4. The Possession of Abundance   101

5. *Couples:* The Loss of the Lover's Vision   106

    PART I: THE PROTAGONISTS
            END THEIR STRUGGLE   106

    1. Piet as Composite Protagonist   106
    2. Death and the System of Imagery   114
    3. Angela and Foxy: The Heavenly Versus the Mundane   120
    4. The Protagonist Accepts Death   122

    PART II: THE MYTHIC UNDERPINNINGS   125

    1. The Demise of Christianity   125
    2. The Vegetation-Fertility Rituals   130
    3. Land, Sea, and Sky Gods   133
    4. Tristram and Iseult: *Love in the Western World*   137

6. *Rabbit Redux:* The Search for Stature   146

    1. America 1969   146
    2. The Sterility of White America   150
    3. Skeeter: The Lover as Militant Minority   155
    4. Vietnam: The Touchstone   160
    5. The Reawakened Sense of Causality   164

7. *Bech's* Comic Realm: The Other Side of the Coin   168

    1. The Nature of the Comic   168
    2. The Landscape of Inaction   170
    3. The Safety of the Comic World   177
    4. Comic Miniaturization   180
    5. The Comic and the Serious in the Other Novels   182

Notes   191

A Bibliography of Books and Critical Essays on John Updike   200

Index   203

Key to Abbreviations

Page numbers given in the text refer to the following editions of John Updike's works chosen for their easy availability, all published by Fawett Crest, New York.

AP	*Assorted Prose*
B	*Bech: A Book*
C	*Couples*
LWW	*Love in the Western World,* by Denis de Rougemont. Translated by Montgomery Belgion. Fawcett Premier
MS	*The Music School*
OTF	*Of the Farm*
PF	*Pigeon Feathers*
PR	Charles T. Samuels, "The Art of Fiction XLIII," *Paris Review*, No. 45 (Winter 1968), pp. 85-117
RR	*Rabbit, Run*
RRx	*Rabbit Redux*
SD	*The Same Door*
TC	*The Centaur*
TPF	*The Poorhouse Fair*

FIGHTERS
AND
LOVERS

Theme in the Novels
of John Updike

Introduction

When I began the preparation of this manuscript four years ago the idea of a book about John Updike still required some explanation; *Couples* had not yet been published, and the critical reaction to Updike's work had been somewhat mixed. But within two years' time. Mr. Updike became the subject of considerable critical attention. *Couples* was written and given surprisingly wide publicity and remained on the best-seller list for months. Feature articles on Updike appeared in popular magazines such as *Life* and *Time,* and critics, although still cautious, labelled him one of the major writers of our time. *Bech: A Book* received lavish critical praise which included belated admiration for previous novels as well. And, while critical reaction to *Rabbit Redux* was less enthusiastic than it was to *Bech* (as a result of its contents rather than its quality, one suspects), the sales of the seventh novel and the amount of discussion prompted by it indicated that Updike had unquestionably become a leading literary figure.

Major sections in critical collections are now being devoted to Updike, and within the past few years three or four book-length studies have appeared. However, most of the studies of Updike have been characterized by either a limited area of concern—including only one or two of the works—or a limited focus of attention—tracing single thematic issues through the fiction. What this study hopes to provide is a broad and extended schematic of the central issues and values which characterize Updike's novels, beginning with the 1958 publication of *The Poorhouse Fair* and ending with the 1971 publication of *Rabbit Redux.*

Of course, in attempting to *characterize* Updike's novels, this study, too, focuses on certain kinds of things which keep

1

recurring in the novels and does not deal with certain kinds of incidentals in theme or form. The three-page description of several hours of radio listening in *Rabbit, Run,* for example, deserves attention and certainly suggests comparisons with Dos Passos. Updike's control of point of view is another point of critical interest. There is also an occasional back-to-Nature motif which was first noticed by Gerry Brenner and later examined at more length in a book by Larry Taylor (see the bibliography). But in this essay, I have omitted such topics in order to study in detail major thematic lines: the flight from death; the need for what I call "Lovers" (characters who can give a feeling of stature and specialness to others); evidence, such as handicraft, of man's impact on his world; the sources of man's sense of importance; man's abilities and responsibilities in relating to the members of his society; and so forth.

It is my thesis that not only does Updike deal with essentially the same problems in each of the serious novels (i.e. excluding *Bech*) but that as a group all demonstrate a progression of approach. The struggles waged by Hook the protagonist of the first novel, *The Poorhouse Fair,* are next observed from two dialectically opposite stances in *Rabbit, Run* and *The Centaur.* Joey, the protagonist of the fourth novel, *Of the Farm,* is given a more defined psychological network of forces which limits and shapes the nature of the struggle; Piet, the protagonist of the fifth novel, *Couples,* carries the struggle to a logical conclusion, ending it temporarily. *Bech* exists in the twilight zone beyond struggle which is created by this loss of stature; it is therefore comic. And in *Rabbit Redux,* the protagonist begins the enormous task of re-establishing a moral arena in which human struggle is meaningful.

The first novel, although it is usually considered an "early work," and not included among Updike's "mature works," establishes with clarity and unqualified definition the dynamics of his vision of man. The old people in the poorhouse are confronted with two kinds of death: their approaching physical death and, much more importantly, the death of dehumanization at the hands of scientific humanitarians like the prefect Conner. Conner becomes the archetype of Updike's central antagonist figure— a well-intentioned but emotionally sterile man who fails to recognize or augment people's sense of their own specialness. He is contrasted to Hook, a type of Updike's major protagonist figure. Buttressed by a belief in Christianity, Hook has a vivid sense of human specialness which he communicates to the people he confronts. He is, thus, a figure of the Lover or Life-giver like Rabbit or Piet, or even Caldwell.

The first novel also examines the roles of myth and handicraft in maintaining man's definition of himself. Religious or historical stories lend stature and identity to man; since they have lost the Christian mythos, Conner and the visitors to the fair must construct their own myths from daydreams or gossip. Handicraft from the older, still Christian generation, such as the finely made poorhouse wall or the artifacts for sale at the fair, show a self-consciousness which goes beyond animal needs and indicates man's special place in creation.

I attempt to indicate the centrality of the first novel to Updike's artistic vision by frequent catalogues of comparative points in the later novels. Except for the role of sexuality— which can only be suggested for Hook—this first work contains a surprisingly complete spectrum of Updike's thematic motifs.

In *Rabbit, Run,* Eccles and Rabbit take up the roles of antagonist and protagonist, Conner and Hook. Although he is a minister, Eccles' social-worker mentality masks an underlying atheism. Rabbit, the only character who believes in a "something" above the natural level, struggles upward towards it, trying to run clear of enmeshing social complexities. Cast into the imagery of basketball, the second novel sees Rabbit as a star player (a Lover) who refuses to be forced into the role of team player, one who has no specialness. Rabbit's obsessive fear of becoming second rate, however, prevents his giving his gift of love to second-rate people without an underlying resentment and disgust. Thus, his ultimate response to social corporation is to reject it totally.

Caldwell, of the third novel, makes the opposite choice. His vision of the supernatural again promotes a solid awareness of human importance. Placed, mythically, in a plane between heaven and earth, Caldwell converts Rabbit's fears of second-ratedness into a wry rhetorical crankiness about his own and other people's incompetence. Pursued by time and death, Caldwell eludes both by offering his life to the community which like a volvox will insure immortality in terms of the whole social corporation. Peter's love of art echoes Hook's love of craft; and the necessity of a mythos is again demonstrated; those without *belief* see people simply as "slippery old fatheads" or "lecherous muddlers." Vision (" ⊚ ⊚ ") makes the difference.

Joey of the fourth novel returns to the farm seeking his mother's myth-making vision which can renew his own sense of specialness. This and the wealth of possession he has in the farm and Peggy promote that sense of being valuable which assures men of their immortality. But, because it is his mother who is the Lover and Life-giver, Joey is trapped by Oedipal conflicts which restrict his own freedom to love others. Rabbit's and Piet's ambivalent relationships to women seem to be given a psychological genesis in the fourth novel. The mother's approaching death and the recent death of the father hang over the novel and add urgency to Joey's struggle to independently assert his selfhood against those worldly forces which seem to diminish one's importance.

Piet of *Couples* inherits the thematic lines carried through the novels from *The Poorhouse Fair* as well as Joey's and Rabbit's complicated psychological restrictions; Freddy becomes the atheistic humanistic social worker. The struggle against insignificance and death is here hyperbolized to its greatest possible degree. Seeking immortality in an upwards reach toward Angela, Piet is repeatedly subjected to symbolic deaths. Although he is a Lover and a Life-giver, his vitality needs the support of belief (as did the previous protagonists) and, deprived of his church at the end, Piet is forced to abandon the struggle, accept satisfaction, and take Foxy, the symbol of a horizontal rather than a vertical orientation. Death will no longer pursue, but he has lost the dignity of fighting it. The tragedy is the *loss* of tragedy. Piet accepts the contentment of "animals who have eaten."

The comedy of *Bech* follows. An absence of human stature, in fact, is one of the marks of the comic viewpoint. Bech has a vivid sense of his ordinariness, his unspecialness, and accepts it. In fact he uses it to protect himself from harm in the form of disappointment or insult. His is a landscape of inaction. Without human significance, actions of any kind become unnecessary, inappropriate, and perhaps impossible. A self-deprecating sense of humor replaces hope and ambition.

In *Rabbit Redux* Updike attempts to rediscover a basis for human stature—for human significance, specialness, and the sense of causality and responsibility that goes with it. Although the novel opens in the amoral realm of *Bech,* the death of Jill and the vitality of Skeeter, an ironic Savior figure, have begun by the end of the book to move Rabbit towards a renewed belief in human causality.

Intrinsic to any discussion of theme in Updike's work is an understanding of how he establishes his framework of values. I think I make this reasonably clear in each explication. However, some broad descriptions are necessary, especially in the light of critical essays which have demonstrated interpretations in considerable conflict to my own. *Rabbit, Run,* for instance, has sometimes been interpreted as the story of a recalcitrant adolescent who refuses the offers of grace made through Jack Eccles. But, although a reader may well find Rabbit unlikable, there is a failure here to respond to Updike's structure of values which clearly establishes Eccles as a force contrary to what is noblest in man.

The use of antagonists is one of Updike's most consistent methods for gaining sympathies which correspond to his intended value system. The old people in the poorhouse can appear sentimental, petty, and nearly senile. Hook's age and his nostalgia might tend to cast doubt on the value of his insights and beliefs. However, the characters of Conner and Buddy, along with the visitors to the poorhouse, are meant to generate disapproval of the alternatives to Hook's mentality. Conner's cold, rational, scientific manner overshadows his good intentions and converts them into "busyness." Since the book invites a choice between Hook's vision and Conner's, the reader is gently led into an espousal of belief in man's specialness, the necessity of myth, the beauty of craft, and so forth.

Similar principles are at work in *Rabbit, Run.* Rabbit is not wholly likable or admirable and at times reader sympathy for him is stretched very thin indeed. But he is thrown into conflict with Jack Eccles whose subtle hypocrisies and fundamental sterility give Rabbit our support by default if nothing else.

Updike can risk an extremely qualified portrayal of his protagonist because the character of Eccles provides a solid touchstone in favor of Rabbit's vision and struggle.

Freddy Thorne, of *Couples,* although a colorful and entertaining figure, is sexually inactive, a symptom of his inability to give life even though he has deep concern for people. His group-therapy church is contrasted with Piet's "real church" and shown to be unsatisfactory. Even Piet's sexual promiscuity, which could act against reader sympathy, becomes, when contrasted with Freddy and the other men (such as Ken), a refreshing vitality, a symbol of the love which members of the community thirst for. Piet's obsessive fear of death, which might seem to be a neurotic handicap, becomes admirable and humanizing when contrasted with Ken's cold glance at a tray of gutted mice.

In *Rabbit Redux* Updike's technique has become so effective that he can use it to disapprove of his protagonist and convert an unlikable antagonist into a savior figure. Skeeter, the black militant, may be foul mouthed, temperamental, unreasonable, and even ludicrous, but compared to the dried-up, emotionally frozen, morally enervated whites (like Rabbit), he has the vitality and system of values necessary to human action and survival.

Another force in Updike's value system is the use of children. The most serious judgment on Rabbit's need to escape social responsibility and on society's unjust delegation of such responsibility is the death of baby June and the lost figure of little Nelson. External to the major actors themselves, the children represent the world of outside concerns which must figure into any personal philosophy of fulfillment. Caldwell's temptation to abandon his suffering is rejected because of his son Peter. Joey's gift of a human and personal response to the world is desperately needed by his stepson, Richard, if Richard is not to become another Conner. The children of *Couples,* Updike says, prevent the scene from becoming a rural idyll. "The distressed and neglected group of children," as Updike called them in *Time*'s article, recall Nelson of the second novel. No solution which fails to offer them love and respect can wholly be approved of by the novel. The group therapy which drags children to cold ski slopes or shuffles them from bed to bed is solidly argued against. The only alternative is Piet's beliefs which lead him to take Ruth to church, comfort Nancy's tearful death fears, and mourn over their sandy sleeping figures when the exigencies of an adult party prevent a bedtime bath. Leaving the children to Angela's serene ministrations is unsatisfactory and provides some of the necessary sadness surrounding an apparent happy ending. In *Rabbit Redux* the failure of Nelson's parents to find a system of belief leaves a melancholy legacy: a lonely, unhappy teenager who fills his time collecting relics of Jill's death and who re-portrays his three-year-old self of *Rabbit, Run*, the old rubber panda now a half-burned guitar.

An interesting aspect of Updike's moral framework is its decreasing force with each subsequent novel until *Bech*. Updike himself admits to a "yes, but" quality in his work, but the first novel offers the most unqualified vision. Conner and the members of his generation seem clearly less than human and undirected by any truly dignifying goals. Rabbit's vision is less certain but is given strength by Eccles' unmistakable wrong-headedness. The Greek myth framework adds a definite and unquestionable framework of values to the third novel but the sheer artificiality of its insertion may hint at Updike's own underlying uncertainties. *Of the Farm* offers only the subtlest judgments: McCabe and perhaps Richard lack human anxieties; Peggy is too much like Foxy of *Couples* to let Joey be the poet he might have become. In *Couples*, even Piet's abandonment of the struggle is not harshly judged. It is grieved over with perhaps a shrug of the shoulders finally: "What else shall we do as God destroys our churches?" said Updike in an interview. Part of the dry humor of *Bech* stems, in fact, from its wry, lighthearted refusal to judge anything as very serious. The need to re-establish a viable moral framework is the central thematic concern of *Rabbit Redux*, and insofar as such a framework exists it drolly approves of a temperamental black militant while deftly putting down a patient, unassuming protagonist.

I have organized my presentation in terms of a thematic approach rather than a discussion of style or technique as such. I hope it is apparent from the frequent quotes, however, that Updike's artistic method is my almost constant focus of attention. His skills with juxtaposition, for instance, are examined in the first chapter on *The Poorhouse Fair*. Alternating between scenes with Conner and scenes with Hook, Updike neatly demonstrates the distinct qualities of their sensibilities. His ability to create affectively colored descriptions is of major concern in *Rabbit, Run* where, for example, the unattractiveness of Rabbit's environment is clearly underlined without going beyond an absolutely ordinary middle-class setting. Updike's tendency to animate inanimate objects bears the most thematic weight in the second novel since it points sometimes to Rabbit's sympathy with his physical surroundings and sometimes to his nearly psychotic sense of claustrophobia and entrapment.

Perhaps Updike's most remarkable artistic talent is his ability to create continuously operative and highly complex systems of imagery. The basketball-net-sex-woman-church structure in *Rabbit, Run* is visible everywhere and is a major force in articulating the thematic lines which explain Rabbit's flight. *Rabbit Redux* uses racial contrasts to set up a basic opposition: white-ice-cold-dryness-moon-technology-sterility vs. black-wetness-Nature-fertility-sexuality. The most extensive pattern is the one in *Couples* which presents a crossweave set of connections between death-greenhouse-parents-sex-flowers. In each case Updike goes beyond simple arbitrary mental associations by his characters or speaker and gives each relationship in the imagery system a narrative support. Rabbit, for instance, had sex after basketball games and offers sex to Ruth while church-goers pass the window. In the later novel Rabbit drinks frozen daquiris while watching the moon shot on television in a cold bar. Piet had the smell of sex on his hands when he received word of his parents' death.

Many of Updike's stylistic characteristics seem to relate to his skills and interests as a graphic artist—a painter and cartoonist. He also mentions an envious appreciation of cinematic art, again because of its visual dimension. He often writes in a highly cinematic style, using the present tense in sections of *The Centaur,* and *Couples* and throughout *Rabbit, Run* and *Rabbit Redux.* Updike discussed briefly his love of the cinematic present tense in his *Paris Review* interview (see the bibliography) and in a review which he wrote on Robbe-Grillet. His sections of pure dialogue in *Couples* seem to be the scenario for internal movies playing on the screen of memory.

"Foxy?"

"Yes, Piet."

"Do you think we're wrong?"

"I don't know. I don't think so."

Updike's graphic tendencies also appear in the strangely spatial quality of his imagery. *The Poorhouse Fair* is designed on the basic metaphor of a patchwork quilt made of a symmetric arrangement of patterned cloths. Without belief, the world appears to be blank cloth to Conner. In *Rabbit, Run* basketball provides the geometry for a spatial system of circles and holes, ups and downs and horizontals, and nets and spaces which project the theme into a physical dimension.

Updike also appears to have a color scheme in mind for his novels, especially surrounding his major characters. Rabbit's colors are blue and white—in the opening scene he becomes a white angel (his arms are "wings") in a blue sky. He drives a blue car, has blue eyes and a white face. As in the case of Angela's blue eyes in *Couples*, blue seems to suggest his spiritual (heavenly) quality. Eccles' colors are green and white; Ruth is always done in red (Updike's sexual color—note Piet's red hair and reddish jacket in *Couples*) and green. In *Couples* Foxy's colors are silver and white. She first appears as a flash of white and is regal in a silver gown at Freddy's party. In her first scene she is bathed in white moonlight. When Piet and Foxy are together, yellow often appears—perhaps a blend of red-orange and white. Foxy's sexuality is "buttery" and she has a lemon-colored dress, a yellow swimsuit and a yellow muumuu. Her hair is honey blond and when she performs fellatio for Piet there is a taste of something "lemony." In *Rabbit Redux*, of course, the color white, a major thematic element, is used throughout to indicate those things which are especially associated with sterile whites. Jill, the hyperbole of the lost and disoriented white society, is always pictured in white—a white sheet, a white dress, a white car. Rabbit is repeatedly described as pale or white. The moon is white (as well as cold and dry), and so on.

Updike's stylistic techniques seem related to his view of reality as "many-layered"—as he described it in the *Paris Review* interview. Mythic underpinnings, a system of colors, interrelations between elements of the environment, the reality of dream visions all reveal aspects of the unsimple nature of our surroundings.

The sudden overlay of two perceptual moments is one of Updike's favorite devices; he seems to identify this experience with our basic human tendencies to be artists. On page 68 of *The Centaur*, for instance, the smell of Peter's hotel room is the same as the remembered smell of his mother's fur coat. Suddenly, he feels "suspended over a canyon of time" much as he did when he found a familiar hometown smell of Essick cough-drops while in New York City. Peter is an artist and such moments are small artistic creations which help him "outmuscle time and tide," the major function of art. Art is valuable because it can freeze a few passing seconds (such as Shakespeare "seals in amber" beautiful scenes for Frank of *Couples*). Peter thinks:

> It was this firmness, I think, this potential fixing of a few passing seconds, that attracted me at the age of five to art. For it is at this age, isn't it, that it sinks in upon us that things do, if not die, certainly change, wiggle, slide, retreat, and like the dabs of sunlight on the bricks under a grape arbor on a breezy June day, shuffle out of all identity. (*TC*, p. 51)

Art's ability to make the fluid universe solid seems not unrelated to Joey's definition of "truth" in *Of the Farm*. It is formed, he feels, from the solidification of illusions. As his wife and mother discuss the past, their voices dive "in pursuit of shadows that I supposed were my father and myself." "Perhaps they were both right," Joey thinks. "All misconceptions . . . have the minimal truth of existing in at least one mind. Truth, my work had taught me, is not something static. . . . Rather, truth is constantly being formed from the solidification of illusions" (*OTF*, p. 100). Updike, manipulating his points of view, often views the same object several times from different directions. The several impressions of Amy Mortis' goiter in the first novel are paralleled in the fifth novel by as many views of Piet Hanema ("that horrid little redheaded man who ran around slapping everyone's behind and doing handstands" is Foxy's mother's impression) or the tip of Harold's nose, described by various characters as a "cleft foot," a "very pale strawberry" and "a bee's behind."

The many-layered quality of reality and its appearance only in "illusions" prompts Updike to go not only to the "gate of horn" for his vision but also to the "gate of ivory." Reviewing Harry Levin's *The Gates of Horn*, Updike quotes the lines from Homer:

> Two gates for ghostly dreams there are: one gateway of honest horn, and one of ivory.

Realistic visions come through the gates of horn; the gates of ivory are the gates of myth and dream. Rabbit's dream in *Rabbit, Run* of the orb of lovely death eclipsing the orb of life is another layer of the truth approached in the basketball imagery or the narrative structure. The mythic aspects of persons in *The Centaur* or *Couples* are the truth seen through the gate of ivory. The novelist, if he can structure his materials skillfully, reveals the layers of his vision. Its arbitrariness fades when its internal intricacies are revealed. When Joey describes his mother's storytelling skills, he seems to present Updike's definition of a novelist: "My mother within the mythology she had made of her life was like a mathematician who, having decreed certain severely limited assumptions, performs feats of warping and circumspection and paradoxical linkage that an outside observer, unrestricted to the plane of their logic, would find irksomely arbitrary" (*OTF*, p. 28). Perhaps the same description applies to this book.

I have divided the chapters into a novel-by-novel approach in the hopes that such an organization would be the most useful to an Updike reader. Each chapter is provided with a brief overview at the beginning to make it possible for a reader to use it individually for the analysis of a single novel in which he has a particular interest. Such an approach also reflects my feeling that each novel is a complete structure unto itself and offers its own dynamics for interpreting its contents. But I also attempt to develop, page by page, a view of the books as a single entity composed of distinct parts. The "entity" implied, I suppose, is

Updike's central artistic vision which in his case is sufficiently narrowly focused to allow such a description to be made.

I have kept the use of outside materials to a minimum, partly reflecting my feeling that they were seldom necessary or useful and partly reflecting my uneasiness with that critical method itself. The notable exception is the second half of Chapter 5, which examines the mythological frameworks of *Couples*. A mythological approach to Updike is suggested by his third novel, by allusions in the other novels, and by several comments by Updike himself in which he mentions a sense of people appearing in mythic "guises." His essays and comments about de Rougemont suggest the role of *Love in the Western World* in the basic Tristram-Iseult story of *Couples;* and the extensiveness of the specific applications of de Rougemont's book to Updike's text indicate its very real participation in the ideas shaping the fifth novel. My method in writing a two-part chapter on *Couples* is intended to reveal a kind of double ideational structure: a form comparable to that of the first four novels and a superimposed form from de Rougemont. Both structures create the same story, as I try to suggest by often using the same quotes and other materials in both sections; they are simply different intellectual and artistic concepts of the vision.

The constant and sometimes intrusive quotes in this analysis are the product of my belief that prose is a quite unsatisfactory medium for discussing a work of fiction which, whatever its appearance on the page might suggest, is *not* prose. Ideally a critic must do more than simply retell the artist's story in analytical abstractions. The most satisfactory critical approach is to select small, manageable portions of the original structure and attempt to reveal the dynamics of idea and technique which give them their meaning. At each moment of the discussion, it is Updike's actual expression which is the focus of my attention.

A remarkably intelligent and highly self-conscious artist, Updike may well become, for future generations, the representative novelist of the sixties. Keenly tuned to the visions and neuroses of middle and upper middle class suburbanites, he has "sealed in amber" the responses of a certain generation to the quiet retreat of its gods.

1

The Poorhouse Fair: Essential Thematic Principles

1. Death and Dehumanization

In his first novel, *The Poorhouse Fair*, Updike uses the format of a utopian novel. He projects onto the arena of a whole society the system of values which later provides the internal dynamics of his subsequent, more narrowly focused novels. An old people's home not only forms a convenient sociological cosmos, collecting as many subjects or types as the author desires, but it also sets in bold relief what Updike sees as the principal fact of human existence: death.

In each of Updike's first five novels the presence of death is manifested in two analogous forms: It appears in its physical form as a threatened or actual death, and it appears in a nonphysical form as the potential destruction of people's sense of their own significance. In *Rabbit, Run,* on the narrative level, the birth of Janice's baby ("'There is no God; Janice can die" [*RR*, p. 165]), the imminent death of Tothero, the death of the infant girl, and Ruth's threatened abortion overshadow all Rabbit's actions. Thematically, the death he fears is dehumanization —what he calls second-ratedness, a loss of *specialness*. Caldwell, in *The Centaur*, fears death from cancer; and the sudden death of the hotel night clerk ominously suggests the closeness of death. Yet the real cancer that threatens him is the poisoning sense of futile service to others, the possibility that he is useless. *Of the Farm* sets unflinching gaze on the mother's gradual death from angina and emphysema in a house which still vibrates with the dead father's lively personality. But Joey faces a more immediate psychological death in his mother's stifling emotional control over him. Finally, in *Couples,* Piet's parents, the hamster, the Kennedy baby, Foxy's unborn baby, John Kennedy, and John

Ong form a virtual procession of dead souls while Piet fights on more abstract levels with a fatal sense of his own insignificance. Jill's death is the central narrative event in *Rabbit Redux;* but, as Mom Angstrom's dream points out, all the white characters exist in a kind of living death.

The people in the first novel's "Diamond County Home for the Aged" all await death in a setting reminiscent of the Pascal allegory which Updike uses in "Fanning Island," seeing in the death of each inmate their own certain fate.

> *Qu'on s'imagine un nombre d'hommes dans les chaînes, et tous condamnés à la mort, dont les uns étant chaque jour égorgés à la vue des autres, ceux qui restent voient leur propre condition dans celle de leurs semblables, et, se regardant les uns et les autres avec douleur et sans espérance, attendent à leur tour. C'est l'image de la condition des hommes.* (PF, p. 166) [1]

It is the fact of death that threatens to make life absurd—meaningless and temporary; yet an awareness of death, an apprehension of death, is a predominant mark of our humanity. Caldwell in *The Centaur* describes man as "flint-chipping, fire-kindling, *death-foreseeing,* a tragic animal" (*TC,* p. 40, my italics). And *Couples* restates: "Man is the sexiest of animals and the only one that foresees death" (*C,* pp. 472-73). Living in expectation of death makes the old people in the poorhouse symbolic humans.

However, although the poorhouse is, by definition, a place to die, it is important to notice that physical death is not the cause of dread for the inmates. They recall Mendelssohn's death, for instance, with tender nostalgia. "In his coffin, I remember saying to Mrs. Haines, he looks like he's come to the end of a prayer, his nostrils still full of its breath. My heart told me to stoop and kiss his hand, but the line was pushing" (p. 22). They also exchange enthusiastic accounts of their visions of heaven. "I've always thought I'd be a beauty and my mother not." "I expect we'll all be about the same age." "Heaven will be . . . a mist of all the joy sensations have given us" (pp. 69-74). Hook uses his approaching death as a cause for increased moral vigilance: "We fellas so close to the Line—have our accounts watched very close" (p. 6). And death creates an urgency to communicate a message to Conner as a "testament to endure his dying in the world" (p. 127). Amy Mortis, whose name suggests she is a friend of death, invokes her own death to fortify her rhetoric whenever she feels attacked. To the antique dealer she threatens, "I doubt if next year I'll be able to find any [patterned cloth] but I'll be dead by then anyway, with luck" (p. 101).

Mendelssohn, the former prefect, understood this essentially sympathetic relationship to death. Unlike Conner who attempts to forestall death with updated health care (his professional success is rated partly by the longevity of the inmates), Mendelssohn encouraged their awareness of death.

> "Can't you picture Mendelssohn now?" Amy Mortis asked at another table. "How he'd have us all singing and shouting prayers and telling us how we all must die?" . . .
>
> They were seeing him now. . . . As the songs grew more religious, the rims of Mendelssohn's eyes grew redder and he was dabbing at his cheeks with the huge handkerchief he always carried and was saying . . . how here they all lived close to death, which cast a shadow over even their gaiety . . . here they lived with death at their sides, the third participant in every conversation, the other guest at every meal. . . . (pp. 56-57)

This death-consciousness is a mark of their intelligence and independence. To remove death—as Conner has done—to the sterile, closed, anaesthetized west wing is to deprive the inmates of the dignity of being death-foreseeing. Conner has been concerned about physical death—which they do not fear—and has failed to consider the death of depersonalization, which is the real threat.

The death the inmates fear, in *The Poorhouse Fair,* is spiritual death—loss of the vision of their significance. In each of Updike's first five novels the protagonists fight to retain a sense of specialness without which they "die"—become simply animals, biological stuff, physical objects. Rabbit equates death with the loss of individuality and heroism in an adult system of group-oriented behavior: "Don't tell me about being mature because as far as I can see it's the same as being dead" (*RR*, p. 30). Caldwell, in the next novel, desperately needs a sense of love and appreciation from students and school officials. Joey, the next protagonist, relies on his mother's view of people (especially her family) as very special beings, and thus he fears the psychological crises her coming death presents. Piet, in *Couples*, uses sex and Christian faith to feel personally special to others and his life "ends" when both of these become impossible at the end. And Rabbit of *Rabbit Redux* has lost this sense of significance and is a kind of walking corpse—cold and white; the action of the novel partly concerns his chances of regaining the self-importance so valuable to the poorhouse inmates of the first novel.

The characters in 'Updike's novels can be roughly divided into those whose vision lends this specialness, this significance, and those whose vision does not. Conner's patronizing regard for the inmates' welfare demeans them to tagged animals. He heads a line of Updike characters including Mrs. Eccles of *Rabbit, Run*, McCabe in *Of the Farm*, Ken of *Couples*, and others whose scientific vision mechanizes human life. Others, like Ted the driver of the soda truck, Mrs. Springer in *Rabbit, Run*, or the couples of *Couples*, simply lack the intelligence, sensitivity and care to focus proper individualizing attention on each person they confront. In *The Poorhouse Fair* Mendelssohn, like the old men, is a type of the Rabbit Angstroms, George Caldwells, Piets (and even Skeeters) who have, as Mrs. Smith tells Rabbit, "the gift of life"—the ability to bestow a sense of significance on others by virtue of their own instinctive belief in that significance.

Updike's prose style—his frequent animation of inanimate objects or converse use of animal imagery for people—indicates the delicacy of the problem. Non-human things can seem dangerously anthropomorphic. Buddy provides an extreme example; sitting in his office, he sees:

> the green steel cabinets, the buried piano, the upright objects on Conner's desk top. These summoned presences intimidated him; he expected at every moment the window to smack its lips, the water cooler to gurgle uproariously. . . .

The bannister uprights and their shadows rapidly criss-crossed in a secret conversation. (p. 39)

Conversely, people are a species of animal—tree shrews with receded snouts and ballooned skulls, as Conner puts it, lemurs with straightened spines (p. 56). Gregg can move like a monkey and Foxy, four novels later, has an ape's slouching gait.

Instinctively men recognize and fear their likeness to non-human matter. They seek confirmation that self-consciousness defines their life in a unique, nonbiological way. Internally the sense of this is vivid; and the characters in Updike desperately look for external evidence of its truth. Thus springs their love and need for the Mendelssohns whose particularizing vision, a mark of faith and love, reinforces a sense of human specialness—that is, gives life. Amy eulogizes Mendelssohn—"Yet he was never too busy to drop a kind word. That's how you know them, John. He had a natural faith. . . You know them when you come across them . . . rare as that is. Oh, we've had our time, John" (p. 22). Mendelssohn's "natural faith" was a vision of men as special to God and thus special to each other.

In structure, *The Poorhouse Fair* can be seen as a series of juxtapositions contrasting characters who have this ennobling vision (Hook, and to a lesser degree the other old people) with characters whose vision fails to individualize or distinguish people as special entities (Conner, Buddy, or the visitors to the fair). In the opening scene Gregg reacts violently against the name tags Conner has put on the chairs, feeling that they reduce the people to animals ("Is he putting tags on us so we can be trucked off to the slaughterhouse?") and are the product of animal-level thinking: "What birdbrain scheme is this now of Conner's?" (p. 5). Conner's unintentionally demeaning act of tagging is contrasted with a long internal view of Hook which shows his thoughtfulness, intelligence, and sensitivity about people. We get, for instance, the beginning of a characterization of foul-mouthed Gregg as Hook sees him—"Gregg sought elevated forms of thought to shape and justify the confused rage he felt toward the world that had in the end discarded him" (p. 6). And Lucas with a line that foreshadows George Caldwell or David's father in "Home" instinctively awards to Conner the human status which Conner's tagging denied the men: "I'll go up to Conner and ask him what his idea was" (p. 11).

The first direct view of Conner reaffirms both his good intentions and lack of vision. He points out that he takes "all complaints seriously" but inadvertently reveals in the same sentence that it is his "duty" to do so. He then gives an explanation of human dignity based on logic and efficient operation:

> Part of my policy has been, within the limits of the appropriations, to give the residents here some sense of ownership. I think especially of men like Hook, who have known a share of respect and prosperity. It strengthens, is my belief, rather than weakens a communal fabric to have running through it strands of private ownership. Lucas, I want to help these men to hold up their heads; to retain to the end the dignity that properly belongs to every member, big or little, of humanity. (pp. 15-16)

Although it is a bit coldly expounded, Conner's statement does seem to recognize, at least in theory, men's sense of their significance. And more importantly his attempt to make a sincere and nonpatronizing communication to Lucas is essentially a humanizing act, as Buddy's jealousy underlines. However, his next statement reduces Lucas to a child. "Mr. Lee . . . took much trouble in fixing each man's favorite chair. . . . This is the reward Mr. Lee receives" (p. 16). And his final treatment of Lucas reveals again the state of Conner's vision. Seeing Lucas scratch a sore ear with a match, Conner reprimands him: "He [Conner] might have been speaking of an animal he had befriended. 'Well, could you go to the west wing *now*, please. And throw the matchstick into the wastebasket. *This* wastebasket. Good God, you'll give yourself otomycoses.' Conner hated, more than anything, pain dumbly endured" (p. 17). People, like animals, have a right to freedom from pain, Conner feels; he shows the same sympathetic concern for the diseased cat.

In counterpoint, the subsequent scene on the lawn portrays animated conversations and clever quarrelling between Hook and the women. The speaker patiently pauses for characterization: "She was a heavy woman whom homeliness had trained to a life of patience and affection" (p. 19). Hook's reactions to subtle implication are also noted. "Uneasiness crept over Hook. The woman's implication—that women did the work of the place—was disagreeable to him." Hook philosophizes in an intelligent, if sentimental, manner and the speaker even finds sexually colored flirtations between Hook and Amy Mortis: "There vibrated between them something of the attraction he had of old exercised on members of the opposite sex" (p. 23).

This scene is contrasted with a view of the west wing of the hospital where people again sink to objects: "The sheets did not seem to have beneath them persons but a few cones, from the points of which the folds sloped apparently to the mattress, . . . parts of bodies—feet, the pelvis, shoulders without arms—joined by tubes of pliable glass, transparent so the bubbling flow of blood and yellow body juices could be studied" (p. 24). This foreshadows Mom Angstrom's dream in *Rabbit Redux* in which she sees a body as "a red puddle . . . connected with tubes to machines" (*RRx*, p. 196).

When Lucas goes to have his ear treated, Angelo, an ironically named doctor, addresses him as if he were a child—"May we see?"—and describes the inflammation to the nurse mechanically: "Right in around here. Between seven and eight o'clock." Even Lucas notes the strangeness—"A queer trick, his making the ear a timepiece. There was something insane in so much explanation" (p. 26). Angelo deals with Lucas' record card, rather than with Lucas himself, and when he explains that Lucas should have a tooth pulled, refers to him as an object containing a tooth: "There are instances of an abscess . . . inserting poison into the bloodstream until the *host* suffers a coronary" (pp. 26-27, my italics). This mechanized environment is followed by a scene of Hook praying.

When Conner joins the people on the lawn, he sees two old men "fumbling," feels that they need "at least advice," and notices that the tables are poorly aligned. Tommy Franklin's meticulously carved peachstones appear to Conner as litter, "strewn on the silver boards like brown pebbles," and the activity is as "ill-planned as that of an ant colony" (p. 36). Hook's view of the same scene ten pages earlier is subtly recalled, in which the intricate purposefulness of the proceedings is apparent.

> . . . two old men were slowly unravelling electric cords,
> cardboard boxes of colored bulbs behind their legs. . . . One
> of the men fumbled at a snarl. . . . The one not fiddling
> with the snag was removing bulbs from their beds of tissue
> paper and laying them, so that no two of the same color
> touched, on the bench. . . . The wooden tables . . . were
> arranged partly along the main walk, but principally in two
> alleys at right angles to the walk, straight across the grass.
> (pp. 19-20)

Conner turns to Mrs. Mortis whom he sees as "unsteady
with her absurd bonnet." He worries principally about her health
("I only thought you looked a little pale.") and tries to encourage her to move into the shade. In explanation he states, "I had
only your welfare in mind," which is more accurate than he
realizes—he considers not people but people's welfare, as Angelo
concentrated not on Lucas but on the card recording his health.
Mrs. Mortis' cautious and annoyed response to Conner indicates
her awareness of the quality of his concern; as a closing comment to him she reads his thoughts about her bonnet: "If you
think up there in the shade I'll take my bonnet off because I
make this place look like a fool, I won't" (p. 33).

Updike also uses figurative language and other special word
choice to reveal the dehumanizing vision of Conner, Buddy, and
visitors of their generation. When Buddy enters the crowded
cafeteria, "one vast bright beast seemed contained in an acoustic
cage" (p. 57). To Conner the crowds entering for the fair "bum-
ble like brainless insects" and form "one living conglomerate,
through whose sprawling body veins of traffic with effort circu-
lated: a beast more monstrous than any he had told Hook of"
(p. 109). David, a youth coming to the fair, recalls seeing the old
people in town where occasionally one "waggled a claw at the
children."

In this regard the description, from the point of view of the
drugged patient, of Lucas (seen as a "bear") catching the para-
keet (seen as a "flower") is more than a verbal *tour de force*.
Robbed by barbiturates of his human vision, the patient represents an extreme form of the dehumanizing point of view of

Conner or Buddy. Like them, he is unable to make the discrimi-
nations which define humans as beings separate from their
biological surroundings, the plants and animals. The animal here,
instead of a tree shrew or a lemur, is a bear and his actions are
as purposeless to the invalid as were the old people's fumblings
to Conner. Yet, like Conner, he has good intentions, and tries
to be considerate.

> The green flower had sprouted unsurprisingly; the appear-
> ance of a bear seemed to follow from that. Now the bear
> growled. It seemed sorry for something, but then he was
> sorry too. . . . The bear pointed; the flower leaped; . . . The
> bear lifted its black arms and sank from view, and the flower
> bloomed on the bed, its bright eye frightening. . . . A chair
> fell lazily and the bear was of course sorry about that, and
> ashamed. Then the bear grew very clever and plucked the
> green flower from a picture on the wall. . . . It occurred to
> him that it all had been arranged to amuse him, and he
> laughed obligingly. . . . (p. 63)

Near the end of the novel, the speaker's voice, in an ironic turn,
imitates the loss of vision:

> . . . health was the principal thing about the faces of the
> Americans that came crowding through the broken wall to
> the poorhouse fair. They were just people, members of the
> race of white animals that had cast its herd over the land of
> six continents. Highly neural, brachycephalic, uniquely able
> to oppose their thumbs to the other four digits, they bred
> within elegant settlements, and both burned and interred
> their dead. (pp. 109-110)

This objective scientific description leads to the speaker's echoic
restatement of Conner's heaven—the highest level of existence
visible within his framework. Conner pictured a place with "no
disease . . . no oppression, political or economic . . . leisure for
recreation. . . . Cities will be planned, and clean. . . . The life
span of the human being will be increased. . . . man will grow

like a tree in the open" (p. 75). The speaker recasts this heaven into a hell where humans, deprived of their unique, nonbiological significance, have only nonlife.

> There was to be no war. We were to be allowed to decay of ourselves. And the population soared like diffident India's and the economy swelled and iron became increasingly dilute . . . and everywhere was sufferance, good sense, wealth, irreligion and peace. The nation became one of pleasure seekers; the people continued to live as cells of a body do in the coffin. (p. 110)

A belief in the significance of life is what creates a recognition of the importance of death. Death loses its terror, for Conner, if it can come without suffering. He foreshadows Ken, of *Couples*, who regards without emotion a tray of gutted laboratory mice. This is a result of their vision of life as biological only, its cessation of no great matter. Mendelssohn's dramatic sermons about death and Conner's peaceful west wing are the keystones of their diametrically opposed views.

Any death, even the death of an animal, invokes the fact of human death to death-foreseeing humans. The death of the cat which Buddy kills and the death of the flying squirrel which Hook had to kill supply two contrasting vignettes of the value of life.

> With a sensation of prolonged growing sweetness Buddy squeezed the trigger. The report disappointed him, a mere slap it seemed in his ears and very local.
>
> If his target had been a bottle, liquid wouldn't have spilled more quickly from it than life from the cat. The animal dropped without a shudder. . . . the gun exhaled a faint acrid perfume. (p. 44)
>
> *   *   *
>
> Breaking up the screaming ring [of children] he [Hook] had found at its center a grey pelt wildly pulsing with the parasitic life that refused to loosen its grip, and had had to dispatch it himself, weeping and trembling, with a hatchet

brought up from the basement. . . . As he had imagined it there had been a storm brooding that day. (p. 34)

The widely differing senses of *life* in the animals, the terror on one hand and the sweetness on the other, and the sense of cosmic importance (a storm brooding) versus a sense of no importance ("a mere slap" and "very local") counterpoint each other. Piet, five novels later, watches a bird die with, like Hook, a sense of its life ("Lifted sheerly by the beating of its heart, it propelled itself to the middle of the lawn . . ." [C, p. 86]) and the cosmic importance of its death ("The bird emitted a minute high cry . . . small as a star . . . only Piet heard this utterance").

2. The Christian Mythos

Since one's assessment of human status depends upon the nature of his total vision, Updike must give to his characters conceptual frameworks appropriate to their treatment of people. For the characters like Conner, a science-oriented vision accounts for their denigration of persons to a zoological category. For other minor characters a simple absence of intelligence or sensitivity reduces their perception of people's inherent importance. But what of the Hooks and Mendelssohns? What system of belief can viably support their treatment and estimate of people as special self-conscious beings deserving of love and understanding?

With reservations that become increasingly obvious in each subsequent novel, Updike has looked to Christianity to buttress his protagonists' instinctive perceptions of people's worth; Christianity assures us of our special place in creation. Not only do each of the protagonists have a basic Christian faith (a denomination is usually not specified although Piet's church is Congregational, and Eccles and Foxy are Episcopalian) but each novel pointedly sets this faith in contrast with surrounding nonbelievers. Hook's debate with Conner is paralleled in *Rabbit, Run* by Rabbit's conversations with Eccles in which Eccles' colder doctrinaire approach is later revealed to mask an underlying lack of belief.

At the funeral, it is pointed out that Rabbit is the only one who believes the words of the service. Caldwell-Chiron's basic faith is the subject of a debate with Venus in *The Centaur* and is contrasted with Peter, Hummel, Doc, and others who lack faith and, appropriately, see Zimmerman, the principal, as just an incompetent old lecher and the students as simply sycophants, hypocrites, and delinquents. In *Of the Farm*, Mrs. Robinson is the only one who wants to go to church on Sunday morning and in *Couples* much is made of the fact that Piet and Foxy are the only ones (except for "the Catholics") who attend church. Skeeter, in *Rabbit Redux* has a vivid sense of God and tells Nelson, "Don't keep the Good Lord out, Nellie. . . . Let Him come." But Nelson, who represents the others, the whites, resists: "I don't want God to come" (*RRx*, p. 262).

The first novel contains the most direct and extensive description of this basic Christian faith. In a debate with Conner (pp. 76-80), Hook outlines his beliefs: God exists; the universe and the interior spokesmen attest to this. Virtue therefore also exists; it is obedience to God's will. Suffering is caused by evil but provides the opportunity for the exercise of virtue, the two fitting together like a carpenter's joints. Without belief, Hook concludes, there are no values for defining goodness; there is only "busyness." Conner, of course, rejects this.

However, it is interesting to note that Conner himself may demonstrate the presence of an "interior spokesman" which he fails to recognize. On page 30 he sees the lengthening vapor trail of an invisible jet. He identifies himself with the pilot (his "fellow modern" and, like Conner, alone) and marvels that the sky is so vast that the pilot's progress would be imperceptible were it not for Conner's vantage point below. Totally separated from the pilot and his movement and able to see the entire sky, Conner can mark the progress of the vapor trail and see the pilot's motion. Is Conner unconsciously positing an analogous Viewer to Whom his own movements in time and space can be seen against the backdrop of the whole cosmos? Ironically in the next paragraph Conner reaffirms his conscious atheism by noting wryly that there is no one an atheist can blame for the coming bad weather.

Updike casts the difference between Hook's and Conner's

worlds into the imagery of the intricately patterned quilts that
Amy Mortis makes. The quilts with their carefully ordered and
arranged design are symmetrical, meaningful, and beautiful as is
a world fashioned by an intelligent Maker. Amy's quilts contain
little worlds—temples and furniture, hills and sky, flowers and
rivers, and children playing. Hook makes the analogy at once and
looking at the quilt, sees himself as a child "wandering among
the rectilinear paths of the pattern searching for the deeper dyed
thread" (p. 21). As a child a quilt symbolized the necessary sleep
after a day's play just as now his faith understands the meaning
of death after the span of life. Eight pages later, when Hook
prays, he becomes "a point within an infinitely thick blanket,"
prayer revitalizing a sense of the world as patterned quilt.

Conner, by contrast, sees himself as living beneath "blank
skies" in the same paragraph in which he admits his boredom
(p. 47). This is an echo of the "plain" cloth which the younger
people prefer but which Amy cannot use in her quilts. Standing
alongside Hook, who frequently makes long, lyrical descriptions
of the view from the poorhouse grounds, Conner sees "nothing,
or what amounted to nothing" (p. 47). Although Hook has seen
and interpreted the thickening cloud patterns, Conner can only
see the western sector of the sky which is "unclouded." This
leaves him unable to understand the thunder as he is unable to
understand the rest of the world which is given meaning by the
pattern in which it partakes.

It is their ability to recognize the world as patterned which
marks humans as special and self-conscious beings. Further, it is
their understanding of their own special place in the pattern
which causes people to love and admire each other. The novel
thus relies heavily on deistic faith as the source of human vision,
dignity, and mutual love. The central irony of the book occurs
when Conner, reading an angry letter from "a Town's person,"
sees her belief in God as *de*-humanizing.

> Their final reward, *this* was their final reward. How much
> longer before people ceased to be fools? It had taken the
> lemur a million years to straighten his spine. Another million
> would it be before the brain drained its swamp? . . . With
> what time-consuming caution had the tree-shrew's snout

receded and its skull ballooned! He could picture the woman
who had sent him the letter . . .—a tree-shrew, a rat that
clings to bark. When would they all die and let the human
day dawn? (p. 56)

Updike indicates the basic need for a mythos by showing
that the major characters who reject Christianity create substitute mythic systems to lend dignity and importance to their
actions. Eccles in *Rabbit, Run* relies on a form of humanism—
group-oriented behavior—to justify or even glorify his coke-shop
teenage conferences or sermon-filled golf games. The couples in
Couples create rituals, go to confession to therapists, and make
"a church of each other."
Conner calls Elizabeth's vision of heaven "tremblings" of her
mind, "shy hallucinations," "cartoons projected on a waterfall,"
for which he has no time. After the discussion, however, Conner
daydreams a far more romantic heaven while listening to music:

grown men and women, lightly clad, playing, on the bril-
liant sand of a seashore, children's games. A man threw a
golden ball, his tunic slowly swirling with the exertion; a girl
caught it. No fear here, no dread of time. Another man
caught the girl by the waist. She had a wide belt. He held
her above his head; she bent way back, her throat curved
against the sky above the distant domes. The man was
Conner. . . . (p. 87)

Later, Walter-Mitty-like, he daydreams again, revealing the need
for romantic heroism which is ignored in his scientific dogma:
"He was sitting at a table of dignitaries, not in the center but
with becoming modesty at one end. He rose, papers in hand.
'My department is pleased to report the possession of evidence
which would indicate,' he said, and paused, 'that the cure for
cancer has been found'" (pp. 108-109). And although he refuses
to believe in Christ—"Can any sane mind believe that a young
carpenter in Syria two thousand years ago *made* those monstrous
balls of gas" (p. 79)—he adopts the very recognizable role of a
Christ figure when he is stoned by the inmates. He feels their
attack is "unjust" but when Buddy arrives to help, Conner huskily

orders "Go away." "Then the least expected thing—he stopped and collected a double handful of the stones that had fallen around him and brought them forward to the wheelbarrow." Buddy asks:

> "What are you going to do?"
> "Forgive them."
> "But at least you could punish their leader."
> "I'm their leader."

As the people begin to arrive for the fair, Conner meditates upon his unattractive and uninteresting job, hoping for eventual promotion. Yet he feels he prizes a useful life over a pleasant life, and just before conjuring a daydream he unconsciously repeats the Christian refrain that requests God's will: "Wherever I can serve," he tells himself. (p. 108). Finally the speaker ends this section by maintaining that as the Christian assurance of a spiritual identity gives life to believers, Conner's substitute myths are the source of his life: "he had been mocked—but within he stubbornly retained, like the spark of life in the shattered cat, the conviction that he was the hope of the world" (p. 109).

3. The Love of Craft and History

When Conner dismisses Christ as a carpenter, Hook responds that there is no profession "so native to holy and constructive emotions or so appropriate for God-made flesh to assume" (p. 79). This statement fits into a continuum of remarks by Hook and the speaker praising the old time craftsmen and recalls another of Caldwell's marks of man: "flint-chipping." As early as page 10, Hook eulogizes skill at crafts:

> "there are no workmen now as there were in my day. The carpenters of fifty years ago could drive a stout nail as long as my finger in three strokes. The joints that they would fit: pegs and wedges cut out of the end of a beam to the fineness of a hair, and not split the wood though they were right with the grain. . . . Then wire became common, and

all their thinking was done for them by the metal manu-
facturers." (p. 10)

Four novels later, Piet similarly admires the old workmen and
therapeutically endeavors to follow their directions (which he
calls "ethical") for an antique-style restoration.

Some of Hook's praise might be written off as empty nostalgia. Holding an oilcloth frill for Mrs. Jamiesson to nail he says,
"The carpenters in my day would drive a coarse nail with three
swift strokes" (p. 19); and referring with some self-satisfaction
to the broken wall he remarks, "Indeed it will cost Conner a
pretty penny to have it repaired; the stone masons nowadays
are used to setting nothing but bricks and the cinder blocks"
(p. 53).

However, many more observations of the evidence of craft
are made not only by Hook but also by the speaker. On page 29,
the intricate decorations of the former ballroom are admired.
"To the credit of the old carpenters their work still appeared
solid, without being thickly made. Along the eaves fancy trim
hung, lace wheedled from pine planking. Five lightning rods
were braced by spirals of hand-forged iron." The desire and skill
to fashion objects which go beyond practical needs into the realm
of decorative beauty and conspicuous care sets humans above
the plane of animals, which only consider survival and comfort.
Even the antique dealer, anxious to buy Amy's quilts, recognizes
the value of handicraft, although he considers people's appreciation of it as vaguely "subversive": "There was a keen subversive
need, at least in the cities, for objects that showed the trace of a
hand, whether in an irregular seam, the crescent cuts of a
chisel, or the dents of a forge hammer" (p. 101).

Handicraft, in *Couples*, forms structures to keep out death
(the Congregational church or the hamster cage)—"snug, right-
angled things" as Piet calls them. Tommy Franklin's peachstone
baskets obliquely perform a similar function. Adults, the speaker
says, cannot appreciate the baskets because they seem neither
useful nor decorative and were "indistinguishable from those
badges and tags given for subscribing to a charity" (p. 103). But
children instinctively comprehend the importance of craft—that
the self-conscious care and skill of it are a mark of humans'

special existence, an assertion against death. "Children however recognized the objects as what they were, *charms*. Children sensed in them the childlike emotion Tommy Franklin had felt making them . . . they were especially pleased by just that place, the hole gingerly widened to make an actual handle free in space, where Franklin in working had himself experienced the most satisfaction" (p. 103). They are hand-formed structures which deny that humans are subject, like unselfconscious animals, to mortality.

In the short story "The Kid's Whistling" a boy Jack, working late hours in a toy store, annoys Roy his co-worker by whistling incessantly. The boy's whistling is described simultaneously with meticulous descriptions of Roy's care and skill in painting signs.

> Then, with no more hesitation, Roy dipped the brush and touched it to the board. The great crescent of the T went on without a tremor. The broad curve capping it had just the proper jaunty hint of a left-to-right downslant. With a No. 2 brush he added the hairlines. He sprinkled Silverdust over the moist letter, blew the loose stuff away, and stepped back, pleased. (*SD*, p. 46)

Both obviously gain satisfaction from the exercise of their talent. But something more is hinted. When, at the end, the boy stops whistling, Roy botches a letter he is painting and feels "something out of place, something askew in his room." The whistling, by filling the room with a human noise, had tamed it, made it a human and secure place, even late at night when the store stood chill and empty. It was not only decorative—a distinctly human consideration—but created a product which, like Roy's sign, pleased its creator.

When the environment is shaped by the work of human hands, work indicating self-conscious care, the world becomes a human place and this permanent evidence of our causality seems to promise permanence to our existence, buys off the finality of death. "There can't be a foot of earth east of the Alleghenies," says Hook, "where a body can stand and not be within hailing distance of a house. We have made the land very tame" (p. 20).

The theme of humanizing the land appears in more philosophical form in the short story "Packed Dirt": "I, David Kern, am always affected—reassured, nostalgically pleased, even . . .—by the sight of bare earth that has been smoothed and packed firm by the passage of human feet. Such spots abound in small towns: the furtive break in the playground fence. . . . The earth is our playmate then . . ." (*PF*, p. 168). It is even hinted here that, as belief in Christianity fades, the sense of making human imprints on the land ("humanized intervals of clay") may be able to replace, to some degree, Christianity's role in giving us a sense of our significance and immortality. The speaker describes a dirt hill left by building equipment:

> . . . children's feet . . . had worn the sharpness away . . . ascent was easier. . . . This small modification . . . seemed precious to me. . . . We in America have from the beginning been cleaving and baring the earth, attacking, reforming the enormity of nature we were given, which we took to be hostile. . . . As our sense of God's forested legacy . . . dwindles, there grows, in these worn, rubbed, and patted patches, a sense of *human* legacy. (p. 169, my italics)

This is to make of the earth itself a protective structure, an artistic product.[2]

In addition to the highly formed product, another aspect of craft becomes significant, especially in Updike's later novels—the idea of the *care* necessary—the high degree of self-consciousness which "care" implies. This shows itself for instance, in Rabbit's extremely self-conscious care at sex or Piet Hanema's meticulous care when he builds. All these indicate a self-consciousness which goes beyond survival needs and thus goes beyond the animal. The tone of any of these passages exudes delight in their observance—the same delight the children felt about the peachstone basket handles.

Just as craft humanizes objects or places, people's history has humanized time. The vapor trail's visibility acted as a mark of the pilot's past and cheered Conner; so too a culture's or a person's memory of the past gives time a visible existence and human appearance. Updike's characters can seek evidence of their identity not only in the physical products of craft or the paths of packed earth but also in their memories of the past—"paths" in time—which preserve in a nonphysical way the marks of their existence. In a sense, Updike even runs time and place together insofar as they supply a basis for one's knowledge of his existence and identity. In his autobiographical prose piece "The Dogwood Tree: A Boyhood" he suggests how the memories associated with his childhood, especially memories of his father, have helped make the geographical area of his boyhood significant. "My father's job paid him poorly but me well; it gave me a sense of . . . *place*. . . . When I walked down the street to school, the houses called, 'Chonny.' I had a place to be" (*AP*, p. 131).

Updike's own use of the past is obvious in the highly autobiographical quality of his work. And even more significant is his tendency to tell semi-autobiographical short stories in the first person and from a point in time much later than the events portrayed, thus automatically superimposing the past onto the present consciousness of the speaker. Nearly half of the stories set in the "Olinger" area are narrated this way. For example, "At the age of seventeen I was poorly dressed and funny-looking . . ." or "I saw him for only a moment and that was years ago. . . .")

Updike has his characters use the past in similar ways. Rabbit needs to revitalize his high-school basketball days; the narrative in *The Centaur* is frequently cast into the memory of the now grown Peter; Joey, in *Of the Farm*, returns home to seek himself in the farm and in his parents, living and dead; the imagery of the greenhouse of Piet's childhod gives form to his perception of the present; and Skeeter's emotional history lectures in *Rabbit Redux* indicate the role of history in his sense of identity.

In *The Poorhouse Fair* the setting and characters themselves are evocative of the past; having come to maturity in a time past, they are living symbols or products of American history. This is why, the speaker explains, the younger generation—for whom "the conception 'America' had died in their skulls"—need to come to the poorhouse fair: to seek to revitalize their sense of their past, to seek to identify themselves.

> They . . . came to the fair to be freshened in the recollection
> of an older America, the America of Dan Patch and of
> Senator Beveridge exhorting the Anglo-Saxons to march
> across the Pacific . . . an America of stained-glass lamp-
> shades, hardshell evangelists, Flag Days, ice men, plug to-
> bacco, China trade, oval windows . . . , pungent nostrums
> for catarrhal complaints, opportunism, churchgoing, and
> well-worded orations in the glare of a cemetery on summer
> days. (p. 110)

The antique dealer stays in business because "in this age there
existed a hungry market for anything—trivets, samplers, whale-
bone swifts, buttonhooks, dragware, Staffordshire hens, bleeding
knives, mechanical apple parers, ferrotypes, weathervanes—
savouring of an older America" (p. 101).

Even the band which supplies the music is becoming an
anachronism. The leader morosely remarks on their dwindling
size and they play old-fashioned parade songs and marches by
Hanson and Sousa. Thus, not only the sights but the sounds of
the older, pronouncedly militaristic America are evoked. "The
music was more than a feature of the fair," the speaker says, "it
was its atmosphere, a ponderable medium through which the
celebrants moved" (p. 104). In the new age of "London Pacts
with the Eurasian Soviet" in which "there was to be no war"
the decline of militarism has left a cultural and emotional blank
spot "new in the experience of America, who had never fought a
war that was not a holy war" (p. 110).

For history-teacher Hook, the past century of American
politics acts simultaneously as his cultural and personal identity.
It replaces the memories of childhood and adolescence in Penn-
sylvania (or Michigan for Piet Hanema) to which the other protagonists—and Updike himself—turn for identity and comfort.
Hook, like the grandfather in "The Dogwood Tree" is solidly in-
trenched in loyalty to the Democratic party. His memory focuses
on the period beginning just previous to his birth and extending,
like the Olinger stories, through the years of his adolescence;
thus his favorite stories begin with Buchanan ("The last of the
presidents who truly represented the *entire* country" [p. 66]),
proceed through Cleveland ("Cleveland had the mettle. He was

no Tilden to let the carpetbaggers steal the office from him"
[p. 105], and to McKinley ("Now that McKinley was nothing
but Mark Hanna's parade uniform" [p. 22]).

During the fair, Hook's stories of Cleveland are set in counterpoint to the snatches of overhead dialog from the fair-goers
who have no vision of the past; their conversation deals exclusively with the present—recent occurrences or plans for the
evening. The most persistent glimpse is an anecdote of a recent
scandal involving a pregnant girl who annoyed a neighbor by
sneaking through his yard as a shortcut home. " 'You know how
when she comes home at night she crosses the Leonards' back
yard to get to her own. I guess she doesn't care in her condition
to walk the full way around' " (p. 111).

There appears to be a pathetic attempt, on the part of the
gossipers, to build the story into a small saga of its own and enter
it into the miniature cultural history of the town.[3] The woman
tries to capture the importance and drama of the event:
" 'Whore?' she says. 'Is that what I am? So that's what you call
me?' And calm as you please she pulls out every one of his
tulips and gladiola, and tosses them into his birdbath. This about
two a.m. in the morning mind you" (p. 117).

In similar fashion, Buddy joins the fair-goers and immediately finds a friend to tell his dramatic story to. "Do any of you
know what the hell happened here this afternoon? The ancients
in residence in this pleasure-palace seized rocks the size of
suckling pigs and brained their shepherd, the reverend Mr.
Conner. Seriously" (p. 119). Buddy also imagines, on two occasions, the story in newspaper headlines with himself being inter-
viewed.

POOR PELT PREFECT
Conner Stoned
On Day of Fair

Deprived of their past (Hook's "farsighted" vision) the modern
generation struggle to construct new sagas, instant history.

4. "Yes but": Thematic Qualification

Of the five novels, it would appear that *The Poorhouse Fair* has the least-ambiguous value system, the least-hedged moral framework. It is the initial definition of people: they are death-foreseeing yet cling to a belief in their significance through a fragile vision of their specialness which must be nourished. Their self-consciousness is evidenced by the products of their craft and by the preservation of their past, both of which disappear in the modern world which also attacks the other supports of their self-image, such as Christianity, which the book itself appears to defend.

However, Updike in an interview for the *Paris Review* said, "my work says, 'yes, but.'" [4] He explained this to mean a qualification in the thematic structure which prevents a clear-cut conclusion. In *The Poorhouse Fair* there are four symbolic moments which intrude a doubt into the tightly woven ethical fabric of the novel. These are four sounds which each act as a 'summons' of some kind to the old people. "As they hastened toward the porch . . . the *fourth noise* of the half hour *summoned* them, encouraging their flight, the ringing of the lunch signal . . ." (p. 48, italics mine). These four sounds are: the shot of the gun, the scrape of the truck, the thunder, and the lunch bell. All of these introduce arguments against Hook's faith and trust in his vision.

The gun brings death to the cat, who like the old people is nearly dead (Gregg's sympathy is a mark of the identification between the two) and who has been cruelly smashed in some violent way. Hook himself sees the cat as a flaw in the world's order ("it was hopelessly out of order") and its existence plays an oblique role in Hook's need to explain to Conner the existence of pain and suffering in the world. The fact of the cat's death presents another theological problem—it appears unjust, even to Gregg, that the life and death of creatures is beyond their own control. And so the first summons is to the problem of suffering and death.

The second sound, the scrape of the truck, breaks open the wall which was constructed by the old-time craftsmen that Hook and the speaker see as so significant. But the wall (like the Congregational Church four novels later) is discovered to be rotten and empty inside. Not only is the product of craft partially a fraud, but it is not permanent. Furthermore, there may be the implication (as there clearly is for the church in *Couples*) that the Christian church is similarly empty inside—just rubble, and only useful for mindless assaults on antagonists. Thus the second summons attacks the basis of man's belief and the products of his intelligence.

The third sound is the thunder, which threatens to destroy the old people's carefully planned and beloved fair. As "God's own lightning" destroys the Congregational Church in *Couples*, so God's thunder can bring the ruination of the work of human hands and prevent the vitalizing products of the human past from reaching others. The third summons is to man's unimportance in the universe.

The fourth sound is the dinner bell which summons the people to a debate in which Conner attacks, intellectually, their belief in God and in the universe of His creation. Although Hook wages an intelligent and emotionally attractive argument against Conner's atheism, he is defeated in the end by Conner's scientific evidence. His response to the case of the girl with the chemically induced vision of God is "shame" and a feeble criticism, "That was a very cruel experiment" (p. 80). After Buddy's story of his brother's slow death from cancer, which acts as a conclusion to Conner's argument, Hook can only invoke the results of destroying Christian beliefs: "There can be no goodness . . . only busyness." This final summons, then, invokes the Achilles' heel of any religion: its ultimate inability to prove its own proofs.

These four thematic qualifications act upon the closing of the book—a scene colored by ambiguity and frustration. Hook wants to give Conner a message—presumably his vision, his natural faith—but the message seems unable to form. Moreover this desire to communicate a message places Hook parallel with Conner himself who had earlier expressed the desire to give Hook such a message, "And he felt, important within him, something he should get across, a *message* . . ." (p. 64, italics mine). As one critic has remarked, these enigmatic closing sentences have become an Updike trademark.[5] But more than a stylistic tendency, the endings of the novels, beginning with *The Poorhouse Fair*, point to the ambiguity, the "yes, but" quality of the conceptual framework in each book. Updike himself claimed that Conner, here an antagonist, reminded him of his father, the lovable protagonist of *The Centaur*. And to what degree does the old people's simple-minded vision of heaven cast doubt on the reliability of their whole system of belief? This seed of doubt continues to gain thematic strength in each novel until, in an apocalyptic burst of flame, the church deserts the protagonist of the fifth novel, leaving him abandoned, if content, on the nearly animal plane that the first novel so persistently resists.

2

Rabbit Run: The Self-Centered Lover

1. The Earth-Bound Humanitarian: Eccles

Deprived of a God, humanitarians [1] like Conner must replace a deistic, upward-directed vision with a social, horizontal
one. God is no longer the ultimate beloved; other people must
provide one's basis for action and finally one's significance. The
socialistic welfare state of *The Poorhouse Fair* is the logical outcome of a totally human-oriented vision: people share responsibilities and problems and devote their lives to community-
directed activity. Updike views contemporary society in *Rabbit,
Run* as resembling the humanitarian, socialistic world of Conner,
though in a less-formalized way. The society in which Rabbit
lives has a comprehensive and complex set of social norms involving mutual responsibility: Rabbit is expected to live with
and support his family; he is expected to keep a job he dislikes
because he is financially responsible for his family; he is expected to consider other people's feelings and not say or do
anything which might upset them, and so on. As Eccles says, "We
are all responsible beings, responsible for ourselves and for each
other" (p. 128).

Updike examines some of the shortcomings of such a view
in *The Poorhouse Fair.* Without a personal relationship to a
supernatural God, a character's sense of his own specialness
dwindles and he lacks the ability to make others feel special.
Moreover, characters like Amy Mortis find the vague promise
of painless community living a poor substitute for the heaven
they expect; as Amy says, "To hell with it!" Conner, the scientist,
must himself turn to romantic reveries to supply the missing
sense of personal importance. In Hook, who has no "downward"
vision but only "far-sighted" (that is, otherworldly) vision, we

find the deistic orientation which supports men's instinctive sense of importance; Hook can then communicate this sense to others. To Conner people are important only as members of a community—they must be kept healthy, satisfied, well-fed, and so on; to Hook they are important as individuals.

In *Rabbit, Run* Updike continues to focus on what he feels are the inadequacies of earth-bound humanitarianism. Here the humanitarian is Jack Eccles, an Episcopalian minister but (as he finally admits) an atheist who represents the belief in mutual responsibility—shared problems and shared guilt. Rabbit is, like Hook (or Piet of *Couples*), one of the life-givers who maintains an upward vision. Although he lacks Hook's solid Christian faith, he has instinctively clung to a sense of God as the "something that wants me to find it." Rabbit's game is basketball—an upward-directed sport—whereas Jack Eccles' hobby is the horizontal game of golf.

Rabbit finds the human net of involvements unsatisfactory because he is unable to relinquish the sense of importance man gains by believing in and looking for the "something"—some more-important figure than Janice as the reason for life's efforts. Involvement with people means involvement with "dumb" (Janice), "soggy" (Eccles), and otherwise "second-rate" people and thus threatens to make the protagonist himself second-rate.

The opening scenes of the novel make it clear that Rabbit's home situation is unacceptable; the reader is given an emotional point of view which makes possible the necessary degree of sympathy with Rabbit's forthcoming desertion of his family. A third-person-limited point of view provides an initial affiliation with Rabbit and we observe that he is sensitive. He sees, for instance, the boys' reaction to his presence at their basketball game: "His standing there makes the boys feel strange." His nostalgic and enthusiastic participation in the game allows the reader to award him an easy affection.

It is then possible for the reader to find Rabbit's home situation—a rather ordinary middle-class apartment—distasteful and unsatisfactory for him. Smallness, a little clutter, the wife's drink, and the television offend Rabbit and (to the degree that we are ready to share his point of view) offend us.

It seems to him he's the only person around here who cares about neatness. The clutter behind him in the room—the Old-fashioned glass with its corrupt dregs, the choked ashtray balanced on the easy-chair arm, the rumpled rug, the floppy stacks of slippery newspapers, the kid's toys here and there broken and stuck and jammed, a leg off a doll and a piece of bent cardboard that went with some breakfast-box cutout, the rolls of fuzz under the radiators, the continual crisscrossing mess—clings to his back like a tightening net. (p. 16)

Janice, who occupies the living room, is neither pretty nor intelligent and the opening description of her, from Rabbit's point of view, hyperbolizes her unattractiveness:

. . . a small woman with a tight dark skin, as if something swelling inside is straining against her littleness. Just yesterday, it seems to him, she stopped being pretty. With the tiny addition of two short wrinkles at the corners, her mouth had become greedy; and her hair has thinned, so he keeps thinking of her skull under it.[2] (p. 10)

Even the descriptive imagery surrounding Rabbit's walk home makes it clear that the unattractive, closely built neighborhood and the house are antagonists. The homes are "fortresses of cement and brick" with windows "like the eyes of an animal"; they are colored "from bruise to dung" and nearly identical. The vestibule is "sunless" but harshly illuminated by a "daytime bulb." The door is shut "like an angry face" and he can smell "the furnace's rusty breath" and "a soft decaying in the walls" (p. 19). Service to this situation seems to offer Rabbit no chance for importance, no chance for dignity, no chance to exhibit the specialness which he feels he has. As he explains later to Eccles, "I once played a game real well. I really did. And after you're first-rate at something, no matter what, it kind of takes the kick out of being second-rate. And that little thing Janice and I had going, boy, it was really second-rate" (p. 90).

As an ambassador from Janice's parents, Eccles represents

social responsibility. He tries to convince Rabbit to return to his wife and attacks his feeling of specialness. "What do you think it's like for other young couples? In what way do you think you're exceptional?" (p. 90). Eccles also attempts to divert Rabbit's belief in God into the earth-bound direction of human relationships: "Do you think, then, that God wants you to make your wife suffer?" (p. 90). And he uses the emotional susceptibility generated by crises—birth and death—to twice pull Rabbit back into the social system: when baby June is born and when she dies.

Eccles represents social responsibility, additionally, in his own behavior. More a social worker than a priest, he views his profession as one of working with people to help them adjust to their various situations. He visits and comforts the elderly and sick, answers teen-age sex questions, and tries to give low-level therapy to the Springers and Angstroms after Rabbit's desertion. He sets up a therapist relationship to Rabbit, trying to talk him through his problems as a way of bringing about his return to society.

Eccles himself, however, is shown to find this horizontal, totally human orientation unsatisfactory. He is bitterly plagued by his own atheism and is twice shown unwilling to pray: once while waiting for Kruppenbach ("he feels an adolescent compulsion to pray but instead peers across the valley . . ." [p. 141]), and once while arguing with Kruppenbach (Kruppenbach: "Will you kneel a moment with me and pray?" Eccles: "No. I won't. I'm too angry. It would be hypocritical" [p. 144]). After an argument with his wife, he wearily admits his lack of belief and the emptiness of his life: "If it'll make you happy, I don't believe in anything" (p. 223).

It is clear that his social work does not offer a substitute for belief. The homes of his parishioners become a wasteland without life-giving water, a confused inferno of lovelessness. When he visits the Springers (pp. 126-133), Mrs. Springer is "a plump dark small-boned woman with a gypsy look about her;" she and Janice have "a sinister aura." She guides Eccles through "a crooked path" in the crowded house. A word becomes a "bat," darting into the air "quick and black," and Mrs. Springer's voice seems to scratch and cut Eccles "like a file." The neighbor's

irritable dog Elsie snaps Cerberus-like at the children; and when
Eccles must journey back through the house without a guide,
he cannot find water because "the kitchen slips by him in the
jumbled rooms."

The Angstroms' house, Eccles' next call, seems an undertaker's parlor full of corpses (pp. 133-140). Though it is day
"several burning light bulbs" illuminate the kitchen and shine
on a sink "full of bloated shirts." Rabbit's father has a "grey,
ragged" look and he "thins his lips over his slipping teeth" like
a skull. "Color has washed from his hair and eyes" and he sits
at a white table in his white shirt. Neither parent shows any
love for their son and although Eccles finally gets a glass of
water, it cannot quench his thirst. This is Updike's version of
the wasteland-limbo-Hades of Eccles' community which seeks to
recapture Rabbit; it is a land of the living dead.

Kruppenbach criticizes Eccles' earthly focus as not appropriate to a minister of God. "Do you think this is your job, to
meddle in these people's lives? . . . You think now your job is
to be an unpaid doctor, to run around and plug up the holes and
make everything smooth. I don't think that. I don't think that's
your job" (p. 142). He attempts to restore Eccles' upward orientation by turning his attention to God and away from people.
"If Gott wants to end misery He'll declare the Kingdom now. . . .
How big do you think your little friends look among the billions
that God sees? . . . I say you don't know what your role is or
you'd be home locked in prayer" (p. 143).

Faith is necessary for the life-giving role of a minister, a
role which, in an ironic turn-about, Rabbit has adopted when he
attempts to give Eccles "the word" feeling that "he really wants
to be told" (p. 112). Eccles feels drawn to Rabbit in the same
way that the parishioners should feel drawn to Eccles—by the
force of his belief. Eccles' duty, Kruppenbach explains, is to
make his faith powerful. "That is why they come." In lines that
echo Hook speaking to Conner in *The Poorhouse Fair*, Kruppenbach concludes, "There is nothing but Christ for us. All the rest,
all this decency and *busyness* is nothing. It is the Devil's work"
(p. 143, italics mine). Failing to turn Eccles' view upwards,
he tries, finally, to direct it downwards. Earthly orientation is
untenable, ultimately—especially for a minister. Without ascent

there can only be descent. "Don't you believe in damnation? Didn't you know when you put that collar on, what you risked?" (p. 144). But Eccles can only scurry to his drugstore haunt, the symbol of his social-worker mentality.

This imagery of ascent and descent permeates the novel, given situational basis in the mountainous setting. It often correlates with whether Rabbit is escaping the restrictions of socially directed responsibility (upward) or being drawn back into the complex system of human involvements (downward). When Rabbit must perform a list of domestic tasks—pick up Nelson, get the car, buy cigarettes—he goes into the center of Mt. Judge and "his progress is always down." Significantly, Updike does not mention the fact that Rabbit must have walked uphill to get home because it contradicts his system of imagery. He simply mentions that "the frame homes climb the hill like a single staircase." On the other hand, the climb up two long flights of stairs to Tothero's room is given several sentences; this is a safe retreat where Rabbit can stay and not be forced back home to Janice. "Tothero leads him to a door he has never entered; they go up a steep flight of attic stairs, a kind of nailed-down ladder. . . . They climb into comparative light" (p. 40).

When at the end of the book Rabbit runs from the funeral, a humanistic ritual of shared respsonsibility, shared guilt, and shared grief—he runs "uphill with broad strength." The angle gets steeper and he goes "always against the slope of the land" because "only by going downhill can he be returned to the others" (p. 245). However, like the car trip, this flight is also unsuccessful in freeing him from people; he runs into the old crumbling house in the woods which "blackens the air with ghosts." Instinctively he sees the significance: it is a world of people and he cannot escape. The "evidence of human intrusion" even here near the top of the hill "tolls bells that ring to the edges of the universe." He begins to feel defeated.

2. Circles and Nets: The Basketball Imagery

The imagery of ascent and descent is part of a complicated system of spatial imagery into which the ideational structure of the book has been cast. Whereas the basic image of *The Poor-house Fair* is the quilt—its patterned symmetry reflecting a meaningful God-created world—the basic image in *Rabbit, Run* combines basketball, sex, and religion into a solid geometry of ups and downs, circles and straight lines, nets and spaces.

Rabbit's high-school basketball provides the framework. The circular hole of the basket is the goal, above the heads of the players and bathed in light. The net surrounds the hole, catching at the ball when it slips through. Net or mesh is also used to trap or cage rabbits, so the images of nets in the novel become associated with threats to Rabbit's freedom or those things which are *not* the goals, which interfere with the goal. Basketball and sex are associated, first through the obvious image of the circle or hole, a female symbol; Rabbit describes the basket as "the high perfect hole with its pretty skirt of net" (p. 35). The rim becomes a "crotch" (p. 7). The net makes "a lady-like whisper." Playing makes his body taut and it feels "like he's reaching down through the years to touch this tautness" (p. 8); thus he becomes the male symbol and can remember fondly a man who used to call from the crowd, "Hey, *Gunner!* . . . shoot! Shoot!" (p. 35, italics mine).

Basketball and sex are also associated specifically by Rabbit when he recalls Mary Ann, the girl he made love to after basketball games. "He came to her as a winner . . . she was the best of them because she was the one he brought the most to, so tired. Sometimes the shouting glare of the gym would darken . . . into a shadowed anticipation of the careful touchings that would come. . . . So the two kinds of triumph were united in his mind" (p. 166).

The light-filled circle of the basket also resembled the circular church window where Rabbit looks for the light which attests to God's existence. God, the ultimate goal, the something-that-wants-me-to-find-it, is the equivalent of *the basket* in life: He is high above the human plane yet provides the reason for human activity; one reaches towards Him only by running to get clear of the other players—clear of their entangling arms—and leaping towards the light.

The emptiness at the center of the circle (basket or woman) transforms the imagery of blankness—a threatening concept in

The Poorhouse Fair—into something attractive which Rabbit seeks. As Hamilton notes in his book *The Elements of John Updike:* "Rabbit's romantic soul has followed the quest of *nothing:* the blank skies of the South, with its huge white sun; Ruth's delicious nothing that she says she does; and the luminous view that concentrates itself into the figure of Lucy Eccles. In his dream this nothingness resolves itself into the less than nothingness of death." [3]

When Rabbit is waiting for his old coach Tothero, he consciously makes the basketball-life metaphor and forms another attractive association with blankness: "the sky of a Saturday morning was the blank scoreboard of a long game about to begin" (p. 37).[4] Threatening the blankness (freedom or goal) is the net. When the route Rabbit has chosen to flee to the blank skies of the South proves futile, it becomes a net:

> At the upper edge of his headlight beams the naked treetwigs make the same *net*. Indeed the *net* seems thicker now. . . . When he strays from the straddling mane of weeds, *brambles* rake his painted sides. Tree-trunks and low limbs are all his headlights pick up; the scrabbling shadows *spider* backward through the *web* of wilderness. (pp. 32-33, italics mine)

This description is parallel with the imagery surrounding his flight uphill from the cemetery. Although he runs swiftly and freely for a distance, the trees and shrubbery thicken and twist around him.

> The trees cease to march in rows and grow together more thickly. . . . Rocks jut up through the blanket of needles, scabby with lichen; collapsed trunks hold intricate claws across his path. . . . berrying bushes and yellow grass grow in a hasty sweet-smelling tumble. . . . Such an unnatural darkness, clogged with spider-fine twigs that finger his face incessantly. . . . (pp. 245-46)

In the midst of this net, appropriately, light appears through *circular* openings in the trees. "Midges circle thickly in the sun-

shine above these holes." When he reaches the openness of the
road, an inner emptiness matches the outer blankness: "he seems
entered, with the wonderful resonant *hollowness* of exhaustion,
on a new life" (p. 247). Similarly, when running from Ruth, he
feels the goodness inside him as a partial answer and his insides
become "very real suddenly, a pure blank space in the middle of
a dense net" (p. 254).

These nets formed intermittently by the physical setting are,
of course, analogues of the basic net—other people with their
sticky web of mutual responsibilities. The apartment holding
Janice "tightens on his back like a net" and the problem of
getting Nelson, and the car, "knits" into a sickening intricacy.
At the end of his car trip he uneasily envisions the social disruptions his flight caused as "a *net* of telephone calls and hasty
trips, *trails* of tears and *strings* of words, white worried *threads*
shuttled through the night and now faded but still existent, an
invisible *net* overlaying the steep streets and in whose *center* he
lies secure . . ." (p. 37, my italics). Appropriately, the first view
of Eccles—the symbol of this human net—contains simultaneously hints of the entangling net and the entangling arms of the
other players: "Eccles' handshake . . . seems to symbolize for him
an embrace. For an instant Rabbit fears he will never let go. He
feels caught. . . . He feels tenacity in his captor" (p. 86).

As in basketball, Rabbit always feels the urge to run clear
of those who crowd and tangle him. After deserting Janice, he
is approached by Eccles. "I've got to run," he tells Mrs. Arndt
when he spots Eccles drawing close. "He feels the green car
crawling behind him; he thinks of throwing the clothes away and
really running" (p. 85). The urge to run, to run from the funeral,
to run from Ruth's ultimatum, is explained by Tothero when he
tells the couples in the restaurant the secret to winning at
basketball, the secret of Rabbit's success. "I had nothing to teach
you," he tells Rabbit, "I just let you run" (p. 52). "Run, run, run.
Run every minute. . . . You can't run enough" (p. 54). This,
and the will to achieve, are the basis of Tothero's early lessons.

What defeats Rabbit in real life is the absence of a counterpart for the basket in basketball. Rabbit loves games because
they create and clearly define the goal, the ways of getting
points, becoming first rate, being a success. But the real world

does not tell him what the something-that-wants-him-to find-it *is*. He has the idea "that somewhere he'd find an opening" (p. 225) but he does not know how to recognize it. So the urge to run and the will to achieve are without specific direction except to move him away from obvious threats and traps which hinder his freedom of motion.

Because of the dynamics of his basketball-sex-religion concept of reality he is attracted to the sexual counterpart of the basket, which *is* definable. It has been noticed by some critics that Rabbit's sexual activity is described as a performance which he concentrates on doing skillfully.

> He makes love to her as he would to his wife. After their marriage, and her nerves lost that fineness, Janice needed coaxing. . . . he sits up on her buttocks and leans his weight down through stiff arms into his thumbs and palms as they work the broad muscles and insistent bones of the spine's terrain. . . . He goes for her neck, and advances his fingers around to her throat. . . . He returns to her back, until his wrists ache. . . . (pp. 71-72)

During sexual episodes he seems most aware of his own prowess. "He stifles his tide of resentment, reschooling himself in her slowness. Proud of his patience, he resumes rubbing her back. . . . is she feeling it? . . . Is he kindling the spark? . . . he is filled with the joyful thought that he has brought her to this fullness. He is a good lover" (p. 205). Here is something which he can do skillfully; here he can be special. And here he often seems close to the larger answer of life. Trying to reach climax with Ruth is a "search" in which they partake together, and the next morning he feels that it would be appropriate to have intercourse while other people attend church. Later, Lucy, "that sweet vanilla cookie," appears in church bathed in light, and Rabbit returns from church feeling he has "something precious for Janice." He later remembers this as a "little flame" which he had "nowhere to put on the dark damp walls of the apartment so it had flickered and gone out." He worries that he "won't always be able to produce this flame" (p. 225).

Yet even sex refuses to supply ultimate satisfaction, refuses to reveal the larger answer. "As they deepen together he feels impatience that through all their twists they remain separate flesh . . . everywhere they meet a wall. The body lacks voice to sing its own song" (p. 72). And sex leads to children, involving Rabbit in new social tangles. Ruth will not let her baby live unless Rabbit formally commits himself to sharing the responsibility, just as Janice's baby dies when he refuses to share the responsibility for its rearing.

Yet the horizontal, social orientation is not satisfactory for some of the same reasons it was unsatisfactory in *The Poorhouse Fair:* it fails to provide the sense of importance and specialness which an upward-oriented, deistic concept of life supplies; it fails to identify any significant goals; and it traps a person into a tightly structured system of mutual responsibility which prevents individual identities from seeking meaning in their own special ways. In the first novel Hook's, Gregg's, Lucas', or Amy Mortis' unique visions are ignored because of the need to regiment the inmates and insure efficient, pleasant operation of the Home. Similarly, Rabbit's desire to free himself and act independently becomes social injustice and becomes a cause, in the system, of personal suffering and death to others.

3. The Lover as Star Player

Rabbit, Run's basic game image provides in the second novel another indication of the inadequacy of the human-oriented society: such a society has no provision for star players; it demands only "team players." In his basketball days, Rabbit was a star player—"Showboat" the man in the crowd called him. He was the shooter, the point-maker. He did not work well with other players, as former team-mate Harrison explains in the bar when he quotes Tothero as saying, "This is in confidence, Ronnie, but I depend on you to spark the team. Harry is not a team player" (p. 148).

The star player and the team players are necessary to each other; and because of his point-making potential the star player is allowed his independence and a certain degree of selfishness. Rabbit naively recalls his record-setting night at Oriole High, for example. The opposing team were poor players and Tothero had instructed his squad to take it easy—"we weren't supposed to try, you know, to *smother* 'em." But instinctively, the star player is a point-maker and not conditioned to pay homage to the other players of either team. ". . . all of a sudden I know, you see, I *know* I can do anything. . . . and these farmers running up and down getting up a sweat, they didn't have more than two substitutes." He then went on to set a scoring record. When he finishes his story Rabbit is puzzled because "he can't make the others feel what was so special." Margaret sarcastically voices a reaction not unlike the reader's—a reaction of one who is *not* a star player, "Yes, sir, Whosie, you're a real sweet kid" (p. 58).

Rabbit is clearly a star off the basketball court, too. Like Hook or Piet he is one of the life-givers, the people who can communicate a feeling of specialness to others. The force of his belief gives people faith—faith in themselves, faith in something beyond themselves. His ability to focus on them as individuals restores their own sense of importance and lovableness. "You kept me alive, Harry," Mrs. Smith tells him. "That's what you have Harry: life" (pp. 186, 187).

Updike repeatedly associates this quality, in his male protagonists, with sexuality. Hook of *The Poorhouse Fair* still manifests sexual attractiveness and inclinations; Piet of *Couples*, Rabbit of *Rabbit, Run*, and even Skeeter of *Rabbit Redux* are highly sexual characters, whose attentions women appear to seek. (Suggestions of this in *Rabbit, Run* are limited to Ruth's initial sexual pleasure and Lucy Eccles' subtle flirting.) It is in sexual relations that Rabbit and Piet try to give the highest degree of personal attention, affection, and individualizing tenderness. Their lust, consequently, becomes a vehicle for communicating the life force which makes them stars in a world of people who desperately want their special skill of love. Even Eccles is touched by Rabbit's power, and in a way not unsexual. He recalls playing golf with Rabbit: ". . . there is the pleasure of hearing Harry now and then cry 'yes, yes,' or 'That's the one!' Their rapport at moments attains for Eccles a pitch of pleasure, a harmless ecstasy, that makes the world with its endless circumstantiality seem remote and spherical and green" (p. 141). (This relation-

ship occurs in *Rabbit Redux* with the roles reversed—the now
dissipated Rabbit finds Skeeter sexually attractive.)

And so, in a meaningful way, Rabbit is, because of his life-
giving ability, not second rate; his natural resistance to second-
ratedness becomes associated with his identity as a star and not
a team player. But it is only by looking above the level of social
responsibility that Rabbit can maintain the vision which makes
him a star. To force him to be a team player, a group-oriented,
responsible, "mature," member of society would be to force him
back to Janice, Magi-Peelers, and "fetching and hauling" where
his special gifts would go largely unused and where a horizontal
outlook would threaten to cloud his awareness of the higher
something-that-wants-me-to-find-it. The novel argues strongly that
society, like basketball, needs stars who look beyond the human
level and remind us that this level is only one of the possible
levels of vision.

At points when Rabbit seems to be the most selfish or irresponsible, he is usually simply using a reasonable and true logic,
but one which does not conform to the conventional norms of
encompassing social responsibility. When Ruth asks Rabbit why
he does not support his wife, he answers "Why should I? Her
father's rolling in it" (p. 122). Readers often react unsympatheti-
cally to that line because it touches—as much of Rabbit's activity
does—on their own expectations of corporate responsibility. Yet
what Rabbit says is true and logical: Janice's father is a successful businessman and much more able (and willing) than Rabbit
to provide for Janice. Similarly, when Ruth tries to force the
responsibility for her baby on him ("You divorce her or forget
me. If you can't work it out . . . this baby of yours is dead too"
[p. 253]), Rabbit finally decides, "Ruth has parents and she will
let his baby live."

At these moments, Rabbit is opting out of the system and
considering in a realistic way the resources which remain to these
people. "Don't you think you're ever going to have to pay the
price?" Ruth asks. "If you have the guts to be yourself," Rabbit
replies, "other people'll pay your price" (p. 125). This answer,
admittedly, is placed in ironic perspective because it follows
Ruth's monolog in which we learn how *she* is paying Rabbit's
"price"; when he says the line, in fact, she is silently crying. But

although it is not said well or sympathetically, this is the position of the star player—the team players pay his price, doing the guarding and making the set-ups for his points.

In addition to being called a life-giver, Rabbit is also called Mr. Death. Ruth calls him this after June's drowning when she considers the abortion of her own baby. Rabbit brings death simultaneously with life because the social system is constructed in such a way that deviations from its regulations cause suffering. Tothero explains: "Right and wrong aren't dropped from the sky. We make them. Against misery. Invariably, Harry, invariably—misery follows their disobedience" (p. 232). Yet deviations from those horizontally geared norms are necessary for a life-giver. Rabbit is a death-bringer because the community has made him responsible for life in more ways than his non-social identity and self-centered personality can support. Leaving the house in an understandable (if not justifiable) temper of sexual frustration leads to the death of his baby because Janice's tendency to drink forces responsibility for the baby's safety on him. Wanting his sex with Ruth to be a fertile and intimate thing (thus psychologically as well as physically life-giving) leads to a threatened abortion because society's rules, which she invokes, require that he assume a husband's role to provide a family set-up for her and her baby.

Rabbit's gardening activities for Mrs. Smith provide him with a contrast to society's belief in ultimate human responsibility. Here one can give life without needing to continually support its existence. Because of his basic maleness (a seed-planter), he finds initial delight in getting Janice and Ruth pregnant ("Great!"). But society refuses to let his role end there. In the garden, however, once the seeds are planted, with love and care, the plants prosper and remain beautiful independent of Rabbit's support. God's presence, it seems, is responsible for them. Rabbit is thus returned to the larger cosmos and is temporarily freed from the smaller human cosmos.

> Sun and moon, sun and moon, time goes. In Mrs. Smith's acres, crocuses break the crust. Daffodils and narcissi unpack their trumpets. . . . He loves folding the hoed ridge of crumbs of soil over the seeds. Sealed, they *cease to be his.*

> The simplicity. Getting rid of something by giving it. God
> Himself folded into the tiny adamant structure. *Self-destined*
> to a succession of explosions, the great slow gathering out of
> water and air and silicon. . . . (pp. 114-15, italics mine)

Here one can give life without the constant potential for giving
death, unlike, for instance, Philadelphia (or Mt. Judge) where
"you can't move without killing somebody" (p: 25).

Society's religion of corporate responsibility is demonstrated
in people's reaction to June's death. They feel Rabbit is to
blame, as Eccles' wife explains, because he "runs off and sends
his idiot wife on a bender" (p. 222). Janice's father finds another source of blame, too—"But you're not the only one to
blame. Her mother and I somehow never made her feel secure,
never perhaps you might say made her welcome, I don't know . . ."
(p. 227). Eccles can also be blamed because if he hadn't brought
Rabbit back to Janice just when she had, as Mrs. Eccles says,
"adjusted" to his absence, "something like this never would have
happened." And when Rabbit's mother arrives at the funeral
she appears to blame the Springers for causing her son suffering
—"Oh, Hassie, what have they done to you?"

Rabbit, on the other hand, sees causes as located in non-
human things. Tothero's explanation of right and wrong ("We
make them.") "chilled" him because "he wants to believe in the
sky as the source of all things" (p. 233). His upward orientation
sees God as the ultimate cause of the baby's death. "How easy
it was, yet in all His strength God did nothing. Just that little
rubber stopper to lift" (p. 230). And insofar as he connects himself with the event, he removes the aspect of voluntariness or
culpability and simply views his personality as an instrument of
fate. "He woke up early enough to go back to Mt. Judge . . . but
something held him back all day. He tries to think of what it
was because whatever it was murdered his daughter" (p. 225).

Rabbit's upward orientation and his need to escape society's
enmeshing system do indeed characterize him as a kind of
mystic, as he himself says only half-jokingly, "I'm a mystic. I
give people faith" (p. 121). Kruppenbach's description of the
ideal minister is that he must strive to be somewhat of a mystic
—not involved with the small daily problems of people but seek-

ing a purer relationship with God which requires a degree of withdrawal from human concerns. The word "saint" is ironically applied to Rabbit on two occasions (Janice: "What're you doing, becoming a saint?" [p. 12] and Eccles: "He [Christ] did say saints shouldn't marry" [p. 107]). Hamilton notes (*Elements,* p. 146) that Rabbit associates himself with the missing Dali Lama —the spiritual leader and mystic.

For Western culture Jesus Christ is the archetypal mystic. He described himself as not of this world and sought to turn people's concerns upward, placing less importance on mundane involvements. The bible says that Peter was requested to leave his fishing (although he was married and therefore a provider) and follow Christ. Christ used the lilies of the field and the birds of the air as examples to restore people's awareness of the larger cosmos—like Mrs. Smith's garden—in which they are not their own ultimate providers.

Ruth says that Rabbit thinks he is Jesus Christ, and when Rabbit goes to Eccles' house he looks at a picture of Christ and sees his own face reflected in the glass. Rabbit promises Ruth the first night, "I am a lover." Mystics are lovers, lovers of the greatest of Beloveds and ultimately lovers of humanity because they attempt to give people the greatest of gifts: a restoration of their relationship with God in which they would become special and infinitely lovable. There is a well-read book about Christ entitled *This Magnificent Lover;* the title itself describes this aspect of mystics. At the end Ruth says to Rabbit, "You love being married to everybody" (p. 252).

Mystics pose a threat to society just as society poses a threat to them. The scene of the funeral is the climactic demonstration of how Rabbit's awareness of God is threatened by other people. Although it is supposedly a religious ceremony, Rabbit is the only one who believes the words Eccles is reading. "The angular words walk in Harry's head like clumsy blackbirds; he feels their possibility. Eccles doesn't. . . . His voice is false" (p. 242). For the others this is a ceremony of shared guilt, shared grief, as Dean Doner points out in his excellent article ("Rabbit Angstrom's Unseen World," see note 1). They have not come to recognize God as their shepherd; they have come to care for each other. "All under him Harry feels these humans knit together.

His wife and mother cling together. . . . she had felt this girl
in her arms as a member with her of an ancient abused slave
race" (p. 241).

While the others feel a closeness, however, Rabbit begins to
draw away from them, "They become remote beside him." As the
words of the ceremony proceed, his sense of God becomes more
vivid, and the surrounding people fade from his awareness. When
the words requesting the baby's entrance to heaven are spoken,
Rabbit mistakenly sees the world and the mourners as sharing
his upward orientation: "He feels them all, the heads as still
around him as tombstones, he feels them all one, all one with
the grass, with the hothouse flowers, all, the undertaker's men,
. . . all gathered into one here to give his unbaptized baby force
to leap to Heaven" (p. 243). This moment of vision is accompanied by the renewal of life and strength drawn from awareness
of divine power. " 'Casting every care on thee.' He has done that;
he feels full of strength. The sky greets him. It is as if he has
been crawling in a cave and now at last beyond the dark
recession of crowding rocks he has seen a patch of light" (p.
244). The "crowding rocks" which stand between him and the
light are the heads of other people which were called "tombstones" in the previous quote. As he turns, Janice's face "blocks
the light"—a forewarning that these people do not share his
vision.

Rabbit's two statements, "I didn't kill her" and "She's the
one" (p. 244), shock the mourners who feel the need of sharing
the guilt and responsibility between them; having no vision of
anything beyond themselves they believe in an obligation to
comfort each other. Rabbit, however, has cast every care on a
divine shepherd and therefore does not see the harm in stating
who was the immediate cause of the baby's death. ". . . she too
is a victim, . . . everyone is; the baby is gone, is all he's saying,
he had a baby and his wife drowned it. 'Hey, it's O.K.,' he tells
her, 'you didn't mean to.' " The shock in the faces of the mourners
suddenly reveals to him their lack of vision. He is not a member
of this community, with its exclusively human focus, and is
despised by them. Freed by their hatred from further participation, he turns and runs *uphill* with "broad strength" and
"exultantly."

The failure of this run to free him from people repeats the paradox which makes Rabbit a tragic and trapped figure. Even though he has upward and even mystical inclinations, Rabbit needs people in the way that a star player needs the team—they are the reason for making points at all. Indeed, Rabbit's central gift—his power to love and make special—is evoked by people. It is only in the arid society which needs the force of his belief that he is a "star" in the first place. The lover needs beloveds. Rabbit eventually returns downhill seeking Eccles and Ruth.

However, this irony becomes a double irony, for even while loving members of this society—Eccles, Janice, Ruth, or even Lucy Eccles—Rabbit is basically rejecting them as not good enough to make *him* special. Making points for a second-rate team makes the star himself second-rate. Furthermore, loving people—although it gives Rabbit life—also threatens him with death in the form of humanistic annihilation, since people associate love with responsibility and feel the right to make demands on lovers. Thus Rabbit brings life and death simultaneously to members of the society, and they bring life and death simultaneously to him.[5] They allow him to love but demean him by seeming to be inferior beloveds.

This contradiction gives rise to a curious love-disgust motif in the descriptions of Rabbit's feelings about other people (and in later descriptions of Joey's and Piet's feelings). The protagonist is conscious of loving an inferior person and actually excites himself by being aware of this. Dignity is thus preserved by patronizing the inferior thing as a means of both loving and rejecting it. After the unattractive opening descriptions of Janice, Rabbit is still shown to love her, "dumb" though she may be. He loves Eccles enough to attempt to comfort him after the funeral, but with the awareness that Eccles is a "soggy" plodding horse who could slow Rabbit's movements. He loves Lucy Eccles "in spite of herself" and while gardening feels affection for a nameless girl who "has a *dumb* girl's sweet piercing way of putting her whole body into one thing at a time" (p 116, italics mine).

The descriptions of Ruth are the most extended example of the patronizing quality of Rabbit's love. Ruth is continually portrayed as physically unattractive in the ordinary sense—overweight, thick ankled, "baggy in nakedness," and so on. In a romantic desire for cleanness and honesty Rabbit washes off Ruth's make-up, and "her wet face relaxed into slabs is not pretty." Ruth's occupation and her crudity make Rabbit's love in some way more satisfying to him because they imply its great depth and breadth. Thinking of her as a whore "makes her seem in terms of love so vast" (p. 65). Yes, he can even love *her*. But there is no escaping that this kind of double-awareness—of lovableness and of inferiority—makes the love patronization and not true attachment of the self to another. In sum, he simultaneously needs the community's people and rejects them.

4. Existentialist Aspects

This constant interplay of contradictions—that love is not love, that life-bringers are death-bringers, that sex invokes an answer but prevents it—is part of the "yes, but" quality of the second novel: the implied qualification which is a part of Updike's themes. Even Rabbit himself is given a characterization so qualified that he, too, becomes a part of the contradictory nature of the book.

Even in the early scene in his apartment, when his home is meant to appear second-rate and not good enough for him, his often crude and inconsiderate dialog tends to associate him with that environment instead of separating him from it. When Janice says that the car is out in front of her mother's, he snaps, "In front of your mother's? That's terrific. That's just the Goddamn place for it" (p. 11). Upon learning that she has bought a bathing suit to look forward to the approaching end of pregnancy, he wheedles, "What the hell ails you? Other women *like* being pregnant. What's so damn fancy about you? Just tell me. What is so frigging fancy?" (p. 13). Thus Rabbit could seem to be a husband appropriate to the setting and not superior to it—as petty and self-centered as Janice is lazy and dumb.

The book denigrates horizontally directed social systems of thought; but it is unable to project a solid religious system of belief to replace them. Rabbit's sense of God is not as conventionally Christian or definite as is Hook's in the first novel. It is an unstructured awareness of a divine power—present in liv-

ing things or even in the moon (which he prays to before entering the hospital at the baby's birth). Although Rabbit feels
cheered by a view of people going to church (as Piet in the
fifth novel is cheered by the construction worker's fear of ghosts),
the church-goers themselves are given a patronizing description
and seem to be somewhat simple-minded; they are "crisply
dressed" and flock like "sheep." The result is a subtle intellectual
nihilism even in the face of emotional optimism. Value systems
themselves become, ultimately, the antagonists. The something-
that-wants-me-to-find-it is never found or even understood, and
Rabbit's mysticism is shown to require the very people who
threaten its existence.

This implied dismissal of known value systems places *Rabbit,
Run* solidly in the tradition of Existentialist novels, a quality
affirmed by critic David Galloway when he included Updike
in a study called *The Absurd Hero in American Fiction.*[6] Tensions and conflicts, he explains, are the only potential source of
meaning in the novel; and there is an unbridgeable gap between
chaotic reality and the human intention to find unity—which
accounts for Rabbit's never-ending search for the "something."
Since value systems themselves tend to become the antagonists,
such a novel often seems like an "anti-novel," attacking any kind
of highly structured insights, even its own.

This may account for the difficulty of maintaining reader
sympathy for Rabbit. His treatment of Janice, in the first apartment scene, his adolescent reaction to Ruth's past relationship
with Harrison, or his indignation when Janice says she didn't
pay rent in his absence ("The trouble with you, kid, is you just
don't give a damn.") all help make Rabbit unlikable. His mediocrity at such times tends to cast doubt on the value of his other
insights, as well. Rabbit's precarious hold on reader sympathy
is reflected in the critical interpretations which see him as a
low-level villain, rejecting the grace offered through Jack Eccles.[7]

The protagonist's rejection of conventional values tends not
only to isolate him somewhat from the reader but isolates him
to an even greater degree from the other characters in the novel.
Just as Mersault in Camus' *L'Etranger* is condemned to death by
an angry society not only for the death of the Arab but also for

institutionalizing his mother, having a mistress, going to a comedy, and not crying when he sees the cross—Rabbit, too, is condemned for the deaths of two babies (Janice's and possibly Ruth's), for criminal negligence, for nonsupport, for having a mistress, and for criticizing Janice's concern about a dress for the funeral. In fact, the degree of society's rejection in both novels is so great that it is a major force in reestablishing reader sympathy with the protagonists.

In addition to the isolation caused by their unpopular value systems, characters in Existentialist novels become isolated by the fact that communication itself is inadequate and suspect. There is the thematic implication that all men are essentially alone. Existentialist novels often contain images of human separation or isolation—such as Mersault's separation from Marie across the jail visiting room or an alcoholic dizziness which prevents his hearing Raymond's conversation. Rabbit watches his son through a window in his mother's kitchen; he cannot hear the conversation, nor can he communicate with anyone in the room. When he and Nelson visit Janice's mother, Rabbit gets sleepy while she is talking, and her "talk leaves his ears like the swirling mutter of a brook. Lulled, he lets his lids lower . . ." (p. 189).

Even the sexual scenes are increasingly touched by this sense of isolation. After the first night with Ruth when there seemed to be some sharing (although Rabbit felt "a wall"), Rabbit's sexual relations with Ruth and with Janice are masturbatory. Ruth can seldom reach climax, and the description stresses his separation from her. "He really hurries now when senses or she tells him *she's lost it*" (p. 125, italics mine). His last sexual encounter with Ruth is cruel and disregards her reluctance for his own pleasure. It is parallel with the only sexual encounter we see with Janice in which she is similarly not a partner but an unwilling masturbatory object. Both Ruth and Janice stress separateness in their Joycean monologues—monologues whose stream-of-consciousness form itself implies emotional isolation. Ruth feels Rabbit "just lived in his skin," and Janice is upset by "this thing of nobody knowing how you felt."

Therefore, although Rabbit, like Hook, is created to be one

of the specialmakers who can see individuals and care about them as such, the novel nihilistically turns upon itself and undermines Rabbit's ability to *know* the people he *loves*.

In Camus' novel, Mersault's essential separation from other people and his mistrust of their value systems leaves him only the plane of solid physical realities and sensuous pleasure upon which to rely. It is an approach to significance based on the objects of the environment themselves—Marie, the ocean, the sun, food and wine, pleasure and rest. In *Rabbit, Run,* too, the physical environment plays an active role. Rabbit's near-mystical sense of the unity of things gives him an intimate and intense relationship with the physical world—sometimes in harmony with it, at other times in conflict with it. His deftness and neatness give him an easy partnership with physical objects; in addition to his grace at basketball he has an agility and a "loving deftness, a deftness as complimentary to the articulation of his own body as to the objects he touches" (p. 11).

A further sense of intimacy with his surroundings is gained through the use of memory in which his previous experiences in the streets or golf courses of Brewer or Mt. Judge make places belong to him, make the earth not only a human place—as described in "Packed Dirt"—but *his* place. It resembles Updike's description of his own home in "The Dogwood Tree: A Boyhood": "When I walked down the street to school, the houses called, 'Chonny.' I had a place to be" (see p. 30, this text).

When Rabbit walks to pick up Nelson, his memories lend a sense of proprietorship—to telephone poles ("He used to love to climb the poles. To shinny up from a friend's shoulders until the ladder of spikes came into your hands"), drain gutters ("He can remember falling in but not why he was walking along this slippery edge in the first place. Then he remembers. To impress the girls—Lotty Bingaman, Margaret Schoelkopf . . .") and the golf course ("He used to caddy over there"). He recalls running through the forests that surround Brewer, and he connects the strip of grass alongside his parents' home with the story of a neighbor's refusal to mow it: "The old Methodist cut exactly his half, one swath of a lawnmower. . . ."

This sympathetic and vitalizing relationship with physical things seems to give them a nonphysical significance for Rabbit.

For instance, he decides from her appearance that Ruth is good natured: "He could just tell from the soft way her belly looked" (p. 79). A physical detail has meaning in a nonphysical matter. There is the repeating pattern (as there is for Piet of *Couples*) of lust preceding love. The physical act of love seems to invoke its nonphysical counterpart. As Rabbit is falling asleep in Tothero's room, sex fantasies about a prostitute lead to a sense of encompassing love: "his heart makes in darkness a motion of love" (p. 42). His knowledge of Ruth's availability and his long careful sexual attentions seem clearly to cause his love for her; and his decision that he loves Lucy Eccles follows a sex daydream about her—". . . a nice low flame in her, lighting up her legs. Those bright white legs. She'd have an anxious little edge and want her own. Cookie. A sharp vanilla cookie. In spite of herself he loves her" (p. 104).

Rabbit does not always enjoy a sympathetic and meaningful relationship with his physical environment, however. Often (such as the times it becomes the net he fears) it reflects the menace he senses around him. It seems to crowd or suffocate him, or like Buddy's file cabinets in *The Poorhouse Fair*, it becomes animate and threatening. A vacant lot becomes "a junkheap of brown stalks and eroded timber that will in the summer bloom with an unwanted wealth of weeds" (p. 18). When he drives south, the highway "sucks" him on and he feels the expressway system "reaching for him." As he runs from the cemetery into the woods "collapsed trunks hold intricate claws across his path."

Whether Rabbit's surroundings are hostile or friendly, however, the novel's stylistic tendency to make the physical environment meaningful in itself seems to correlate with the simultaneous tendency to denigrate abstract value systems. It is a small move in the direction of Mersault's immersion in moment-to-moment physical impressions with a disavowal of any abstract level of meaning beyond them. J. A. Ward (see note 1) describes the scene leading to Rabbit's flight from Brewer as an example of the substitution of sense impressions for moral sensibility. "No thinking occurs," Ward says, "and none is described. There is merely a flood of images, then action: Rabbit begins to run" (p. 33).

The second novel, therefore, while it reaffirms and develops the criticisms of atheistic humanitarianism which Updike began in *The Poorhouse Fair,* seems to show an Existentialist coloration which enormously magnifies its "yes, but" quality to the point where it attacks itself almost nihilistically. Ward says, "Since all attempts to find order and all social postures are shown to be absurd, illogic becomes logic, irresponsibility becomes responsibility, and escape becomes a discovery. Essentially then this novel is existentialist. It is truly an anti-novel . . ." (p. 36).

While Rabbit is reaching for a level of meaning above the human plane, the style is suggesting a level of meaning below it in physical objects and impressions. Although he may be running toward the "something," he is also running away from trees that reach out and houses with menacing faces. And although he is a Lover, one of society's star players, he is also locked inside his own skin, isolated from his beloveds, and ultimately forced to reject them as second rate.

3

The Centaur: The Altruistic Lover

1. The Use of Mythology

The Centaur generated considerable interest upon its publication in 1963 because of its overt use of Greek mythology. Critics, by and large, were suspicious and uneasy with the mythological elements, asserting that they added nothing essential to the novel and were an affectation. Updike, however, has continually experimented with the form of the modern novel, not writing any two with the same method (except for *Rabbit, Run* and *Rabbit Redux* which he clearly wants to function as a set).

The Poorhouse Fair is a utopian novel, highly ideational, with the characters often little more than spokesmen for ideas. In structure is is basically a series of discussions and debates counterpointing opposing viewpoints. *Rabbit, Run* was originally subtitled, "A Movie," and a movie of it was in fact made in 1969. It is written in the present tense, with behavioral descriptions of Rabbit's appearance or mood which frequently sound like stage directions, and it includes a highly cinematic auto trip. Updike said he pictured the credits playing above the opening scene of the basketball game. (See his *Paris Review* interview, p. 110). *Of the Farm* is dramatic in structure and in presentation. It could be neatly divided into three acts and takes place—excluding two small and highly expendable scenes—entirely in the farmhouse in Firetown. It contains, proportionally, more extended dialog than the previous novels and follows the familiar format of group psychodrama. *Couples* would appear to be the most conventional in form of Updike's six novels; yet like *The Centaur* it is steeped in myth and ritual. The basic Tristram-Iseult story has been remarked on by critics and by Updike himself; there are also structural lines borrowed from Catharism, a neo-Manichean heresy of the Middle Ages, and mythic parallels for the main characters—Angela, for example, is often a sky-goddess and Freddy an androgynous sea monster. *Bech: A Book* is structurally a series of short stories, loosely connected by their protagonist and their chronological arrangement. Together they outline the internal process of Bech during a certain period in his life; but the chapters are often begun *in medias res*, as it were, with little reference to the previous pages. The impression is that of a series of slides or letters containing only small moments of the whole. Plot, as such, scarcely exists. In fact many of the chapters appeared first as single short stories.

The Centaur, therefore, is one of a series of structural experiments. The mythology affects the form of this third novel in two major ways: It contributes a separate mythological narrative at points, which is intended to be loosely parallel to what might be called the realistic narrative level; and it colors the realistic level with narrative and descriptive details which evoke the mythic presence indirectly. While the straight mythological narrative is unique among Updike's novels, the use of highly allusive imagery in the narrative and descriptive details has been a characteristic of the author even in his relatively early work. The critics' charge of "over-writing" and the tendency to see Updike's work as allegorical have been encouraged by Updike's constant tendency to invoke Christian or Greek doctrine or his whimsical urge to give characters symbolic names like Angstrom (Angst), Eccles (ecclesiastical), Conner (a con-man), Angela, or Foxy.

The Centaur is characterized by descriptions such as the following one which transforms Minor's cafe into the maze on Crete which held the Minotaur.

> It was a maze, Minor's place. So many bodies . . . I felt in this clouded interior a powerful secret lurking whose nostrils exhaled the smoke and whose hide exuded the warmth. . . . I pushed my way through the bodies as if through the leaves of a close-set series of gates. (p. 91)

However, such metaphorical description is paralleled in other Updike novels, though in less-extended form. In *Rabbit, Run*

when Rabbit and Eccles get out of a car, Eccles' head "across
the top of the car looks like a head on a platter." John the
Baptist? Joey's mother, in *Of the Farm,* looks through the screen
door and her head becomes "the head of a goddess recovered
from the sea," whereas Peggy "seemed a doe of my species,
grazing immune in a thicket." (Richard is earlier called a "faun"
appropriately.) Freddy Thorne in his skin-diving suit is "disturbingly androgynous: he was revealed to have hips soft as a
woman's and with the obscene delicacy of a hydra's predatory
petals his long hands flitted bare from his sleeves' flexible
carapace. This curvaceous man had arisen from another element"
(*C*, p. 239). Teresias? Poseidon? Updike himself mentions a
larger structural use of the St. Stephen story for *The Poorhouse
Fair,* Peter Rabbit for Rabbit Angstrom, and the story of Lot
for Piet Hanema. Thus, although *The Centaur* uses mythical
allusions more consistently and frequently than the other novels,
the novel's use of myth does not separate it from Updike's other
work. The third novel simply exploits to a greater degree myth's
potential for lending significance to reality. The allusions suggest
by their ubiquitous presence a viable system of belief.

Man's need for some sense of myth is introduced in *The
Poorhouse Fair* where Hook's knowledge and love of American
history gives him a sense of identity and lends stature to his
society. The people who visit the fair are shown to be without
a sense of this American myth; they try to revitalize it with
antiques and old-fashioned handiwork or attempt to create their
own myths in their gossip about dramatic local happenings. Joey
Robinson of the fourth novel returns to the farm partly to recapture a sense of myth about his own earlier life through the
memories of his mother whom he describes as having a myth-
making vision.

> "Yes," my mother said . . . "we used to make this sophisti-
> cated young Harvard man and his refined wife from Boston
> go out along the road with a board and two trestles and
> peddle berries to the Sunday traffic!" It startled me to hear
> how Joan and my earlier self had become part of my
> mother's saga of the farm. (*OTF*, p. 24)

The speaker of the short story "A Traded Car" recalls his mother's description of his father hurrying home the night of his birth. "The story of his all-night ride," he realizes, "was the first myth in which I was a character" (*PF*, p. 187).

In *The Centaur* Peter is moved by hearing his father tell the story about Doc Appleton's wife and Zimmerman. He ponders the narration with silent excitement: "*Alive or dead, made love, before you were born*—these phrases, each rich with mystery, rendered the night brimming around us terribly deep . . ." (p. 105). The story becomes a small local myth giving Peter an added sense of his genesis. However, in this case, the novel's overall mythic framework can make the story more significant than *The Poorhouse Fair*'s gossip because the Corinna story is merged by allusion with the story of the Greek deity Coronis so that the two mythic levels become stylistically one. An impression is created of values and human importance that over-arch time.

The use of myth in *The Centaur* is made viable, additionally, by employing a Joycean range of stylistic levels from the conventionally realistic to the fantastic to the purely mythical. An example of this versatility is the opening scene which metaphorically couples the levels in a manner not repeated in the book. As George walks down the school corridor with the arrow in his ankle

> he tried to keep that leg from touching the floor, but the jagged clatter of the three remaining hooves sounded so loud he was afraid one of the doors would snap open and another teacher emerge to bar his way. . . . His bowels weakly convulsed; on the glimmering varnished boards, right in front of the trophy case with its hundred silver eyes, he deposited, without breaking stride, a steaming dark spreading cone. His great gray-dappled flanks twitched with distaste, but . . . his head and torso pressed forward. (p. 10)

Here the visual image of a centaur is drawn, but George is called Caldwell, not Chiron, and the setting remains in the building of Olinger High.

When George teaches his class in evolution (pp. 31-40), a scene that has become famous for its sheer brilliance of style, the setting remains in the classroom and George, Zimmerman, and the various students do not take on the Greek names of their mythical counterparts. But living trilobites are released on the floor, and a girl who is "a huge purple parrot" takes one in "her painted beak" and chews it; Zimmerman sits with Iris Osgood (Io) and undresses her; and Deifendorf is described as having hooves instead of feet. My students in recent classes have often seen that this is partly stylistic hyperbole to convey George's sense of confusion and disgust; but it can be placed within a spectrum of increasing hyperbole which leads to the level of the purely mythical scenes.

A higher degree of fantasy, with correspondingly less co-herence, is found in the description of Peter's second day at school during their three-day sojourn (pp. 134-44). Again Peter, his father, and Peter's high school friends retain their names but the action often describes Prometheus chained to his rock and visited by various mythic personages. The chapter opens "As I lay on my rock, various persons visited me." A mythical figure called "The Town" talks to Peter; Peter's shirt disintegrates; and a line of students forms and passes by, staring at his psoriasis. Mixed with these mythic scenes, we see confused and dreamlike glimpses of Peter's classes—social science, gym (in which Peter cannot catch a ball because his wrists are chained), lunch, Latin, and natural science. As in the classroom scene this is certainly stylistic hyperbole to show Peter's tiredness and anxiety about his father's health. But it continues to thin the line between the mythical and the real.

For this novel Updike appears to have expanded his allusive style to include, in subtly varying degrees, narrative details of pure fantasy, such as the trilobites, which clearly do not occur on the factual level. Stylistically these shrink the gap between the real and the mythical and thus create that strange "boundary between heaven and earth" in which the opening Barth quotation places man.

Heaven is the creation inconceivable to man, earth the

creation conceivable to him. He himself is the creature on the boundary between heaven and earth.

Karl Barth

Within this dimension a view of the realm of cultural tableaux—the realm of myth—becomes possible.

The difference in *The Centaur*, then, is partly one of degree. The mythical allusions in the realistic narrative level are more frequent and systematized than in other novels and bear a greater thematic burden because their coherence implies their reliability as evidence of man's stature—an invisible world of timeless meaningful dramas in which persons have a more clearly defined significance.[1]

It is the level of the pure mythic narrative—where the Greek names are used exclusively—that distinguishes the book stylistically and structurally and which provides the most puzzling analytical problems for the critic. What point of view, what temporal and psychic standpoint is implied in superimposed scenes of Chiron and Caldwell? Man as the creature between heaven and earth might sense both realms, and a third-person-limited viewpoint (Caldwell's or Peter's) does prevail in the novel. But the question of vision is confusing enough that at least one critic has assumed that the mythic elements exist in George's imagination.[2] Scenes of pure myth occur only in Chapters I, III, and IX where George's viewpoint seems dominant. However, this turns George into a schizophrenic who mouths complaints about his inadequacy but, Walter Mitty-like, entertains fantasies of his own grandeur. It would contradict his view of all humans as victims needing help beyond themselves and would thus erase the logic whereby his final sacrifice is meaningful. It would also fail to account for the chapters which use an omniscient point of view (such as VII) or Peter's viewpoint (such as IV) but attest through allusive imagery to the mythic level.

How, then, are we to understand the scenes of Chiron's story? First, they make explicit what is only hinted at metaphorically in other places and are thus a logical extension of Updike's style. A solid existence is given to a system of archetypal dramas which are at the basis of the highly allusive prose style. Because these dramas characterize men and give them importance, they can form the basis of men's evaluations of themselves and each other. *The Centaur* attempts to offer this basis to the reader explicitly.

In *The Poorhouse Fair*, for example, Conner's vague resemblance to St. Stephen may contribute a slight coloration to our judgment of him, but the St. Stephen story itself is never vitalized or confirmed. The story of Peter Rabbit is assuming the status of a folk tale, but Rabbit's possible similarity to Peter is important only if we feel that Peter Rabbit's story is real or meaningful. But Chiron becomes real; his suffering is attested to; and his death becomes significant in an existing world. It is not simply a psychic symbol from the world of Jungian archetypes. Our vision of this world solidified, we gain a sense that the metaphoric devices which associate Minor's cafe with the Maze reveal something meaningful about the definition of the lunchroom, that they do more than simply delineate the picture more vividly. The reader is given a basis for sharing Caldwell's sense of mysterious but effective forces which bear upon human lives, his sense of a real realm of significance not clearly perceived by man, but certain.[3]

In terms of theme, the inclusion of direct mythic narratives unquestionably "loads the dice"—making certain value judgments explicit. The emotional ambiguity which troubles a reader of *Rabbit, Run* can scarcely exist when Caldwell and Zimmerman are the noble Chiron and lecherous Zeus. My students often mildly complain, for instance, that Caldwell is a bit too much the anti-hero to be likable or admirable; nonetheless, the reader knows intellectually that Caldwell is heroic because he is Chiron. His irritating or embarrassing character traits can only be mere humanizing qualities, a psychological analogue of Chiron's lower half.

In *The Poorhouse Fair* it is not impossible to read Conner sympathetically (Updike once said he was a preliminary study for Caldwell) and Hook, consequently, as a lovable but imperceptive old man; and in *Rabbit, Run* it is possible to read Rabbit as a psychotic and Eccles as the instrument of grace (see note 7, Chapter 2). But in *The Centaur* no such character ambiguity is possible, no such thematic ambivalence is allowed. Direct narration of mythic scenes makes definite what even metaphorical use of myth leaves vague: specific character judgments on the personages of the drama. Theoretically, Zeus can be either a noble father figure or hen-pecked lecher; a Centaur might be a wise teacher or a lustful troublemaker; Venus is sometimes the totally desirable female, at other times a petty, whorish girl. In *Couples,* such ambiguity serves Updike's purpose, but in *The Centaur* he chooses to make identities clearer by delineating them in mythic scenes. It is Zeus, the lecher, Chiron, the teacher, Venus the whorish girl—Zimmerman, Caldwell, and Vera.

This is not to suggest that there is no ambiguity in the novel. Although Updike has chosen to let us view his mythic realm directly, there is some uncertainty in the relationship between the earthly happenings and the Olympian. Sometimes the mythic narrative seems an extension and elaboration of events in Olinger; but at other times it acts as an ironic contrast. The degree of irony, furthermore, is never precisely clear.

What, for example, is the relationship between the scene of Chiron entering his class (pp. 74-78) and the class that George is about to teach? Most obviously there is an ironic contrast drawn between Chiron's students who "all hailed him gladly" with faces "unanimously hushed and attentive" and George's class with their baying, hooting, laughter, and disorder. Yet the feelings of expectation and satisfaction attributed to Chiron apply to George as well. "His students completed the Centaur. They fleshed his wisdom with expectation" (p. 78). This seems not to be irony but the truth beneath George's rhetorical crankiness.

It is also in this section that George's reaction to Peter's scolding about the hitchhiker is described, this time from the father's point of view. "When she [Ocyrhoe = Peter] taunted him, however shrilly and cruelly, he felt no rage, and submitted meekly, hoping to earn her forgiveness for his inability to work her cure" (p. 76). Here the myth is a direct parallel, revealing what George's feelings were. The mythic analogue to George's class, then, is both satirical and serious. It offers the suggestion that George's class is like Chiron's on its deepest level of significance even though its appearance seems quite different; yet it also hints at a comic but sad disparity.

The Olympian scene of Chiron and Venus (pp. 22-29) seems to be simply a mythic reproduction of an incident between George and Vera Hummel in the locker room of the school. Replace the gods' names with their earthly counterparts and the story is revealed. However, from what we see of George's relationships to people—the hitchhiker or Hester—it does not seem likely that he would manifest Chiron's cool suavity or his gentle but firm command of the situation. The scene thus seems partly a gentle satire of George's affectionate clumsiness in social situations.

Thus, the overt use of myth in this manner allows Updike to control the extent and direction of his ambiguity in such a way that it contributes to his theme. Value judgments remain certain; for example, George is heroic and has a meaningful and valuable view of reality. But the relationship between appearance and reality is vague. George's feeling that we remain somewhat helpless in an inscrutable world is given credence.

This particular effect of the use of myth offers me a chance to comment on a related critical matter. The sense that the world is enriched with mystery and invisible meaning makes it clear, I think, that this is certainly Caldwell's story, and not Peter's. The employment of an external frame in which a thirty-five-year-old Peter recalls parts (or all?) of the story tempts some critics to consider the book as a species of *kunstlerroman.* But Peter's artistic tendencies antedate the period of the narrative (he has long been interested in Vermeer) and seem to be touched by his father's character in only one aspect: that art can soothe the anxiety wrought by the facts of time and change —facts which deeply trouble George. Peter's sense of the "stage resonant with metaphor" is only verbally attested to, and we never learn anything of Peter's philosophy of art or his style other than the facts that he considers himself "a second-rate abstract expressionist" (p. 81) and that art can offer a "potential fixing of a few passing seconds" (p. 51). We learn nearly as much about Caldwell's influence on Deifendorf whose mixture of affections for the teacher led to his becoming himself a high-school teacher "from whose breast pocket the pencils and pens thrust" in unintentional mimicry of George.

2. The Character of George

The character of George Caldwell, which is at the thematic center of the novel, is based on Updike's father, Wesley Updike, a high-school math teacher. The personality appears early in Updike's fiction, recognizable by the self-demeaning remarks, brusque prose style, and exaggerated concern with people's opinions. It is interesting to observe the frequency of the father's appearance in Updike's stories and his remarkably consistent presentation.

The short story "Pigeon Feathers" offers one of the most extensive portraits. Discussing farming methods with his wife, the father (who is called George) says, "Elsie, I *know*. I know from my education, the earth is nothing but chemicals. It's the only damn thing I got out of four years of college, so don't tell me it's not true" (*PF*, p. 87). To David, the son, he says, "You can't argue with a femme. Your mother's a real femme" (p. 87)— the exact comment he makes in *The Centaur* (p. 57). Later during a family argument, George intones the Caldwell incantation: "This reminds me of death" (*PF*, p. 91). Of farmers he says, "In this day and age only the misfits stay on the farm. The lame, the halt, the blind. The morons with one arm. Human garbage. They remind me of death sitting there with their mouths open" (*PF*, p. 93). When his wife complains that her own father was a farmer, he gives the Caldwell term of affectionate dismissal: "He never knew what hit him," prefiguring the remark about the hitchhiker on page 73 of *The Centaur:* "That poor devil never knew what hit him."

The problem of death is at the center of the short story, as it is of the novel. His pocket bristling with pencils, the George of "Pigeon Feathers" discusses his death with his son: "I'll be lucky if I live till tomorrow . . . if they'd taken a buckshot gun and shot me in the cradle I'd be better off. The *world*'d be better off. . . . Get the garbage out of the way. If I had the man here who invented death, I'd pin a medal on him" (*PF*, p. 99). "Biff bam," says the George of the novel, "Next stop, the dump." Of David's reluctance to shoot pigeons, his father says, "Kill or be killed, that's my motto," the same motto Caldwell adopts in *The Centaur* for dealing with students.

In "Flight" the father is called Victor but he's easily recognizable. Meeting his son after a debate tourney he says, "Well, you won one debate, Allen, and that's more than I would have done. I don't see how you do it" (*PF*, p. 51). He gives a similar self-demeaning compliment in "A Traded Car." "I don't know how you do it, David. I couldn't do what you're doing if you paid me a million dollars a day. I don't know where the kid gets his ideas. Not from his old man, I know that. I never gave that poor kid an idea in my life" (*PF*, p. 184). The church visitor in his hospital room gets the same kind of effusive praise. "That's *aw*fully nice of you. I don't see how you people do it on the little money we give you. . . . You're a wonderful woman to be doing what you're doing" (*PF*, pp. 186-87).

The father of "The Traded Car" also finds "wonderful" people in the hospital. "I love this place. There are a lot of wonderful gentlemen in here" (*PF*, p. 185). The father in "Home" finds "interesting" people with "interesting" information. "That was a very interesting man." "That was very interesting" (*PF*, p. 109). Similarly, in *The Centaur* Caldwell returns late to the hotel room to tell Peter, "I was talking to an awfully nice gentleman downstairs in the lobby" (p. 128). When an irate driver in "Home" shouts something inaudible, the father calls back, "I'm trying to understand you, mister, but I can't catch your meaning. I can't get your point." Later he complains, "That man had something to say to me and I wanted to hear what it was" (*PF*, p. 116). It's the same father who listens, in *The Centaur*, to the hitchhiker and the drunk.[4]

On one level, the constant self-deprecations and prophecies of doom are a kind of superstitious ritual—a way of hoping for their untruth by buying off the gods with verbal homage, as it were. The man who says he is sure he will miss the train is unconsciously waging war with the possibility, preparing for the worst as a way of insuring something better. But on a deeper level, closer to the thematic network of the book, George is affirming other people's importance and worth, while simultaneously attesting to his own unspecialness. This is a reversal of

Rabbit's instinctive feeling that he is special and that other people are not good enough to maintain his first-ratedness.

3. The Volvox: Altruism, Death, and Time

Many critics have already pointed out that Updike uses *The Centaur* as a kind of companion piece or perhaps a reply to the second novel. Here the volvox is the central thematic image—individuals giving up immortality and freedom to create a community:

> the volvox . . . interests us because he invented death. There is no reason intrinsic in the plasmic substance why life should ever end. Amoebas never die. . . . But the volvox . . . by pioneering this new idea of *cooperation,* rolled life into the kingdom of certain—as opposed to accidental—death. For . . . while each cell is potentially immortal, by volunteering for a specialized function within an organized society of cells, it enters a compromised environment. The strain eventually wears it out and kills it. It dies sacrificially, for the good of the whole. (p. 37)

What Rabbit feared unconsciously, Caldwell confronts openly: Involvement with people is killing him. But this fact in the volvox story becomes admirable, not demeaning.

Rabbit wanted to be first-rate, to be a star; he felt that being a team player (the equivalent of a volvox member) deprived him of this specialness. Caldwell becomes a star (literally) by accepting totally and lovingly the very thing Rabbit avoided: social involvement. In this way paradoxical problems created by Rabbit's personality and vision—needing people but rejecting them, loving people but rejecting love's responsibilities—are resolved. "In giving his life to others Caldwell entered a total freedom" (p. 220). Whereas Rabbit dreaded being mediocre, Caldwell theoretically approves of it and verbally feasts on it. "You deserved a winner," he says to Peter, "and you got a loser" (p. 116).

The third novel also reworks some thematic threads from

The Poorhouse Fair. There the humanitarians—the Conners who devote their lives to creating better social corporations—lack a vision of people's specialness because of their horizontal orientation. Although Conner may have been, in Updike's mind, a preliminary study of George, he lacks George's most prominent characteristics: his constant focus on death and his nearly neurotic concern with each individual he meets. George thus partially resolves one of the problems of the welfare state—that its providers are not true lovers but only caretakers. His sense of the mystery, the invisible meaning in the world and his consequent sense of helplessness which encourages belief in a divine Provider, have maintained his sense of people as special things. "God made man as the last best thing in His Creation" (p. 52).

However, although Caldwell theoretically admires the fact that living beings are willing to give up immortality and freedom to make a better life for each other, his sense of approaching death and his reluctance to die indicates that altruistic sacrifice of life causes great suffering for individual members. They die, he notes, because of "the strain." Moreover, the "compromised environment" which is killing each individual member makes each moment of life a constant reminder of death. Thus the death motif which characterizes the two previous novels is now given a more solid thematic perspective: life as a community member means living with the fact of one's death ever present.

The death motif in *The Centaur* is introduced at once when Caldwell is shot with the arrow. After this he carries the arrow's poison—hate—in his system; he feels it eating him away like cancer.[5] (During the three-day confinement in Alton and Olinger, Caldwell also awaits the report on X-rays which may diagnose actual cancer.) His car is a black hearse, its broken grille a mouth of jagged teeth. The school is part of the compromised environment causing his death and its lower floor is, appropriately, Hades: Each trophy in the case contains "ashes of a departed spirit" (p. 88); Heller finds seeds resembling a pomegranate's; and amid sulphurous fumes (from room 107 where chemistry is taught) the janitor harvests all the "flecks and flakes and bits and motes and whatnot that go to make up a universe" (pp. 165-66). In the school gym Caldwell sees the "living corpses" and "dead meat" of former students who return year after year to watch games. The land of the farm—a compromise for his wife—is also an image of death. "I hate nature. It reminds me of death" (p. 216). Unwilling to be dependent on a car for transportation (a necessity if they live on a farm), he feels threatened when it breaks down; in the gas station he says again, "This reminds me of death."

Such instances represent death not only because they portray the compromised environment which kills, but also because they hint that even in his sacrificial life he's a failure—a poor teacher, a poor father, and an inefficient provider. Death can be made meaningful, in the volvox world, by making good and useful contributions to the society, since this is the reason for entering into the compact. What Caldwell fears is that instead of teaching his students, for instance, he's breeding their hatred and that perhaps his own wife and child would do better without him. "My father died at forty-nine and it was the best thing he ever did for us" (p. 47). His claim of mediocrity—which is partly an affectation and partly a necessary sense of inadequacy and ordinariness—becomes double-edged: In addition to being a vent for frustration, it also invokes the possibility that he is not even performing his roles very well. It begins to appear to him that his living sacrifice is worthless and that his death would serve the community better.

However, Caldwell decides while talking to the drunk that he is not ready to die, that even "a ninety-nine year old Chinaman with tuberculosis, gonorrhea, syphilis and toothache" is not ready to die. And he recognizes his rejection of death at that moment even though the drunk is, on the mythic level, Dionysius, a symbol of resurrection, of death creating new life. (According to tradition he is buried to insure that grape vines will grow again in the spring.) The end of the book suggests that Caldwell does finally believe in his own abilities. He does not want to die physically so that he can "sustain" the joy of his family "for yet a space more" (p. 220). "I can't afford to die," he tells Hester (p. 146). And he again resolves to accept the death-in-life of the compromised environment—the farm that reminds him of death ("this paralyzed patch of thankless alien land") and the school where the students' apparent hatred is poisoning him: "He saw now that this was the mouth of a tunnel he must crawl through; the children he was committed to teach seemed in his brain's glare-struck eye, the jiggling teeth of a grinder, a multi-colored chopper" (p. 221).[6] His comment to Peter, "Kill me, that's the cure-all" and Peter's consequent dream of Sybil's parallel cry "I want to die. I want to die," are converted in the end to this second kind of death—the continual dying which sustains other life. From his motto "Kill or be killed" Caldwell has chosen the second alternative.

The recurring focus on *time,* in the novel, is a correlative to the focus on death. The fact of death is what creates time and what makes the passage of time meaningful and ominous. Caldwell's sense of this appears early when he feels time passing while Hummel removes the arrow. "His sense of time passing was working on Caldwell's bowels, making them bind. 'I got to get back,' he said. . . . A clock in his head was ticking on" (pp. 17-18). Throughout the novel this feeling of being *late* persists in Caldwell's mind. He hurries Peter to school in the morning (pp. 43-55): "Hey Cassie, tell the kid it's seven-seventeen." "Hey, Cassie: what time is it?" "We gotta move." "Jesus kid. . . . It's ten to. I'll lose my job if we don't move." During this onslaught he expresses annoyance at the maxim that "Time and tide for no man wait." He feels that since man is superior to the rest of creation he should not be subject to time. Appropriately, during this conversation he is considering the fact of his own death which he feels is drawing near. Death, of course, is what makes man subject to time.

After school that day, this *existential* lateness—the fact that for mortals time is always growing shorter—is directly connected with ordinary anxiety about being late. Peter suggests to his father that perhaps he should get out of teaching. " 'Too late. Too late,' my father said, 'Too late. Too late.' He looked at the clock and said 'Jesus, I'm not kidding—I'm late. I told Doc Appleton I'd be there at 4:30' " (p. 87). For humans it is always late; on Caldwell's creation clock death would be only a split second away.

The two clocks in George's house may suggest this frustrating aspect of time for the mortal. Kronos' clock (Grandpop's) says there is plenty of time; but the human clock (George's) says they are late. Cassie, nearly hysterical about her husband's possible death, tries to rip that human clock off the wall and stop its movement. But then, in tears, she resignedly hugs it. Zeus (Zimmerman) can tease George maliciously about being late because he himself is not subject to time; a master control in Zimmerman's office moves the clocks in the teachers' rooms.

Change and death mark the passage of time. The volvox changes constantly as individual cells die; this allows the community to continue to exist. However, this makes the fact of change and the resultant accumulation of death frightening to individual community members who see in it the image of their own approaching death. Caldwell's class in evolution makes explicit the time-change-death association by the use of the Creation Clock. The clock is meant to be a teaching aid, reducing enormous numbers of years to something more manageable ideationally. However, reducing the history of the world to three days and the history of man to one minute conjures up the disturbing realization that, in relation to the eternal cosmos, beings in the temporal world could be considered to have only a momentary existence.

The discussion of evolution, with the volvox as its central aspect, also stresses the fact that the existence of living things today—of human beings—depends upon eons of death, death of individual members and whole extinct species. George expresses his uneasiness with such a picture when he tells Diefendorf that he would just as soon not teach such a course. "Who cares about dead animals? If they're dead, let 'em lie; that's my motto. They depress the hell out of me" (p. 79). When Peter recalls visiting the Alton museum as a child, he envisions it as a place of death, "stuffed creatures" and a "noiseless mummy." Echoing Dante, he comments, "So much death; who would dream there could be such a quantity of death?" (p. 199).

The changes wrought by time are a guarantee of hope for the community but a guarantee of death for individual members. Thus, when Judy Lengel asks if *time* might be an example of an erosional agent, Caldwell feels struck. "My father looked up and seemed to have taken a blow. His skin was underbelly-white beneath his eyes and an unnatural ruddy flush scored his cheeks in distinct parallels like the marks of angry fingers" (p. 84).

Time's erosion is measured by deaths of living creatures like George.

Peter's love of art stems from the human anxiety change creates. "It sinks in upon us," he muses, "that things do, if not die, certainly change, wiggle, slide, retreat, and like dabs of sunlight on the bricks under a grape arbor on a breezy June day, shuffle out of all identity" (p. 51). Art offers, he feels, "a potential fixing of a few passing seconds." In the Alton museum art collection, which contains paintings that radiated the "hope of seizing something and holding it fast," he is fascinated by the fountain—a statue of a lady about to drink from a shell spilling water. The moment of her pause before drinking has become unending, but not being mortal she can remain contentedly expectant and patient.

4. The Vision of Love

In the community of humans heavy with their own death George is, like Hook or Rabbit, a life-giver. Like the previous two protagonists he has a sense of meaning in the world that makes people the "best thing" in creation and thus in some mysterious way suggests that they are in the protective gaze of the divine. "Don't worry about your old man, Peter," he says. "In God we trust" (p. 128). "Heaven protects the ignorant," he tells the hitchhiker. "If heaven didn't look after fools I'd be in your shoes" (p. 70). Caldwell's instinctive faith communicates to Peter, as it communicates to others he loves. When Peter tells Minor that no one believes in God, he senses "an abysmal betrayal of his father" (p. 154). He assures his mistress "It [life] was good. . . . We lived in God's sight" (p. 57).

In their book, *The Elements of John Updike*, the Hamiltons interpret the repeating images of eyes (☺ ☺) as symbolizing this "sight" of God. They refer to lines 267-73 from Hesiod's *The Works and the Days* in which Hesiod says that the eyes of Zeus see everything and will not let unrighteousness go unpunished forever (Hamilton, p. 164). However, although George feels protected by a vague divine benevolence, he is not reassured by a sense of being in God's *gaze*. When George-Chiron fails to serve Vera-Venus sexually he feels "a painful, confused sense of having displeased through ways he could not follow, the God who never rested from watching him" (p 29). This scene is followed by the scene of Zimmerman cruelly watching George's chaotic class in evolution. George likes being in school when it is empty after the snowstorm because he does not feel "like there's somebody sitting on the back of my neck all the time" (p. 207). Chiron, at the end of his story, has found no solutions and is weary of searching. He has consulted the gods and has received no answer. The eyes are drawn here to depict a watching which is sterile and unconcerned. "Must he wander forever beneath the blank gaze of the gods? 👁 👁 " (p. 219).

The symbol of the eyes is more directly related to George's own vision. It is first introduced with reference to one's own eyes, one's own vision: "Protect your 👁 👁. You won't be given another pair." George's life-giving potential comes partly from his vision of human importance and human lovableness, and from his simultaneous vision of a divine power which, as Kruppenbach saw in *Rabbit, Run*, diminishes earthly problems, the problems of individual community members like himself. Although George's ankle is desperately painful, for instance, the pain is dwarfed by the larger cosmos when he steps outdoors. "Outdoors, in the face of spatial grandeur, his pain seemed abashed. Dwarfed, it retreated to his ankle . . ." (p. 11). The pain had almost gotten up to his heart a moment before.[7]

When the students shoot the arrow, they threaten George's vision of people as lovable, as the best thing in creation, as members of a volvox-community for which he is sacrificing himself. Thus the arrow is described as "an optical defect in his lower vision"—the part of his vision that sees people. Limping to find Hummel, he first sees the sign "Protect your 👁 👁 ." The pain moves upwards and seems "to be displacing . . . his heart" (that is, the source of love). Hummel's kindness and affection remove the threat to George's vision. Later, when the students throw BB's at the teacher, Updike again uses the picture of the eyes. In order to be a life-giver, George must not lose his vision of people's worth or lovableness even in the face of what ap-

pears to be mindless malice from others. He must protect
his 👁 👁 .

The students' treatment of Caldwell contributes to a motif
of love-rejection similar to the one found in *Rabbit, Run* where
Rabbit loves "dumb" girls or "soggy" ministers. The animal imagery that often surrounds George's students and their cruel
treatment of him enhances the fact of his love for them, just as
in *Rabbit, Run* Ruth's unattractiveness makes her seem "vast" in
terms of love. The hostility from the students also recalls the
short story "Alligators" in which Updike demonstrates that what
appears to be rejection can be love in disguise. Although the
fifth-grade students in Olinger grade school appear to hate Joan
Edison, a new girl, the protagonist discovers at the end that "far
from hating her, everybody loved her" and that she was the
"queen of the class." Thus it is possible that the kind of treatment George gets from his students may be affection. Cassie tells
him, "It's not hate, George; it's love" (p. 42). And in the lunchroom, after the students have traded gently demeaning humorous
anecdotes about the teacher, they tell Peter only half-sarcastically,
"You got a great father there, Peter" (p. 95).

More puzzling is Caldwell's own version of the love-rejection
motif. Although we feel that his interest in people and his affection for them is real, he often follows praise to their face with
dismissive criticism behind their back. After calling the hitchhiker "an artist," "a man I admire," and "a gentleman," he later
tells Peter "That poor devil never knew what hit him" (p. 73).
He hints away the coming quiz to Judy Lengel and tells her
"Don't get buffaloed. After Wednesday you can forget all about
it and in no time you'll be married with six kids." When she
leaves the room, Caldwell says, "That poor femme, her father'll
have an old maid on his hands" (p. 85). To Doc Appleton,
George concludes, "You're a straight shooter and I'm grateful"
but outside he complains to Peter, "See, Peter? He didn't tell me
what I want to know. They never do. . . . That's how he keeps
his reputation" (p. 105). He compliments the gas station man
after their car breaks down. "You've told me what you think is
the truth and that's the greatest favor one man can do for another." But when they leave the station he confides to Peter,

"That poor devil didn't know what he was talking about, Peter" (p. 119). The "awfully nice gentleman" George was talking to in the lobby (p. 128) becomes in the next sentence a "bastard" who would "walk over your dead body to grab a nickel."

Such instances are not meant to cast doubt on Caldwell's basic affection for other people. Rather, they are a manifestation of his general sense of inadequacy, which he assumes other people share. His complaint in the cases above is usually that the person involved is not intelligent enough to be a success. The hitchhiker "never knew what hit him." Judy cannot pass the quiz and probably cannot even land a husband; Doc Appleton does not know enough to diagnose George's ailment; the gas station man "didn't know what he was talking about."

The important thing to note in such cases is that George usually includes himself in the denigration. Of the station attendant he admits, "I've been a bluffer all my life so I can spot another. . . . He acted just the way I feel half the time." Of Deifendorf, Caldwell tells Peter, "He's dumb, Peter. I feel sorry for him. It takes a rat to love a rat" (p. 87). And later to Foley, the other swimming coach, he complains, "He's dumb, Bud. D-U-M-B. The poor devil has no more brains than I do and I hate to bawl him out" (p. 111). Even the word "poor" which often occurs implies the sympathetic equality Caldwell feels. Most people including himself are poor devils who never knew what hit them. This view of humans forms the counterpart of George's sense that people need and have protection beyond themselves, that "heaven protects the ignorant." This gives George a remarkable double vision in which he can see simultaneously people's inadequacy (what Rabbit saw) yet love them all the more because they continue to attempt to cope as successfully as they can. The novel makes this clearer by offering a direct contrast. Zimmerman lacks this necessary sense of inadequacy, Doc Appleton says, because he "never had adversity." This makes him, even in Doc's eyes, a tumor "like a cancer": "He's not a man to trust" (p. 103).

Like the others, George's lower half "is heavily sunk in a swamp where it must eventually drown"—the same primordial swamp that Conner waits for us to drain from our brain. But his top half is "all afloat in a starry firmament of ideals." So he is able to accept human inadequacy (Rabbit's second-rate world) without feeling, as Rabbit did, that it traps and humiliates him. In fact, through volvox-sacrifice, it leads to the star status Rabbit always sought.

5.   Peter: Rabbit and His Search, Continued

Many of Rabbit's character traits appear in the third novel in the character of Peter. As Rabbit would do, Peter calls Penny "my poor dumb little girl" (p. 93), but after she promises to pray for his father, he says of her as Rabbit says of Ruth, "You're good." Peter is described as seeing other people "as an arena for self-assertion," as Rabbit clearly does. And though it has only a slight relationship with the theme in the third novel, the association between religion-sex-love that characterized *Rabbit, Run* appears in Peter's reactions. The "crucified brown skeleton" of a rose vine (a Christ image) reminds Peter of "ambrosial thoughts of undressing Vera Hummel." His love of Penny is manifested sexually, and even his love of his father can have sexual expression. Worrying about his father while sitting at the table with Penny, he slips his hand between Penny's thighs. Like Rabbit, Peter feels in sex a mysterious power, "the secret the world holds at its center" (p. 184).

Peter also prefigures the connection between sex and death which characterizes Piet, a character similar to Rabbit in many ways. Seeing Dedman's pornographic cards or touching Penny's crotch reminds him of his father's death. "Where her legs meet there is nothing. Nothing but silk and a faint dampness and a curve . . . yet even here . . . the blunt probing thought of his father's death visits him" (p. 184). Rabbit's "I'm a lover" and Ruth's parallel "You want to be married to the whole world" are re-echoed in Peter's sexual love scene with the whole city portrayed as a mythic female. Standing at the hotel window, he thinks: "Alton seemed herself already bathing in the lake of the night. . . . Her shining hair fanned on the surface of the lake. My sense of myself amplified until, lover and loved, seer and seen, I compounded in several accented expansions my ego, the city, and the future . . ." (pp. 126-27). But like Rabbit he is afraid of the personal involvement and sacrifice love demands. He is described by Penny as "so wrapped up in your own skin you have no idea how other people feel"—precisely what Ruth says of Rabbit. (It is also what Skeeter says about himself and Rabbit at the end of *Rabbit Redux*.)

Peter thus functions as a kind of thematic counterpoint to Caldwell. He hates the hitchhiker, the drunk, and the students who harass Caldwell, feeling that they are sucking the life out of his father. "Deifendorf had stolen his strength." "Deifendorf was attempting to leave, sated. He all but belched getting up from his chair" (pp. 81-82). Peter, like Rabbit, instinctively dislikes demanding emotional relationships, "He is overswept . . . by a wave of distaste for all this mediocre, fruitless, cloying involvement. Somewhere there is a city where he will be free" (p. 156).

Like Rabbit who was seeking an "opening somewhere" (the something-that-wants-me-to-find-it), Peter must find "the clue." Caldwell remarks that "the poor kid doesn't have a clue" (p. 185), and Peter feels that there is "a clue" to fastening the tire chains but he cannot figure it out. In the course of the book, several messages are given to Peter, but he cannot understand them. When he steps into Doc Appleton's office he sees a picture which he cannot interpret. The "representation seemed to contain a message for me which I did not wish to read" (p. 98). It may be a depiction of the flaying of the satyr Marsyas. Is it a warning to Peter who, like Rabbit, tends to reduce everything to the physical?

Peter feels he hears another message in the swimming pool. "Cecrops! Inachus! Da!" They are words of no language Peter knows but seem to be "answers to a question I had unknowingly asked" (p. 110).[8] When he goes to school the next morning a whirlwind speaks another "senseless word" and Johnny Dedman turns the ace of spades upside down in a suggestive way, but Peter sees nothing except "an apple with a thick black stem." The "clue" might mean a sharing of Caldwell's vision of meaningful reality and the existence of the divine—that invisible world just around the corners of our eyes which Peter senses. But, as in the second novel, the character involved in the search (as well as the reader) fails to identify the object of the quest.

The adult Peter appears, in his cynicism and modest self-deprecation, to realize that he has failed to find the clue. His life seems to be somewhat aimless and empty. As in adolescence he finds pleasure in sex and (as in each of the middle four novels) there is a long sensual description of a woman he loves. But he is "second rate" and his painting materials, he says, are "oddly worthless when transmuted into art" (p. 200). Thus he adds a touch of irony to the novel's central volvox theme. "Was it for this," he asks, "that my father gave up his life?" (Nonetheless, one feels certain that the Caldwell we know would say, "You've done a hell of a lot more than I ever did, kid; you're an artist.")

The irony of Peter's second-ratedness is part of the "Yes, but" quality of the third novel. Updike himself mentions that the book says "yes to self-sacrifice and duty, but—what of a man's private agony and dwindling?" (*PR*, p. 100). Can Caldwell's acute suffering be justified? The mythology, too, may introduce hidden qualifications. The use of mythology—both directly and indirectly—lends that invisible depth of meaning to visible reality; it allows the reader to share Caldwell's sense of helplessness in the face of strong but little-known powers; and it may represent a quality of hyperbole in Peter's affectionate memories. But, along with Peter's disappointing adult life, the myth works in a certain way against the novel's thematic impact by making obvious the element of artifice, artifice not in the area of plot or description where its use is expected and appreciated, but on the deeper level of the framework of values upon which the theme gains its degree of truth. It suggests the necessity of a certain intricately structured ideational realm without which the novel's thematic lines collapse. If, to the contrary, Caldwell's story can gather its impact apart from the mythical analogies—as it does in the short-story versions of Chapters II and VIII—then there is the possibility of a bifurcation in the conceptual materials of the work.

It may be for this reason that in the next novel, *Of the Farm,* Updike avoided, almost entirely, the elements of mythic tableaux and confined his vision to a smaller dramatic setting, sacrificing the size of his cosmos to produce a more independent, dramatically supported set of ideas.

4

Of the Farm: Psychological Considerations

1. The Character of the Mother

As *The Centaur* focused on the father, the fourth novel, *Of the Farm*, features the mother. Her character, like his, appears repeatedly in Updike's earlier fiction, although neither has made an extended appearance subsequently. (The mother in *Rabbit Redux* is recognizable but too incapacitated by illness to provide much dialog.) However, whereas George's mannerisms and brusque prose style are consistent and easily recognizable throughout Updike's fiction, the younger mother of the protagonists' adolescence—in "Pigeon Feathers," for instance—is considerably different from her older self in *Of the Farm* when she is a widow and her son middle-aged.

The younger woman of "Pigeon Feathers" shares Mrs. Robinson's feelings against working on Sundays and her sense of the farm as a person: "The land has a soul" (*PF*, p. 87). Both women sense God's presence in the land. In answer to her son's doubts of God, the short-story mother says, "But, David, you have the *evidence.* Look out the window at the sun; at the fields" (*PF*, p. 98). But she lacks the older woman's wry, sarcastic, artificially self-demeaning manner, and her assertiveness and strength. The mother in "Pigeon Feathers," *The Centaur,* and "Flight" has a pleading manner, a besieged look; she seems harassed and defeated; her prose style has a slight whining quality.

> "George, don't you read the papers? Don't you know that between the chemical fertilizers and the bug sprays we'll all be dead in ten years?" (*PF*, p. 88)

84

"You're killing *earth*worms, George!" (*PF*, p. 90)

"Your father was a disappointed *man*. Why should *you* be disappointed?" (*TC*, p. 47)

"Mother, stop hanging on my *back!* Why don't you go to *bed?*" (*PF*, p. 91)

"Pop, can't you wait until they're out of the house before you start tormenting the bread?" (*TC*, p. 56),

Yet she has already developed the skill in family drama that marks Joey's mother. Angry at her husband's attitudes toward farming, David's mother bangs a cup in the kitchen and cries, "You talked Pop into his grave and now you'll kill me. Go ahead, George, more power to you." (*PF*, p. 91).

We see her a few years later as Allen's mother in "Flight." The pitch of her whine is changing, becoming sharper. "You'll never learn, you'll stick and die in the dirt just like I'm doing. Why should you be better than your mother?" (*PF*, p. 42). And the hostility towards her son's female friends has emerged with bitter force. "Don't go with little women, Allen. It puts you too close to the ground" (*PF*, p. 51).

The short story, "A Traded Car" views the household at a time a few years prior to the setting of the fourth novel. The son is married but the father is still living, though hospitalized with chronic heart disease. In this story we seem to see the mother in transition between the younger, weaker woman and the assertive elderly widow. Blushing and embarrassed, she tells her son, visiting because of his father's illness, "Daddy says he's lost all his faith." But the son notices the authoritative way she leads him through the hospital corridors. Her coming widowhood is altering and strengthening her character. "My mother's shoulders seemed already to have received the responsible shawl of widowhood" (*PF*, p. 183). Her sarcastic humor is also beginning to develop. When her son asks about an old girl friend, she replies in mock disappointment, "Oh, dear, I thought you came all this way to see your poor old father and all you care about is seeing ——" (*PF*, p. 183). Her husband fears she will crack up the car and worries, "I don't want anything to happen to your mother." "The car, you mean," she jibes; "It's a sin, the way he worships that car" (*PF*, p. 184). By the time she appears in *Of the Farm*, her personality has matured into the tough-spoken but thin-skinned Mrs. Robinson. Forced into the man's role of head of her house and property, she has even borrowed some of her husband's personality, such as his strange self-deprecatory but bullying manner. When Joey teases her about not working on Sundays she retorts, "That's right, poke fun of an old woman's superstitions" (p. 69).

Rabbit's mother, too, although she is not the farmhouse woman of the Olinger stories, is a recognizable version of the mother figure. In *Rabbit, Run* she complains to Eccles that her son's wife tried to talk her into buying a washing machine just as Joey's mother recalls of Joan. Mrs. Angstrom betrays the younger mother's tearful sensitivity about her family but shows the older mother's facility with direct, biting insults. Of Mr. Angstrom's hopes that Nelson will imitate Rabbit's basketball success, she says, "He can't, Earl, he has those little Springer hands" (*RR*, pp. 190-91). Of Rabbit's wife, Janice, the mother says blithely, "Just to look at her you know she's two-thirds crazy" (*RR*, p. 134). Eccles, the minister, aptly describes Mrs. Angstrom in words which fit Mrs. Robinson two novels later: "Eccles realizes that this woman is a humorist. The difficulty with humorists is that they will mix what they believe with what they don't; whichever seems likelier to win an effect" (*RR*, p. 134). As Mrs. Robinson might, Rabbit's mother wryly designs a maxim about the expected roles of men and women, "It's what they keep telling you in church. Men are all heart and women are all body. I don't know who's supposed to have the brains. God, I suppose" (*RR*, p. 135).

The thematic and structural position of the mother in *Of the Farm* is much more complicated than the position of the father in his novel *The Centaur*. For, whereas Peter is a secondary focus in his father's story, lending counterpoint and some irony, Joey is much more central to his novel and the mother becomes, to a certain degree, the antagonist. When Joey returns as an adult to the setting of his adolescence, the reader is offered a kind of psychological case history—the simultaneous visions of what the child experienced and what the man has become. We never get such a view of the adult Peter.

The first three novels seem to deal primarily with the system of values pertaining to the protagonists—the role of Christian faith, the human need for importance, the need for star and team players, the inevitability of personal suffering, and so forth. But the fourth novel appears to turn its attention inward to the smaller cosmos of psychological realities. Having explored the *external* directives of human behavior—beliefs, insights, goals, ideals, and values—Updike now explores the *internal* directives —the real psychological needs and restrictions which determine how one responds to the external directives. The character of Joey's mother and the relationship between the son and the mother are revealed to have a great bearing on Joey's behavior.[1]

Thus, although the mother in *Of the Farm* is the central character of that novel because she is central to Joey's interest, Joey himself is central to the reader's interest. *She* is the focus of attention, as it were, but *he* is the focus of concern. The last line is spoken by him and the various speculations about the future concern *his* future, his freedom of action, and his possibilities for happiness. Joey and his story are formed by the mother's character, but the thematic lines have an ambivalent relationship to her. Insofar as she is a myth-maker, a special-maker like Hook, Rabbit, or Caldwell, she bears a protagonist's relationship to the theme; but insofar as her emotional relationship to Joey threatens his freedom of action, she is an antagonist. (A similar but less-severe role ambiguity appears in Skeeter of *Rabbit Redux*.)

2. The Lover as Myth-maker

Mrs. Robinson, like Hook, Rabbit, Caldwell, and Piet, believes in God and goes to church; and like them, she senses the presence of the divine in her surroundings. "I see and touch God all the time" (p. 55). To a reader familiar with Updike, this immediately suggests the possibility that she is one of the people who are able to make others feel special, who see them as important, and give them a renewed sense of their identity. The only characters in Updike's novels who keep their Christian faith in some recognizable form are these "life-givers," as Mrs. Smith calls Rabbit. The uniqueness of their belief is always made obvious: Hook's belief is counterpointed by Conner's militant atheism; Rabbit is said to be the only person at the funeral who believes the words; Peter teases his father about being "superstitious"; and Mrs. Robinson is the only one at the farmhouse who wants to go to church Sunday morning. (In *Couples* Piet's church-going is described to new-comer Foxy as "neurotic" and somewhat humorous. And in *Rabbit Redux* Skeeter's faith contrasts with the whites who, as Nelson says, do not want God to come.)

Mrs. Robinson's similarity to the other life-givers is somewhat disguised because Joey is her son and would naturally be important to her and dependent to a degree on her vision of him. And her relationship to Peggy is too much colored by hostility to be easily seen as vitalizing. Yet even in her reaction to Peggy as a threat ("She'll have me dead within a year" [p. 103]) Joey's mother awards her daughter-in-law more respect than does Joey with his patronizing and very physical affection. Her long arguments with Peggy and her tendency to allow herself direct insults evince the implicit flattery to an opponent whom one respects as an equal. If she really judged Peggy as "stupid," "not subtle," and "vulgar," she would be more polite and less honest.

Mrs. Robinson also awards this kind of respect to Richard, not in the form of insults but in the way that she treats him as an adult, pouring him coffee or suggesting that he run the tractor. "My mother," muses Joey, "has a dangerous way of treating children as equals" (p. 22). He recalls the morning that his mother gave his little two-year-old son Charlie a whack with a yardstick because the boy, as she put it, had "been giving her the eye" all morning and was putting her "to the test" (p. 22).

Joey sees these reactions to people as part of a larger vision, a religious sense of purposefulness in the universe. He describes this, with a Peter-like rejection of such belief himself: "As primitive worshippers invest the indifferent universe with pointed intentions, so my mother superstitiously read into the animate world, including infants and dogs, a richness of motive that could hardly be there . . ." (p. 22).

Although Joey verbally dismisses his mother's sense of a mythic universe, it is to that vision and to the memory of an earlier life with his mother that he returns, seeking a renewed sense of his identity and significance. Beginning a new life, attempting to relate to a new lover, he needs to reestablish his own sense of self. His mother is capable of providing identity and importance; her memory of the stories surrounding his life, along with her ability to invest these stories with drama and significance endows him with definition and stature.

After she tells Peggy about how Joey and Joan had to sell the farm's strawberries at a roadside stand, Joey thinks, "It startled me to hear how Joan and my earlier self had become part of my mother's saga of the farm" (p. 24). Her stories recall the mother in "A Traded Car" who tells her son about the night he was born. "This is like when you were born. Your father drove through a snowstorm all the way from Wheeling in our old Ford" (*PF*, p. 187). Even less-pleasant myths are restorative and aggrandizing to Joey. When his mother says she sees her son's "ruin" in Peggy's eyes, Joey notes, "*Ruin*. It pleased me to feel myself sinking, smothered, lost, forgotten, obliterated in the depths of the mistake which my mother, as if enrolling my fall in her mythology, enunciated . . ." (p. 104).[2]

This sense of the importance of things allows Joey's mother to form highly personal relationships not only with people but with other living things in her environment, apparently feeling in them that divinity and importance which the minister explains in his sermon: "Does not some glint of God's original intention shine out from the eyes of the dog, the horse, the heifer even as she is slaughtered? Has not Man, in creating civilization, looked to the animals . . . for inspiration, as in the flight of the birds and the majesty of lions?" (p. 111). Or perhaps, more properly, she approaches *everything* as if it had a soul—in contrast to the new wave of Richards, Conners, and Kens who feel that *nothing* has a soul. "The farm," she says, "is just like a person, except that it never dies, it just gets very tired" (p. 24). Richard is impressed that Mrs. Robinson "knows the names of everything," echoing the sermon's point that "language aerates the barren density of brute matter with the penetrations of the mind, of the spirit." When Richard asks about a purple flower he once saw,

Mrs. Robinson responds using a personal pronoun for the flower: "The purplest thing around here is joe-pye weed. We can look *him* up and see if he has any relatives" (p. 90). She can start the tractor (described, metaphorically, as a large animal) because she possesses an instinctive knowledge of its rhythms (Joey calls it the "prehensile tact of the mechanically blind"), again foreshadowing the minister's description that women and creatures were "turned to the same rhythms" by God's creative hand. Mrs. Robinson's relationship to the things around her is one of love; Joey notes, "My mother's method when she mowed was to embrace the field . . . I imitated war, she love" (p. 47). This is not just the love resulting from possession, but the love resulting from knowledge and appreciation.

Joey inherits to a degree his mother's ability to establish a personal relationship to the surroundings. He envisions the tractor as a mule and sees the butterflies and earth as a "mute concubine" and "her giant lover." Whereas Richard can only approach the science-fiction stories from an objective, scientific viewpoint, Joey is able to identify personally with their descriptions. Richard wants to explain that the end of one story depends upon the changing positions of the stars: "Some day Arcturus will be the North Star." But Joey wants to personalize the story. "Richard, do you ever at night, just before dropping off, feel yourself terribly huge? . . . Well, that's how that man must have felt lying there in the water dying, don't you think?" (p. 44).

Joey also inherits some of his mother's love for the farm, partly because he sees it through her eyes and partly because he can find in it a reservoir of the myths of his earlier life; it is a place to identify himself and feel significant. The objects on the farm are rich in memories and personal to him for that reason. The privet bush near the house bears a split which contains a story.

> A Mennonite dairy farmer rented our meadow for a small herd that included this rust-colored bull. . . . He pranced up into our yard, snorted, attacked the little round bright green bush. . . . Flapping the apron and speaking to him . . . my grandmother—the rest of us cowering and shouting in the kitchen—protected the bit of privet, a transplant from

her beloved Olinger yard, until the Mennonite's hired hands arrived with ropes. (p. 16)

Pictures of the younger Joey are everywhere. His book collection remains untouched in his room. "Nothing's been moved," his mother assures him. The lamp Richard reads by is the one his father would "sleep directly under while it burned" (p. 25). "Things lasted forever here," Joey notices. There is a "rhomboid of sun" on the kitchen floor just as it had been "twenty years ago, morning after morning" (p. 31). The rock Joey scrapes with the cutter is the big one his father hit when he mowed. "That big one. Daddy always took a piece out of it" (p. 49). And so as his mother finds comfort from the presence of the divine in the land, Joey derives comfort from its ability to conquer time like Peter's art work in *The Centaur;* it preserves the stories and objects which attest to his special existence.

This aspect of the land is enlarged upon in the short story "The Family Meadow." Generation after generation the family holds reunions in the meadow. The permanence of the meadow seems counterpart to the permanence of the family; though children continue to be added, the old ones like Aunt Eula, mummified and shrivelled, keep returning. With the meadow, it seems, they could exist forever. "When they tap their quoits together decades fall away" (*MS,* p. 175). They take photographs which (like the ones in *Of the Farm*) freeze time and promise to ignore change. But just as the end of the farm is predicted by Joey's inability to care for it and his possible need for the income it would bring, the demise of the family meadow is also near. Encroaching housing has polluted the creek. The young people no longer feel at ease on the meadow, thinking instead of luncheonettes. When Uncle Jesse takes the group picture, he cannot keep the new ranchhouses out of camera range. "Sell," they say, "sell." Joey's mother feels the same mounting pressures to sell. "The vultures are gathering," she tells Joey (p. 30).

The value and importance of the meadow or the farm is made obvious by the approach of its destruction; and the satisfaction of possessing it is increased. Its preservation of a family's heritage and its attractiveness to other people give it value: "Land is cheap until people make something of it" (*OTF,* p.

56). This lends stature to those who possess it. Possession, in fact, is in itself an important form of comfort. The sermon describes man as the caretaker of the beasts, of the fields and, to an extent, of his woman. In both Joey and his mother this protector-ship has developed into a fierce possessiveness. In Updike's earlier novels, too, the special care that the life-givers feel for the per-sons they love often includes possessiveness. Watching Ruth swim in *Rabbit, Run*, Rabbit thinks, "The solid sight swells his heart with pride, makes him harden all over with a chill clench of ownership. His, she is his" (*RR*, p. 120). The first paragraph, Joey driving into the farm, is marked by possessive pronouns: "Our barn," "ours," "his land . . . our land." "You own both sides of the road?" Richard asks. "Oh sure, originally Schoelkopf's farm was part of ours," Joey proudly replies. "It's probably the biggest piece of open land left this close to Alton."

Joey's possessiveness is exhibited to a greater degree for his wife, Peggy. Possessing her lends him the stature which pos-session of the farm lends his mother. Each exhibits their posses-sion with pride. While his mother describes the farm, Joey watches his wife sleeping in the chair. "She overflowed the chair, and I felt proud before my mother, as if, while she were talking of the farm, I were silently displaying to her my own demesne seized from the world" (p. 30). Peggy herself recognizes Joey's possessiveness about herself and the farm. "You like it in the same way you like me. It's something big you can show off" (p. 91). In fact, she may earlier have used his love of proprietorship to encourage his affection. He recalls her saying, "You act as though you own me. It's wonderful" (p. 63). As the descriptive imagery surrounding Peggy makes clear, she is his farm. "My wife is wide, wide-hipped and long-waisted, and surveyed from above, gives an impression of terrain, of a wealth whose ownership imposes upon my own body a sweet strain of extension" (p. 39).

The mother's possessiveness about the farm is first chronicled in "Pigeon Feathers" which records her desperate wish to buy it even though her husband hated it because it reminded him of death. Her need to own the farm may even have hastened his death because of the emotional and practical burdens it created. Joey's mother is also possessive about her son. She associates the two emotions, claiming that she wanted to move back to the farm for Joey's sake: "You were becoming something very tame before I brought us back to the farm. That's why I did it" (p. 115). In a certain sense, then, she sacrificed her husband for her son; and in an indirect way she wants the reciprocal sacrifice from Joey: the recognition and admission that Peggy is not competition for her.

3. Oedipal Conflicts

In one way or another Updike's first five novels all chart the lives and problems of protagonists with the vision that makes special, the love that gives life. But in the fourth novel a paradoxical situation is explored: Because it is a mother who bears such a relationship to her son, his love and need for her (which is analogous, on one level, to the love and need people in the other novels feel for the protagonist) seriously restricts his life at the same time that it promises to vitalize it. In creating a form of Oedipal conflict, the son's love for his mother prevents his forming adult and life-giving relationships with other women. Like Paul in Lawrence's *Sons and Lovers*, Joey has already given up the intellectual woman for the purely sexual one, and the novel leaves uncertain whether Peggy will be any more successful in satisfying Joey than Clara was with Paul Morel.

The mother's jealousy towards her son's girl friends, which is like the jealousy shown by Paul's mother, first appears in "Flight." The mother sees her son with Molly Bingham and insults her. When her son tries to ward off her criticism, the mother turns to the father and creates an implied choice between the girl and herself: "You see, Victor," she says to her husband, "he defends her. When I was his age that girl's mother gave me a cut I'm still bleeding from, and my own son attacks me on behalf of her fat little daughter" (*PF*, p. 51). When Allen continues to date Molly, the mother cries and creates scenes. Allen recalls, "I've never seen so many tears as I saw that winter." She waits up for his return from a date to ask, "Well, how was little hot-pants?" (*PF*, p. 55).

It is clear that Joey's mother did not like his first wife and Joey accuses her of poisoning his first marriage. "Why did you dislike Joan so much? In the end you made me dislike her" (p. 102). Her hostility towards the second wife was first manifested at the wedding when Joey found her cool and angry. Her first words to Peggy, during the visit, are polite barbs, "Oh, I didn't *mean* that Peggy looked tired. I've never seen Peggy look anything but cheerful" (p. 15). During their first chat at the kitchen table, the mother talks about earlier days when Joey was married to Joan—a subtle dismissal of the second wife.

By suppertime, Joey himself is beginning to dismiss Peggy and focus his attention wholly on his mother. Peggy seems to him "dense" when she does not understand his mother's remark about the grandfather being "a pretty ugly customer"; and as his mother talks Joey becomes more and more deeply engrossed in her myths of the farm and his own history. It offends him when, after supper, his mother "docilely" carries dishes to Peggy who has the "dominant" position at the sink.

When Peggy falls asleep, Joey carries her up to bed. But his mother does not say good night to him "as if I were certain to return." Seizing the role of lover, the mother expects her son to come back down and be with her alone—the way young lovers wait for their parents to retire and leave them alone. When Joey returns she is ready for bed, her hair down and, he notices, one strap of her nightgown awry. She uses her illness to elicit feeling from him. "I think I've overindulged." "Do you feel funny?" "Queerly, as Pop would have put it" (p. 34). After this maneuver, she casually gives tacit permission for him to have sex with his wife, deftly paralleling it with kindness to the animals, "Don't worry yourself, just give the dogs their water and take your wife to bed" (p. 34).

When Joey returns from feeding the dogs, the mother viciously insults Peggy, saying she does not seem bright. "I'm surprised at you . . . that you would need a stupid woman to give you confidence" (p. 36). Yet even after this, Joey has to control an urge "to keep myself from conspiring with her." The ensuing sex with his wife is only implied by oblique metaphors.

When Joey awakes the next morning he adopts the role of his father, wearing his pants and shaving with his razor. "Its angle scraped and burned and, just as my father had always done, I nicked the curve of my jawbone" (p. 41). In coming to mow for his mother, he has taken the role of her husband.

When Joey enters the kitchen, the three others are already seated; but he only has eyes for his mother. "Something in the deliberate way she was holding the cup eclipsed the others for me . . ." (p. 42). Peggy looks provocative in shorts and pigtails, but Joey only wonders if "my mother found the hairdo presumptuous or too assertive or condescending." His mother did not sleep well and perhaps inadvertently elicits Joey's guilt about sex with Peggy by saying, "Everything wakes me now. Even your bed seemed noisy to me last night" (p. 43).

From atop the tractor, later that morning, Joey watches both women walk away from him and feels masculine pride about them both. "I noted with pride that both women were tall." Yet his mother's disapproval of his wife and her greater hold on Joey begin to tell in his feelings for Peggy. He learns that Peggy's ex-husband slept with her after the divorce and begins to see "a whorish little twitch in her hips." Beginning to believe that McCabe was glad to get rid of her, that he had wanted the divorce, Joey feels deceived and trapped.

Mrs. Robinson's treatment of Richard, in addition to being flattering and respectful of him as a person, may also be motivated somewhat by jealousy. She attempts to win Richard over by suggesting that he ride the tractor when she already knows that Peggy is opposed to it. "Let the boy take a few turns. . . . If he can ride a bicycle in New York traffic he can do this. . . . How can Richard manage my people sanctuary if he can't drive a tractor?" (p. 70). Peggy, sensing what is taking place, disarms the attempt by making it obvious. "He's not going to manage anything for you. He's not going to be another Joey." (Joey considers this a "ruthless and needlesss" response.) Her maneuver exposed, Mrs. Robinson retreats. "Dear Peggy, one Joey is enough for me."

The ensuing two scenes are effectively juxtaposed. In the first, Joey accuses Peggy of being whorish. He objects to her sleeping with McCabe after the divorce; and to her question "Don't you feel that I love you?" he replies, "I feel you as a loving woman and I happen to be next to you in bed" (p. 72).

In the second scene he and his mother sit together shelling peas and talk about his (their) children. Peggy becomes an outsider and knows it. "Please don't talk about the children as a way of getting at me," she says. "It's too hard on Joey" (p. 79).

Later when Peggy and Richard play Parchesi in the living room, Joey tries hard to hear his mother's motions in the kitchen instead. "I wanted to hush the rattle of the dice and the click of the counters . . . my mother's sullen clattering in the kitchen seemed a monolog I must listen to instead" (p. 86). To assure herself primary attention in Joey's thoughts, Mrs. Robinson throws a tantrum; she smashes two plates and cries "in a semblance of agony"—"What's this whispering?" Peggy rises to the competition, "You're throwing a sulk and worrying your son." She understands how Mrs. Robinson can use her moods on Joey. Earlier she remarks, "She turns it on and off, she uses her temper as a weapon" (p. 57). When Peggy leaves in a huff to begin packing, it is Richard who goes to mollify her. Joey remains with his mother, talking. When Richard returns, they pull apart "guiltily."

The second evening the two women argue about men while Joey, in retreat with a book, only watches from the sidelines. But when Peggy gets sleepy and goes upstairs, he again remains downstairs alone with his mother to talk. They wait until Peggy leaves the bathroom and is out of earshot. Then the mother calls Peggy "vulgar" and "not subtle" and eventually gets Joey to agree with her. " 'She *is* stupid.' I am always a little behind my mother, always arriving at the point from which she has departed. She smiled, seeing me sitting upright, excited like a boy by my discovery of the obvious. 'Remarkably stupid' " (p. 104).

But even though she has his betrayal of Peggy, the mother remains a mother and cannot assume the position of lover. She changes the subject to her own approaching death. Joey reacts with jealousy. "I was angry at the ease with which she had accepted my betrayal of Peggy, had absorbed it . . . devoting her innermost thought not to me but to her farm" (p. 105). Her ensuing conversation is perceived by Joey to be "one of those sharp withdrawals by which she kept me in the end at a son's distance." He goes upstairs to Peggy but refuses her offer of sex, still meditating on what he considers her promiscuity. "So you laid for a Yalie. I'll be damned."

In the closing scene, Joey rewards his mother's nominal acceptance of Peggy; Mrs. Robinson tells Peggy, "I'd like you to go and have your picture taken for me." Joey responds by agreeing to become a sharer with his mother in the farm: "*Your* farm? I've always thought of it as our farm."

The supposed behavioral manifestations of the Oedipal complex are familiar enough that they need no repeating here. But it is interesting to note that the protagonists in many of the short stories, as well as in novels like *Rabbit, Run, Of the Farm,* and *Couples,* seem to see themselves as low in some kind of sexual power structure. All must woo the wife or lover, must make polite requests for sexual favors, must expect the possibility of being turned down, and once received must seek to please the other to show their gratitude. A general relationship of little boy and mother is recognizable. Although Peggy is generous with sex, it seems clear that she largely controls their sex life. She can encourage ("Shall I do anything?") or dismiss ("You smell like hay. You'd make me sneeze"). When Richard offers to act as peacemaker between his mother and Mrs. Robinson, Joey is jealous of his little-boy identity. "I wanted to go to her myself and was jealous. More precisely, I wanted to be his size and go to her" (p. 88).

Joey can conjure up an early memory of his mother as a young, slim woman. The memory is sensual and describes her as a lover: "I seemed to be in bed and a tall girl stood above me, and her hair came loose from her shoulder and fell forward filling the air with a swift liquid motion, and hung there, as a wing edged with light, and enclosed me in a tent as she bent to deliver her goodnight kiss" (p. 94). Appropriately his dream about Peggy makes her into his mother, himself a little boy:

I was home on the farm. I stood at the front of the house looking up over the grape arbor . . . at the bedroom windows like a small boy, too shy to knock at the door, come to call on a playmate. Her face appeared in the window, misted by the screen. Peggy was wearing, the straps a little awry on

> her shoulders, a loose orange nightie . . . she was so happy
> here . . . so in love with the farm and so eager to redeem
> with the sun of her presence, the years of dismal hours I
> had spent here. (p. 40)

The woman in the farmhouse with the loose nightgown straps
who looks down at the little boy and wants forgiveness for the
hours of boredom is Joey's mother, not Peggy. The similar roles
of the two women, as mother-lovers, is demonstrated in their
final mutual approval: "He's a good boy," says Joey's mother;
"He *is* a good boy," agrees Peggy (p. 127).

Since a mother cannot give sex to her son, men like Joey
forever feel defeated in the sexual power struggle and their relations with women are complicated by an exaggerated sense of
the female's sexual power. Little boys like Richard and scientific,
impersonal men like Ken of *Couples* (and possibly McCabe)
have a power over themselves and their women which hyper-
sensitive men like Joey lack. Joey cannot outgrow his original
sexual put-down by his mother. Of that young mother outsprint-
ing the father to the barn, he complains, "I had felt this woman
within her and had felt she withheld her from me as punishment" (p. 122). The resulting view of sex as the woman's approval and reward is clearly seen in Rabbit, Joey, Piet, and
several men in the short stories. Oddly, however, Updike seems
to admire the hypersensitivity in these men which makes them
subject to a woman's sexuality. Men without it—the McCabes,
Conners, Richards, Kens, and Eccles—although they seem conspicuously well-adjusted and content, are presented as something
less than human, scientific hybrids of a sterile age.[3]

Joey's inability to be an adult male is made worse by his
return to the farm. The identity which the farm's timelessness
preserves is his little-boy identity. He is again reduced to performing chores for his mother while the women assume the tasks
of proprietorship—cooking, cleaning, and surveying the grounds.
During their arguments, he remains respectfully and humbly
silent, like a well-trained child. Although at the beginning of
the book his mother does not know what to call him ("She
studied me, still searching for my name."), by the end even
Richard calls him "Joey." Therefore, although the farm appears

to offer him life and vitality, he can gain a necessary freedom only when the farm and his mother cease to be part of his life. Like the man struggling to get to the sea, his mother's death will be the source of new life.

The co-existence of life and death sources is a repeating thematic concern in Updike's novels. Rabbit is both a life-bringer and a death-bringer. Caldwell, although he vitalizes his environment, also conspicuously brings the fact of his own death wherever he goes. Piet in *Couples* brings life to Foxy but death to her unborn child, just as the greenhouse, the symbol of life, reminds Piet of funerals. Skeeter's life-giving vitality in *Rabbit Redux* sacrifices Jill's life. Similarly, Joey's relationship to his mother may be life-giving, but it is also existentially stifling and confronts him with her approaching death.

The mother as simultaneously figuring life and death is referred to obliquely in *Rabbit, Run*. Rabbit has an anxiety fantasy that the woman who gave life could take it away: ". . . he began in her stomach and if she gave him life she can take it away" (*RR*, p. 239). Piet, although he pictures his mother planting growing things in the greenhouse, is obsessed by the fact of her violent death in a car accident, seeing in it a symbol of his own death. In *Rabbit Redux*, the dying mother becomes a symbol of the ebbing cultural vitality—both are central life sources whose loss is imminent. Similarly, Joey experiences a brief death fantasy involving his mother. During a silence in the conversation he feels "her soul plunged backwards from her eyes and mouth and revisited the darkness in which but for her grace, I would be buried unborn" (p. 28). The mother's obvious approaching death intensifies the threat. Joey appreciates a moment of laughter because it relieves "the darkness that had come upon her since her health had weakened. Her spirit had acquired a troubling resonance, a murky subtlety doubly oppressive out of doors" (p. 16). Returning to the farm, then, becomes for Joey a confrontation with death as well as life.

The farm as a place of death becomes a central imagistic motif in the book, echoing the father's impression of it in "Pigeon Feathers" and *The Centaur* as well as *Of the Farm* ("I hate nature. It reminds me of death.") Joey feels that his mother permeates the land of her farm. "In being surrounded by her farm we had been plunged into the very territory of her thoughts" (p. 16). The mother keeps the things of the farm alive; her death seems to invoke the fact of their death, too. As she lies sleeping after her heart attack Joey feels "a thousand such details of nurture about to sink into the earth with her." Her death seems to him "a defect she had overlooked in purchasing these acres, a negligible flaw grown huge" (p. 122).

On the farm the presence of Joey's dead father is also especially vivid to Joey. "I listened for his footstep to scuff on the porch. . . . It did not seem incredible that he would walk into the living room. . . . But he did not; the four of us were alone" (pp. 17-18). Waiting for the doctor to answer the telephone, Joey studies the barn, noticing that the overhang has been removed. The barn's appearance "had something dreadful about it, and it came to me that the barn had been my parents, and my father was gone" (p. 120). The missing overhang, like the missing father, admits a vision of death to the surroundings. "Where the overhang had been I could look through to a . . . stand of sumac with a few leaves prematurely turned red, as if individually poisoned, and there was no answer." The closing four words refer on one level to the ringing telephone, but are an example of a trick with language Updike frequently uses. There is no answer explaining death, either. Caldwell's response to the farm ("This reminds me of death.") seems repeated in his son.

The novel introduces one other element of death which is developed further in *Couples:* the connection between death and sex. When Joey's mother cries that her death is almost upon her, Joey's throat engorges "as if I had surprised my parents in coitus." And when she has her attack in the car her gasps "parted her lips as if alert to be kissed," foreshadowing Freddy's concept of death in *Couples* as a giant lover, "Big Man Death."

Paradoxically, the sermon suggests that sex comforts the anxiety wrought by death. Man can turn towards woman's warmth "wherein his tensions find *re*solution in *dis*solution" (p. 112). Motherhood, he says, "answers concretely what men would answer abstractly"—the very name *Eve* means *life.* Allen in "Flight" seeks comfort from Molly after being badly beaten in a debate tourney. "For the first time on that ride home, I felt what it was to bury a humiliation in the body of a woman" (*PF,*

p. 50). Peter in *The Centaur* thinks of his father's illness and possible death on two occasions while stroking Penny. And for the men in *Couples* (excluding Piet), sex lends a feeling of immortality. "A bed," says Foxy's riddle, "is bigger than mortality." Joey, returning to the house in which his mother may be dying, strokes Peggy's back and crotch. "I touched first the damp base of her neck and followed her spine with my fingers and went beyond to where the curve curved under into the crotch of her pants. I felt this long living line as a description of grief . . ." (p. 119).

The sermon divides men into two separate halves—a death-seeing half and a sexual half—and in that sense it may oversimplify. It would appear, rather, that man's need for sex is directly related to his vision of death. It may be Rabbit's fear of death, for example, that makes him so sexually active; in *Rabbit, Run* he parallels sex, at one point, to church-going. When Harold makes love to Janet in *Couples*, he feels as if "a glowing tumor of eternal life were consuming the cells of his mortality." And clearly, by coupling with an Angel, Piet is also seeking to escape death. Especially for men like Joey whose mother relationship inhibits intellectual masculinity (that is, their ability to relate to women intellectually, their power as an adult male person, not just a male body)—sex provides for these men a reassuring situation, offering a sense of competence, of at least physical masculinity, and of importance. The approval that sex implies to them militates against death in the same way that the intricacy of the pigeon feathers reassured David of his immortality: It promotes a feeling of being valuable.

4. The Possession of Abundance

Joey's mother also turns to a lover to assuage the fears of death: She turns to the farm, her "giant lover" as Peggy calls it. Like her husband, the George of *The Centaur*, she feels her death approaching—from heart trouble, and from Peggy: "That woman. She's fierce. She'll have me dead within the year" (p. 103). When she has an attack in the car she cries, "Get me onto my land." Her land gives her a place to "touch God" just as sex invokes a sense of divine love for the men in *Rabbit, Run* and *Couples*. Paradoxically, the source of Mrs. Robinson's comfort, the farm, reminds Joey of death—just as his source of comfort, Peggy, signifies death to his mother. Their reciprocal agreement at the end is to accept the death images they fear in order to continue to have each other: Joey must accept the farm to have his mother; she must accept Peggy to have her son. Again, the sources of life also bring death.

Mrs. Robinson's love and need for the farm is never fully explained, except insofar as it is a place where God's presence is evident. The farm's ability, like the meadow's, to conquer time and preserve the elements of one's own special myths is never shown to be as important to her as it is to Joey (or as it would be to Peter of *The Centaur* who fears things losing their identity). But, like her, the David of "Pigeon Feathers" also finds comfort against death on the farm and since his story is more fully explained it can, perhaps, offer suggestions about her feelings, too. When he looks at the dog's intricately colored hairs, or sees the pigeons' unbelievably complicated color patterns, which decorate every tiny feather, David suddenly feels that a God with such an abundance of skill, such generosity in His creation, and such infinite love would not kill.

> The feathers were more wonderful than dog's hair, for each filament was shaped within the shape of the feather, and the feathers in turn were trimmed to fit a pattern that flowed without error across the bird's body. . . . And across the surface of the infinitely adjusted yet somehow effortless mechanics of the feathers played idle designs of color, no two alike, designs executed, it seemed, in a controlled rapture, with a joy that hung level in the air above and behind him. . . . [W]ith a feminine slipping sensation along his nerves that seemed to give the air hands, he was robed in this certainty: that the God who had lavished such craft upon these worthless birds would not destroy His whole Creation by refusing to let David live forever. (*PF*, p. 105)

Peter gets a similar feeling in *The Centaur* when he watches the complex patterns of millions of tiny snowflakes and their shadows. He seems near some great truth. "It fascinates him; he feels the universe in all its plastic and endlessly variable beauty pinned, stretched, crucified like a butterfly upon a frame of unvarying geometrical truth" (*TC*, p. 191). When Joey watches the patterns of rain on a window, he gets this same sense of divine benevolence, and he becomes a child of God. "Its panes were strewn with drops that as if by amoebic decision would abruptly emerge and break and jerkily run downward, and the window screen . . . was inlaid erratically with minute, translucent tesserae of rain. A physical sense of ulterior mercy overswept me . . . I went into the living room, in search of other children" (p. 80).

What is felt here is abundance—countless tiny structures, limitless creations which suggest a magnanimous creator. It is the farm's *size* that Joey first brags about in the opening description. "The acres," he says, "flowed outward from me like a foam of boasting" (p. 10). What the mother fears for the farm is not so much that Joey will have to sell it, but that he will have to cut it up into sections. She even offers a compromise: "You could sell the small flat field off in half-acres, I guess my ghost could put up with that, and use the money to keep the rest intact" (p. 30). She wants to preserve this elemental evidence of divine magnitude. Thus Mrs. Robinson's vision of the importance of living things on her farm—their reflection of "divine intention"—and her appreciation of their *abundance* convinces her, as it convinced David, of her own value and her consequent claim on the Creator's generosity in giving life.

Although Joey is losing his mother's instinctive faith, he still shares her need for this abundance, as shown in his fascination with the rain and the size of the farm. In Peggy, the death-diminishing comfort of sex and of abundance come together. Moreover, Peggy skirts the potential obstacle of his Oedipal emotions because Joey envisions Peggy as land—which his mother loves and which he is therefore permitted to love, too. Joey's first description of Peggy notes the "pelvic amplitude" the "sense of space between her thighs." He develops this more fully in the metaphorical love scene that night. "My wife is wide, wide-hipped and long waisted, and surveyed from above gives an impression of terrain . . . entered she yields a variety of landscapes,

seeming now a snowy rolling perspective . . . now a taut vista of
mesas . . . now a gray French castle complexly fitted to a steep
green hill . . . now something like Antarctica; and then a receding valleyland . . ." (p. 39). Mowing gives Joey an erection which
he "idly permitted to stand" imaginatively transferring it to
Peggy, "My wife is a field." Later the clouds also seem to take on
the shape of her body. "A luminous forearm seemed laid in sleep
across a distorted breast" (p. 63). The mother confirms Joey's
semiconscious analogy between Peggy and the farm: "You've
bought an expensive piece of property," she warns (p. 103). Both
mother and son are proud that other people covet their property.
"The vultures are gathering." the mother says, referring to eager
buyers. And Joey admits that one of the forces leading him into
marriage was the feeling that everyone wanted Peggy: "I . . .
felt the world to be full of resolute men who . . . would carry
her off forever" (p. 85). Peggy is aware of these feelings too.
"You like it [the farm]," she tells Joey, "the same way you like
me. It's something big you can show off" (p. 91).

The sense of sadness in the book is parallel to the sense of
sadness at the end of *Couples* when Piet, like Joey, exchanges
an intellectual and difficult relationship for a simpler more sexual
one: Angela is relinquished for Foxy as Joan is relinquished for
Peggy. With Foxy, Piet stops fleeing death, just as Joey finds
in Peggy's spaciousness the comfort against death which he could
not find in Joan: "I felt in danger of smothering in her," he says
of Joan (p. 39). Death dismissed, the question of God's existence
"ceases to be a problem" as it similarly ceases to be for Piet.
Nevertheless, the divorce was *a fall:* "I had the sense of falling,
of collapsing, at last, into the firm depths" (p. 14). He still loves
Joan, his "true," his "inner" wife. "It was a mistake," he tells his
mother, referring to the divorce. Joan "was what my life had
been directed to go through. In leaving her I put my life out of
joint" (p. 102).

Joey's mother feels that what he loves is the "poet" he could
have become with Joan but can never become with Peggy. "With
Joan you still had the space to be a poet" (p. 103). When man
finds a way to stop grappling with the problem of death he loses
two of Caldwell's marks of man: death-foreseeing and tragic. Piet,
too, stops being an architectural artist when he marries Foxy

and only works with army prefabs; he has lost the space to be a poet because he has found, in Foxy, as Joey has found in Peggy, a comfort against death.

The word "space" seems to echo the Sartre epigraph on freedom.

> Consequently, when, in all honesty, I've recognized that man is a being in whom existence precedes essence, that he is a free being who, in various circumstances, can want only his freedom, I have at the same time recognized that I can want only the freedom of others.

Joey's freedom of action is restricted by his mother and the farm; both offer him vitality and identity, but the identity ultimately hinders his movement. Peggy may never, in her more simple maternal, sexual identity, force Joey to become a man in any other arena but the bedroom. Joan's "smothering" may ironically have offered greater freedom insofar as it did not remove the vision of death which drives men to the heights and depths of their humanity and makes them poets. And Joey's mother who now acts as the source of his life may, like the man in the story, have to die in order to give the possibility of life and freedom to her offspring. As in the case of Peter and Allen, the chance for freedom lies for Joey in the city which is urging him home at the end.

5

Couples: The Loss of the Lover's Vision

PART I. THE PROTAGONISTS END THEIR STRUGGLE

1. Piet as Composite Protagonist

Updike's fifth novel, *Couples,* bears the same relationship to the previous four novels that novels like *Rabbit, Run* and *The Centaur* bear to several short stories which precede them: the later works are an elaboration, intensification, and expansion of themes and characters exercised and aired first in the shorter works. Rabbit first appears as Ace Anderson in "Ace in the Hole." George Caldwell can be recognized as a major or minor character in several previous pieces, including the *New Yorker* short stories which became part of the novel itself.

Similarly, the character of Piet may be recognizable as the father in the short story "Music School"; but more importantly he is an older, wiser Rabbit, and a more mature but also more troubled Joey. Like Hook, Piet has a need for prayer and a love of fine carpentry. Like Rabbit, he uses sex for love and communication and needs it for a sense of importance. Like Caldwell, he brings to the story a sense of all-encompassing death. Like Joey, he demonstrates an unresolved mother relationship and the consequent need to leave the challenging woman for the simpler one. And, like all the protagonists, his unique faith in a Christian God is correlated with a life-giving but death-fearing vision.

Piet's story, unlike most of the previous narratives, ends with a situation that is static but difficult to evaluate. Thematically, the journey of the protagonists is brought to a rest. Unlike Hook

106

who still searches for the message, or Rabbit who is "still fighting," or Joey who is still left to struggle with his mother's death, for Piet the struggle is ended; and this ends, too, the identity of "protagonist"—literally, *one who struggles*. He has lost the fears of death and ordinariness which have harassed the major characters throughout the novels and has accepted a comfortable, unspecial life with Foxy as just "another couple." His satisfaction, Updike has explained, marks his loss of tragic status and, consequently, his loss of human status, too. "A person who has what he wants, a satisfied person, a content person, ceases to be a person. Unfallen Adam is an ape" (*PR*, p. 101).

The impression that Updike intended his fifth novel to provide a culminating, comprehensive view of his previously worked materials is strengthened by the completeness with which Piet portrays the characteristics of his fictional predecessors. Hook's description that prayer makes him feel as if he's in a "warm blanket" is recast into *Couples'* recurring hamster image; Piet thinks, "When it [prayer] worked, he seemed, for intermittent moments, to be in the farthest corner of a deep burrow, a small endearing hairy animal curled up as if to hibernate" (p. 23). Piet also shares the need of the old people in the poorhouse to believe in a life hereafter. Depressed by a day seemingly full of death, Piet is cheered by the sight of the Protestant cemetery, a testament of people's trust in an afterlife. "Order reigned," he thinks (p. 89). The world is made orderly if man is immortal. Similarly the operator of the bulldozer unknowingly cheers Piet again when he suggests that he fears human ghosts:

> "What do you do when you see them [bones]?"
> "Man, I keep movin'." (p. 93)

Piet tries to soothe Nancy by explaining to her that her soul will not die but go to heaven; and he feels, as does Hook, the enormity of death of any kind—hamsters, birds, or people. Hook's chilling memory of the death of the flying squirrel (see p. 22, this text) is matched by Piet's recollection of the dying robin, struggling to fly: "The children, bored by the bird's poor attempts to become a miracle, wandered away. So only Piet, standing helpless . . . witnessed the final effort, an asymmetric splaying of the dusty wings and a heave that drove the robin's beak straight down into the sweetish shadowy grass. The bird emitted a minute high cry, a point of noise as small as a star, and relaxed. Only Piet had heard this utterance" (p. 86).

Conner becomes Ken in *Couples*—well-intentioned, hard-working, self-righteous and moralistic, scientific, emotionally sterile, and unimpressed with death. He is the new wave predicted in *The Poorhouse Fair;* as Foxy says, "The future belongs to him" (p. 449). On the day Piet is upset by the hamster's death, Ken views in his lab a whole tray of upturned gutted mice, and hearing of Piet's sadness wonders "how some men still could permit themselves so much sentiment" (p. 109). His expectations of other people are a logical extension of his own austere morality; like Conner he is unable to understand illogical human needs or ingratitude. He doubts a rumor of a colleague's broken marriage because "how could any woman leave so good a man?" (p. 105) and thus forecasts his own dismay when Foxy betrays him. His atheism, asexuality, and corresponding scientific sterility form a counterpoint to Piet as Conner formed a counterpoint to Hook.

Piet also displays Hook's admiration for the old craftsmen, seeing, in their dedication to quality, evidence of some basic human morality which separates men from animals. Piet calls the carpentry specifications "ethical" and feels, watching the meticulous labors of the old carpenters, Adams and Comeau, "as if he had been handed a flower" (p. 94). Hook liked to recall that carpentry was Jesus' profession, but God Himself seems to Piet to be a carpenter Who "nails His joists of judgment down firm, and roofs the universe with order" (p. 418). Piet loves looking at the workmanship in the Congregational Church:

> Alabaster effects had been skillfully mimicked in wood. Graceful round vaults culminated in a hung plaster ceiling. A balcony with Doric fluting vertically scoring the parapet jutted as if weightless along the sides of the sanctuary and from under the painted Victorian organ in the rear. The joinery of the old box pews was still admirable. Piet seldom entered the church without reflecting that the carpenters who had built it were dead and that none of their quality had been born to replace them. (p. 22)

But when the church burns down at the end it is discovered to be rotten and hollow within, as was the poorhouse wall which Hook had admired. The wall and the church, like Hook and Piet, belong to a dying era—"a miracle it had not collapsed of itself a decade ago" says Piet, referring to the church (p. 478).

The similarity of Piet to Rabbit Angstrom has already been alluded to by several critics.[1] The highly sexual orientation of the two protagonists is their most obvious similarity. Their identity as life-givers is depicted in this sexuality: It is a fertile sexuality, attractive to women; and in both cases it results, symbolically, in pregnancy. Both Rabbit and Piet feel a relationship between sex and their Christian faith. The imagery of *Rabbit, Run* associates the circular church window with other sexual circles; and Rabbit wants sex with Ruth when he sees people going to church. Piet's prayer-masturbation association also appears first in the second novel when, for example, Rabbit feels aroused by Lucy Eccles in church. In *Couples* this pattern is carried to its logical extreme: Christ's cross is X-shaped (p. 26) like Georgene's "X-shaped red cleft, wet"; and Foxy's God, Piet tells her, is between her legs. The fact of their Christian belief, moreover, is related to both protagonists' ability to love, an ability often expressed as sexual energy. Appropriately Piet defends his church-going to Angela by explaining, "It's the source of my amazing virility" (p. 12).

Eccles, the atheist-priest in *Rabbit, Run* who has replaced religion with psychology, is reincarnated as Freddy Thorne, an atheist who acts the role of priest and replaces Christianity with group therapy. Like Eccles he is asexual or bisexual, a symptom of his inability to give life. Instead of giving life Freddy, like Eccles, tries to help people accept the fact of death. The socially oriented, horizontal outlooks of both men make them, in contrast to the protagonists, depressing people who defeat their own good intentions by hinting through their atheism at people's basic insignificance. (They thus foreshadow, in a sense, the comic realm of *Bech: A Book* and the early sections of *Rabbit Redux*.)

Nevertheless, their sense of the magnitude of death and their sensitivity towards people places Eccles and Freddy thematically closer to the protagonists than is either Conner or Ken. In fact, in both *Rabbit, Run* and *Couples* it is suggested several times that the priests are alter egos of the protagonists. Both

Eccles and Rabbit comment on the similarity they see in each other; and Freddy describes feelings of brotherly love for Piet. Freddy and Piet are paired at the end of the novel by the equation that "hate and love both seek to know" (p. 417), a description which might also fit Skeeter and Rabbit in *Rabbit Redux.*

Both Piet and Rabbit have the ability to love. Rabbit's "I am a lover" and Ruth's "You love being married to everybody" are echoed by Foxy's description of Piet: "He loves us all" (p. 294). Nevertheless, both men are selfish and consequently strangely separated even from their lovers. Ruth's complaint that Rabbit cannot see outside his own skin and the masturbatory quality of his sexual relations appears again in Piet. He uses Bea sadistically to excite himself and release guilt feelings, is glad Georgene can "find her way by herself," and enjoys Foxy's oral ministrations in bed. Angela says that she feels he does everything alone. He left her most alone, she complains, when he made love to her (p. 445). Ruth's sarcastic flattery of Rabbit— "Oh, all the world loves you. What I wonder is why? . . . What's so special about *you?*"—becomes Georgene's argument: "What's so special about you? What makes you such a playboy? You don't even have any money" (p. 199). Rabbit carelessly abandons Ruth when the situation seems to warrant it, telling his mother, "She can take care of herself." Piet also believes this about Georgene, even though she pleads for his return. "Piet had tested her strength before and knew she could withstand all pressure of grief" (p. 256).

George Caldwell's preoccupation with death, the focus of the third novel, is also the central characteristic of Piet, and a major focus of his novel. The fifth novel's more extreme viewpoint sees all living things as symbols of death. Caldwell's vision of death-in-life is framed, in *The Centaur,* into the volvox image where life in a society equals death for the individual. Piet's obsession is explained by the fact of his dead mother, simultaneously the symbol of life and meaningless unpredictable swift death. Both novels encapsule this thematic element in the photosynthesis-respiration equation: $C_6H_{12}O_6 + 6O_2 = 6CO_2 + 6H_2O + E$. Growth and decay are equivalent. Caldwell teaches it in class; Ken meditates in his lab on the "lone reaction . . . that reverses decomposition and death" (p. 10). Freddy, too, knows from his medical school training that life means decay; and Angela recalls Freud's theory that "we all carry our deaths in us—that the organic wants to be returned to the inorganic state" (p. 384). Physical death is ever present in *The Centaur* in the form of Caldwell's possible cancer. Physical death in *Couples* is structured into a veritable procession of corpses: Piet's parents, the hamster, the Kennedy infant, the president, Foxy's unborn baby, and John Ong.

Piet himself is not a remake of Caldwell; he bears a closer relationship to Peter. Peter, the David or Allen of the short stories, portrays the adolescence of the protagonist figure who becomes a Rabbit, Joey, or Piet. Caldwell's story does not need to grow further in the way that Rabbit's, Joey's and Peter's stories do. Insofar as it is Caldwell's story, *The Centaur* is thematically the most resolved of the first four novels; Caldwell accepts the answer he has found and the fate it defines. But his sense of death-in-life is inherited by his son Peter, the David of "Pigeon Feathers," who sees earth's beautiful life forms as "an ocean of horror" if we, like they, die. It is this unresolved struggle that the character of Piet takes up, as he takes up Hook's yearning to communicate, Rabbit's quest, and Joey's struggles with mother-fixation.

A general narrative connection between *Of the Farm* and *Couples* would be apparent to anyone reading through the Updike canon: Piet is the slightly older Joey whose mother has died; and as might be predicted of Joey, Piet is still deeply troubled by the fact of her death. However, Piet is still married to his first wife, the intellectual and evanescent Angela who resembles the Joan we never see in *Of the Farm*. Thus, the novels, in a sense, act as companion pieces: *Of the Farm* gives us a direct view of the mother-son relationship which, though it may not be the same as Piet's, helps explain the suggestions of his mother-fixation; and *Couples* allows us to see Piet turn from the intellectually superior but unsatisfying woman to the simpler, more physical, and soothing one, which we were unable to see happen in Joey's story.

Since the fifth novel includes only a few recalled glimpses of Piet's mother and does not deal with the quality of his feeling for her when she was alive, the author is forced to construct his mother-fixation by means of a few directly stated Freudian maxims. Explaining to Piet what neurotic means, Angela says, "You sleep with women when you're really trying to murder your mother." "What if your mother's already been murdered?" Piet asks. "Then maybe you're trying to bring her back to life" (p. 218). Georgene restates this from the point of view of an abandoned mistress: "You're making me suffer because your parents were killed" (p. 231).

Gallagher gives an Oedipal interpretation of Piet's attitudes, too. When Piet tells him he would like to watch another man have sex with Angela "while sprinkling blessings on his hairy back," Gallagher explains, "Mother and father. . . . As you described that I pictured a child beside his parents' bed. He loves his mother but knows he can't handle her so he lets the old man do the banging" (p. 232). Piet jokingly concurs when he talks to Bea after his separation from Angela. She teases, "Everybody's sure you're keeping a nest of women down there." "Everybody's wrong," he replies, "I only liked married women. They reminded me of my mother" (p. 441). The reader gets an early hint of this fact when Piet, making love to Georgene on her sunporch, "kissed her belly, flat and soft and hot and remembered his mother's ironing board and how she would have him lay his earaches on its comforting heat" (p. 53). After sex with Georgene, Piet feels as "weak and privileged as a child." When he dreams, like Joey, he dreams of being both a little boy (one still attached to his mother) and his father (his mother's lover): "He was a little boy, in fact his own father" (p. 450).

Love of the mother theoretically breeds subtle enmity with the actual father, whom the boy unconsciously assumes will punish him. Piet feels uneasy around Gallagher whom he compares with his father—"that ghost patiently circling in the luminous greenhouse gloom silently expecting Piet to do right" (p. 101). When Piet gets Foxy pregnant, it is Ken's wrath that he unconsciously fears, as he formerly feared Freddy when Georgene was his mistress.

Piet saw that he lived in a moral world of only men, that only men demanded justice, that like a baby . . . he had fallen asleep amid women. . . . In Piet's mind there was no end of Ken. . . . His father potting geraniums with stained thumbs, the perspective of the greenhouse implying an infinity of straight lines. He had preferred as a child the dead-ended warm room at the end where his mother sat. . . . There was a mandate in his father's silences he had shied from. (p. 362)

The possessiveness—for both property and women—which was so apparent in Joey and formed a central motif in *Of the Farm* appears again in Piet in his sense of proprietorship as a builder and in his relationships with women. Even in the first scene he sees his house as representing "how much of the world he was permitted to mark off and hold" (p. 9). His love for Foxy is spurred partly by the fact that as he rebuilds her house he gains a sense of possession about it which eventually transfers to her. "It gave Piet pleasure to see Foxy, pregnant, reading a letter beside a wall of virgin plaster, her shadow subtly golden. And he wanted her to be pleased by his work. Each change he wrought established more firmly an essential propriety" (p. 207).

As Peggy did, Foxy responds to Piet's need to feel ownership of his women. Peggy's compliment, "You make me feel as if you own me. It's wonderful," is repeated by Foxy after lovemaking: "Oh Piet I've never felt so taken." (p. 456). And he rejoices in this ownership: "Ah, you're mine" (p. 459). Angela on the other hand struggles to maintain her freedom and calls Piet a bully. Piet sees her as "seeking to salvage something of herself, her pure self" from men (p. 365). Joey's first wife, Joan, who "never came out from behind those blue eyes" to really look at Joey, had a similar remoteness and unpossessable appearance.

The most prominent feature of Piet's character, therefore, is that he hyperbolizes the characteristics of the previous protagonists. Although he is not old like Hook, he is repeatedly called an "old-fashioned man" whose virtues are "obsolete." He shows an even greater dependence than his older predecessor on the Christian church, and when it burns down he feels that "his life in a sense had ended," whereas Hook has managed to endure into a churchless age. Piet intensifies Rabbit's sexual promiscuity; and his relationships in the light of his stabler home and professional life are more clearly undirected, purposeless, and confused. His sense of all-encompassing death is more vivid and painful than Caldwell's and in no way connected with physi-

cal illness or hypochondria which might suggest that the obsession is temporary. And his mother's death intrudes an even
greater amount of death-anxiety than did the coming death of
Joey's mother.

2. Death and the System of Imagery

The sense of pursuit by death, which marks all of the novels,
reaches its highest degree in *Couples*. It exercises its formative
influence on the patterns of imagery, the overall character structure, and the plot. Almost no detail of the novel is not heavily
colored by it.[2] In an early scene Freddy, the high priest of death,
invokes the Pascal allegory which Updike used in "Fanning
Island." (See p. 14 of this text for its application to *The Poorhouse Fair*.) "We're all survivors," Freddy announces, "a dwindling band of survivors" (p. 37).

Piet's obsession with this viewpoint seems to have begun
with the sudden, senseless death of his parents in a highway
accident: "Since this accident, the world wore a slippery surface
for Piet; he stood on the skin of things in the posture of a man
testing newly formed ice, his head cocked for the warning crack,
his spine curved to make himself light" (p. 24). He sees in the
death of his parents, as Pascal's condemned men saw in each
other, his own certain fate. "From the odd fact of their deaths
his praying mind flicked to the odd certainty of his own." Piet's
death litany, one of the novel's finest moments technically, includes primarily sudden violent deaths like that of his parents.
"The shotgun blast purging the skull of brains. The massive
coronary. The guillotine. The frayed elevator cable. The boom-
ing crack and quick collapse of ice. . . The threshing machine.
The random shark . . ." (p. 273). It is only after the slow death
of John Ong that Piet realizes that death can be a daily mundane
thing on a plane with "the arrival of the daily mail" (p. 448).

Although the parents and their death are mentioned only
a few times in the novel, the major imagery pattern takes its
form from them and attests to their centrality in Piet's subcon-
scious. He associates his parents with the greenhouse. It is a
life-holding structure, giving the plants warmth (what Piet feels

when he prays) and light (what he reaches toward in women). It keeps out the cold and snow, and so it is also a structure which protects from death. Thus the greenhouse becomes in the novel the archetypal structure. Piet, as a builder, wants to build similar dwellings to provide security against death. The opening scene tells us that Piet loved "things that enclosed." The Hanemas' snug bedroom, for example, seems to Piet "safe." When he builds Foxy's house he pictures it as guarding her. "He envisioned her as protected and claimed by sentinels he had posted . . ." (p. 207). He loves the church because it is a house built against death. The "white well-joined wood and the lucent tall window beside him airily seemed to deny [the fact of his death]" (p. 24). He loves Foxy's growing tummy because it is a life-holding structure.

The novel pauses to describe in detail Piet's building of the new hamster cage. Built after the first hamster's misfortune, it will be a house to keep out death. It is beautiful to Piet and his hands shake with excitement. The novel has already repeatedly associated him with the hamster ("Pet. Pit." anagrammatically equals *Piet* for example), and so the dwelling has a high symbolic value as well. He pictures Nancy crawling inside, and the reader understands at once why: She, too, is terrified of death.

This is one of a series of parallel narrative patterns which depict Piet's losing struggles to escape death. Nancy becomes frightened of the cage, mistaking it for a prison—just as Piet's fear of death imprisons him. Foxy's tummy flattens, depriving him of its comfort; and at the end Piet is forced to leave his snug house as Foxy is forced to leave hers. Ultimately the central symbolic structure—the church—burns down, too. The future offers only Gallagher's prefabs, built for a sterile, modern generation which has no dread of mortality.

In addition to being a life-holding structure, the greenhouse also symbolizes death because the flowers grown within it are cut and used for funerals. Moreover all the buildings constructed against death symbolize death because they recognize its existence. So the greenhouse as a structure supports the thematic note that symbols of life are also symbols of death. Piet recalls the backroom office where "carnations being dyed and lovely iris and gladioli leaned, refrigerated, dead" (p. 17), and the mem-

ory disturbs him. "Piet tensed and changed position and erased
the greenhouse." These flowers, intended for death, become all
flowers, all growing life. The spring itself seems to Piet "a tangled hurrying towards death" (p. 85).

The novel's complex system of imagery also makes an association between death and sex. This is forecast by the minister's
sermon and the imagery in *Of the Farm* (see p. 100 of this text).
There, as here, sex is an antedote for death. In *Couples,* Harold
feels immortal when making love to Janet and sex reverses time,
recapturing her beauty of fifteen years earlier (p. 147). Foxy
says that a bed is bigger than mortality and quotes a friend's idea
that "man is the sexiest of the animals and the only one that
foresees death" (p. 473). On a day seemingly filled with death,
Piet wants sex so much that in Foxy's absence he goes to Georgene (p. 238).

In the tightly interwoven imagery of the novel, the death-
allaying power of sex is related to the security of dwellings.
In sex a man enters the enclosing female structure. Not only is
Foxy's womb a dwelling, but Bea and Piet discuss Bea's body
as a house. Veiling his sexual offer for the sake of propriety, Piet
asks Bea if he may come over and look at her "house." "Once,"
Piet prompts, "you would have liked me to." "I would like you
to," Bea replies, looking into his eyes, "It's just—a house, you
know." "I know it's a house. A lovely house" (p. 342). After
passionate sex with her, "death no longer seemed dreadful" (p.
352).

But the fifth novel also makes a less-soothing connection
between sex and death that more closely resembles the one Peter
felt in *The Centaur* when he felt guilt and anxiety over his
father's coming death while touching Penny's crotch: Sex *recalls*
death. Again the parents act as the point of contact for Piet.
When Piet received the phone call announcing their accident,
he had just returned from a date "that left his mouth dry and
his fly wet and his fingertips alive with the low-tide smell of
cunt" (p. 334). Thus the connection is made and a recurring
motif appears in Piet's thoughts: parents-greenhouse-sex-death:

> He rolled over on his stomach and the greenhouse washed
> over him. . . . He surveyed the party for a woman to bring

home and picked Bea Guerin. *Dear Bea, of course I want to fuck you . . . Now spread your legs. Easy does it. Ah.* The moisture and light within the greenhouse had been so constant and strong that even the weeds grew; . . . He saw them, his father and mother, *vader en moeder,* moving gently in this receding polyhedral heart of light carved from dank nature, their bodies transparent, and his mind came to a cliff—a slip, then a skidding downward plunge. (pp. 20-21)

The narrative structures also take up the association between sex and death. Piet's sex reverie about Georgene ("sashaying from the shower nude, her pussy of a ferny freshness") is interrupted by a view of Kennedy's casket being unloaded from the plane (p. 326). The plot as a whole demonstrates the sex-death connections, too. When Foxy becomes pregnant by Piet, sex has brought life but it is a life which Piet sees as death—"a disaster identical with death"—and which results in death when Foxy must get an abortion. (Similarly, in *Rabbit Redux*, Rabbit is in bed with Peggy when he learns of the fire in which Jill has died.)

Freddy makes explicit the identification of sex with death: death he tells Angela, is "being screwed by God." Death excites Freddy sexually, and he tells Angela that God is "Big Man Death." When Freddy discusses the abortion with Piet he uses a sexual expression to describe Foxy's possible death: "If she's had it, son, she's had it" (p. 393). Piet reacts to this expression with uneasiness: "The ambiguity of 'had it' the suggestion of a finite treasurable 'it' that Foxy could enclose and possess, as one says 'had him' of sleeping with a man . . . sent ghosts tumbling and swirling through Piet." It echoes Joey's impression in *Of the Farm* that his mother, while having her heart attack, looked as if her lips were parted to receive a lover's kiss. (See this text, p. 100.)

The network of imagery is drawn closed by the association of sex and flowers, since flowers also recall the parents in their greenhouse and the funerals they supplied. Piet's most frequent sexual metaphor describes women or sex organs as flowers. Trying to fall asleep in the first scene, he daydreams about sex. Egyptian handmaidens are a "single lotus, easy access"; his unerect penis feels like "wilted camelia petals"; he recalls his appearance after ejaculating as "a waxworks petal laid out pillowed in sensitive frizz." At later points Foxy's pubic hair is "fuzz on a rose"; her crotch is a "pansy shape"; her milk seems "roses." He imagines Bea's body as "just about all lillies." Thus the pattern is knit closed: parents-greenhouse-flowers-death-sex-flowers-greenhouse-parents.

Just as Caldwell's awareness of death makes time important in *The Centaur*, the focus on death in *Couples* intrudes the element of time into that novel, too. Piet recalls the house of Angela's parents as filled with clocks. "In the house there had been many clocks, grandfather's and ship's clocks, clocks finished in ormolu or black lacquer, fine-spun clocks in silver cases, with four balls as pendulum" (p. 8). Safe in their divinity (Angela's father and other relatives are called gods in the imagery), Angela's family is not threatened by time and even seem to control it. When Piet courted Angela "time came unstuck" and "all the clocks hurried their ticking, hurried them past doubts, around sharp corners" (p. 8).

Piet feels that the fireplaces (openings) in his snug, death-proof home are "entryways into a sooty upward core of time." The green in the center of town is hourglass shaped, suggesting its temporal existence; but it is overshadowed by the Congregational Church whose promise of immortality should overcome time. Frank and Marcia, who find sex immortalizing, can make love with a clock visible (Frank learns to leave it lying "discreetly visible") but Piet's awareness of time drains some of the pleasure from sex. Outdoors with Georgene he feels that the birds' chirping "had become a clock's ticking" and after lovemaking with Bea the reader is told that "with each woman his heart was more intimidated by the counterthrust of time" (p. 352).

Angela who is free from anxiety about death loves the stars because to her they seem an eternal and unchanging realm —symbols of an infinite universe which will last forever. But to Piet the stars are a giant clock and thus forecast change and death to mortal creatures. It is he, appropriately, who goes out very late and discovers the star patterns moved out of their expected positions. "The rigid cascade of stars had been dealt a sideways blow: Vega the queen of the summer sky no longer reigned at the zenith . . ." (p. 286). The movement of the stars represents the passage of time which will eventually witness Piet's death, while they themselves seem infinite. Thus they doubly accentuate his own small mortality: "His gaze, followed shortly by his death, would travel outward in an eternal straight line. Vertigo afflicted him. Amid these impervious shining multitudes he felt a gigantic slipping . . ." (p. 286). The feeling makes Piet desire Foxy, one of his comforts against death.

Later that night when the stars represent, by their further changed positions, the still distant winter, Piet feels time suddenly collapse: "So the future is in the sky after all. Everything already exists." Thus numbed by a sense that his existence is both eternal and momentary, he decides that henceforth he will need Foxy less.

Nancy, who shares Piet's fear of death, becomes hysterical in a planetarium exhibit which makes the stars move. "Mommy," she cries to Angela, "the stars went round and round and round" (p. 445). The symbolic passage of time upsets her as it upset Piet in the above scene.

Piet's fear of death is mirrored by Freddy's fascination with it. Alter-egos, Piet and Freddy manifest two sides of the same coin, what Freddy describes as a male and female relationship with death. "Piet spends all his energy defying death," Angela remarks to Freddy, "and you spend all yours accepting it." "That's the difference between us," Freddy explains. "Male versus female" (p. 388). As the ending says, "Love and hate both seek to know." Both Piet and Freddy seek to know death; both men see living things as symbolizing death; and both know that it is the only important fact of life. They both sense, furthermore, that sex and Christian faith provide comfort against death. Although Freddy is an atheist and asexual, he explains to the couples: "In the western world there are only two comical things: the Christian church and naked women. . . . Everything else tells us we're dead" (p. 155).

3. Angela and Foxy: The Heavenly Versus the Mundane

The power of sex as a comfort from death is less effective
for Piet, not only because of his direct association between the
two but also because the very physical quality of the act is a
subtle reminder of the mortality to which all physical things are
subject. Thus, although he attempts to escape his death anxieties through sexual activity, it is not a satisfactory refuge. Angela, for this reason, becomes the ideal sex object for Piet because
she is unphysical. She is portrayed as divine and spiritual—an
angel.

The opening scene describes Angela as a filmy transparent
spirit for whom even air is a relatively corporeal medium (it is
"loosely packed with obstructing cloths"). She is "fair and fine"
compared to Piet's coarse body and has "tipped arms" which
are "simple and symmetrical" like wings; indeed her whole shape,
Piet says, seems geared for "some undeniable effort of flight" (p.
14). Although the others feel the loss of Kennedy after his
death, Angela feels nearer to him. "He's right here. Don't you
feel him?" (p. 322). As Angela speaks, songs about stars play
softly on the record player. The heavens are her domain.

Angela represents Piet's attempts to strive upward and seek
confirmation of his own supernaturalness. Rabbit's sense of a
basketball hoop—a goal—far above the heads of the players,
and Chiron's half-divine nature are portrayed in Piet's upward
reach towards Angela. Piet feels with Angela "a superior power
seeking through her to employ him" (p. 4). When angry with
her, Piet sarcastically describes exactly the quality in her that
he needs: "You are so fantastically above it all . . ." (p. 217).
"You're too good for this world" (p. 222).

Angela's unphysical existence is the true symbol of life—life
that does not equal death. Her scent is "absolutely good, like
water, or life, or existence itself" (p. 321). Like the stars which
are her symbol, she contrasts with earthly life which is not eternal, but which is "the predominant vacuum *between* the stars"
(p. 321). Sexual coupling with Angela symbolizes triumph over
death, a resurrection from death's domain. When Piet makes
love to her, her nightgown becomes "transparent, rotten, sliding

and falling from her flesh like deteriorated burial cloth from a body resurrected in its strength" (p. 205).

Since Angela's companionship promises Piet his immortality, separation from her means facing the fact of his death. "Don't make me leave you," he begs, "You're what guards my soul. I'll be damned eternally" (p. 425). Marcia sees this, too. "Without Angela," she tells Piet, "you'd die" (p. 325).

Piet's sense of his wife's angelic identity, however, does violence to her as a person. He prefers her sexual frigidity and her difficulty reaching orgasm because these attest to her unphysical nature. "You enjoy making me feel frigid," she complains (p. 434). He does not want her "cured" by psychotherapy since this would threaten her emotional and physical aloofness, which is necessary for his security. Piet's necessary vision of her as superior leaves her feeling alone and unloved. "I adore you," he offers. "Yes, that says it," she retorts. "You adore me as a way of getting out of loving me" (p. 434).

One of the most carefully and intricately worked portions of the novel is the portrayal of Foxy as the appropriate lover for Piet if he can relinquish his upward struggle from mortality. As Updike said, she is "in some obscure way turned on the lathe for him" (*PR*, p. 101). The first two scenes of the novel depict Piet and Foxy each returning home from a party and a careful parallelism is drawn between the two. Like Piet, Foxy is an orphan—"the couple Foxy's parents had been had vanished" (p. 47). (Foxy and Piet later describe themselves as "a pair of orphans.") Like Piet, Foxy returns from the party overexcited. She would like to make love with Ken, as Piet would with Angela, but neither spouse is interested and neither has offered sex in the recent past. Ken does not want children; Angela wants no more; and Foxy and Piet both suffer insomnia beside soundly sleeping partners. When Piet catches a glimpse of Foxy leaving church, several days later, she is "a piece of white that by some unconscious chime compelled focus" (p. 28). She is meant for him. She is, as the palm frond points out, Jesus coming to Jerusalem.

In contrast to Angela's unphysical imagery, the imagery surrounding Foxy is richly sensuous. The first detail we learn is the color of her beautiful oak and honey hair, and even her eyes look like "brushed fur." Hair, in all of Updike's novels, is the indication of physicalness and sexuality. (Freddy, consequently, is bald and Angela's hair is almost never mentioned.) In her kitchen after a party, Foxy hungrily gobbles a bowlful of crackers and milk while the cat rubs against her ankles. "While the glow of the heater and the begging friction of fur alternated on her legs, she spread butter thickly on spongy white bread, tearing it, overweighting it, three pieces one after another, too ravenous to bother with toast, compulsive as a drunk. Her finger-tips gleamed with butter" (p. 51).

The gleam of butter appears again in a description of Foxy's thickly grown backyard, a symbol of her sexuality: "More sun by the sea. More life. Tiny wine-colored cones that in weeks would be lavender panicles of bloom. Drenched. Dew. Salt. Breeze. Buttery daffodils trembled by his cuffs . . ." (p. 102). Foxy's pregnancy gives her a life-holding identity and a maternal identity, both important to Piet. After the birth of the baby, her breasts become ripe and full of milk and Piet wants to nurse from them, seeking the sense of life and mothering he craves. But after her abortion Foxy loses her full-stomached, large-breasted maternity and Piet abandons her, turning to Bea who can never repeat Foxy's offer of maternally enriched life.

4. The Protagonist Accepts Death

Foxy's name implies her symbolic role for Piet: In contrast to Angela's spirituality, she is an animal—she exists only on the animal plane of creation. She could satisfy Piet only if he were willing to abandon his upward struggle, only if he could cease running from death. Consequently, the action of the novel is geared to frustrate Piet's struggle to the point where he does abandon it. He is subjected to a series of increasingly significant and devastating symbolic deaths until, no longer maintaining a sense of immortality, Piet admits that his life has "ended."

The hamster, conspicuously marked with male genitals and rusty red hair, is the first Piet-figure to undergo death. Like the hamster Piet is frustrated by his cage—Angela. When she complains one night that he is like a "caged animal" he cries, "But,

Angela, who made the cage, huh?" (p. 217). However it is a cage that, like the hamster's, protects him from death. When the hamster attempts to escape its cage, death overtakes it. Piet pictures it in heaven and misses the comforting squeaking of its wheel with which he used to try to match his own breathing.

Next, Kennedy's death is visualized by Foxy as Piet's death. She pictures Kennedy, pouchy-eyed like Piet, as a man "with whom she could have slept," and then it seems that "the cocky pouchy-eyed corpse had been Piet" (p. 309). Both are Christ figures—note the fear that Kennedy would be "crucified" if he became too liberal. Both are given active, promiscuous sex lives. The night of Kennedy's death Freddy threatens Piet with knowledge of Piet's affair with Georgene and promises, "I'm going to hurt you." Ominously, it is then that Marcia warns, "Without Angela, you'd die." Thus, on the day of Kennedy's death, Piet's spiritual death is forecast.

Piet's next symbolic death is caused, significantly, by himself: He arranges for the death of Foxy's unborn infant. This is tantamount to killing himself, since it is life he created. He changes the Our Father—a prayer asking for life—into a death prayer and it is noted that the seed which he will kill "bore his face." It is himself. Yet afterwards, he seems less troubled than one might expect, and he and Foxy are described as "complacent —like animals that have eaten." His gradual acceptance of her animal level of existence is beginning.

The final death of the part of Piet that sought immortality occurs when the church burns down. God Himself appears to end the age of the Christian church with flames whose description invokes an ironic apocalypse:

> by now the tall clear windows along the sides had begun to glow, and the tar shingles of the roof gave off greasy whiffs. The fire had spread under the roof and through the double walls and, even as the alien firemen smashed a hundred diamond panes of glass, ballooned golden in the sanctuary itself. . . . the Doric fluting on the balcony rail was raked with amber light; the plush curtain that hid the choir's knees caught and exploded upward in the empty presbytery like a phoenix. (p. 463)

Only the Golden Cock remains, a sexual pun recalling the maxim that we have only sex when God is gone.[3] (Freddy describes the time as "one of those dark ages that visits mankind between millennia, between the death and rebirth of gods, when there is nothing to steer by but sex and stoicism and the stars" [p. 389].)

Even the work of the old carpenters, with whom Piet identifies, is shown to be disappointing: "structurally unsound: a miracle it had not collapsed of itself a decade ago" (p. 478). Piet is released from servitude to hope. He "wondered at the lightness in his own heart, gratitude for having been shown something beyond him, beyond all blaming" (p. 464). Yet, he realizes that "his life in a sense had ended." The sky is "empty" without a church spire and Angela unknowingly makes the thematic judgment: "The fire's nearly out," she observes, "the best part is over" (p. 465).

Thus, killed several times over, Piet is purged of the desire to escape mortality. He can find satisfaction with Foxy and can accept it. The final description of their love-making focuses on her animal identity—"the goosebumped roughness of her buttocks, the gray unpleasantness of her shaved armpits." In contrast to Angela's doe-like feet with uplifted little toes, Foxy is flat-footed and walks like the animal counterpart of man, the monkey. "Her flat feet gave her walking movements . . . a slouched awkwardness" (p. 454). Unlike Angela's serene sleep, Foxy snuffles, crowds, and struggles against nightmares. She awakens hungry for sex; her stomach growls with emptiness.

Angela's promise of immortality among the stars had prevented Piet from settling for the joys of the physical realm "beneath the stars." "There was a silver [Foxy's color] path beneath the stars. Obliviously Angela barred his way" (p. 223). Now with Foxy he empties his chest of a soul with loud animal groans and joins Foxy in that sub-stellar plateau. "Each groan felt to be emptying his chest, creating an inner hollowness answering the hollowness beneath the stars." "Ah," he realizes, "you're mine." She puts her face against his and "the tip of her nose was cold. A sign of health" (p. 459).

Emptiness is the final picture. The sky, like Piet's chest, is now empty. Stripped of the possibility for tragedy, Piet's life is emptied of moral significance. Contentment is Updike's mark of the loss. Yet, as Updike himself saw, "it is Foxy that he [Piet] most deeply wants" and "what else shall we do, as God destroys our churches?" (*PR*, pp. 100, 101). There is no thematic judgment here; Piet is not condemned by the novel's value system for abandoning his flight from death. There is simply a sad sense of loss. The next stage is surely the world of Bech where fear of death and consequently death itself is largely absent and, in the nature of comedy, nothing matters very much. Such a world is not unpleasant, *Couples* suggests. But it lacks the artists and lovers who give testament to human importance.

PART II. THE MYTHIC UNDERPINNINGS

1. The Demise of Christianity

When the church burns down at the end of *Couples*, it is shown to be weakened and rotten within and should have collapsed "of itself" earlier. The image, of course, is boldly allegorical to what the novel has portrayed about Christianity itself. The forms of Christian ritual and dogma appear in dissipated, oddly transmuted shapes, empty of the belief which gave them meaning for an earlier age. The all-powerful, all-seeing God Whom children were earlier taught to fear and respect is tamed into a golden rooster ("the rooster was God") whose bright eye seems vigilant but is found to be only as big as a penny. It is a weathervane, changing in the wind, and at the end it is brought down among the children to serve as the occasion for a holiday, a parade, and a newspaper feature—another golden calf. Pedrick's sermons, too, seem directed at a Mammon-like deity for whom financial terms are more appropriate than spiritual ones. "The man Jesus does not ask us to play a long shot . . . he offers us present security, four and a half percent compounded every quarter!" (p. 26). As in Joyce's short story "Grace" this is the god the age demands.

When the couples gather for Easter-eve dinner, there is a "bump of silence" replacing grace. The only angels are ironic ones who warn when adultery is being too pointedly mocked. " 'By the year 1990 they're going to have one [a television] in every room, so everybody can be watched. . . . nobody could commit adultery.' An angel passed overhead" (p. 35). Lamb is served at the Paschal dinner but no mention is made of the reason; the logic of its appropriateness has been forgotten. A death is discussed but it is the loss of the submarine *Thresher*. There is a reference to God but it is Ken's patronizing remark about the complexity of organic chemistry: "If a clever theologian ever got hold of how complex it is, they'd make us all believe in God again" (p. 38). A crucifixion is mentioned but it is Kennedy's, should he become too liberal. New life is promised, but it is only Foxy's pregnancy which is, during the party, making her queasy and irritable. The temple's torn veils at the moment of Christ's death become Foxy's memory of the "tearing of veils inside her" when she performed fellatio for Peter.

Piet, too, although he represents an "old fashioned" believer, goes through the ritual forms unconsciously and meaninglessly. In church he daydreams about sex: "Funny how fucking clears a woman's gaze." On Palm Sunday the palm frond becomes, metaphorically, the symbol of the coming of one who will teach him to accept death, not One who will teach him to conquer it: His daughter presents it to him as he catches sight of Foxy, dressed in white (p. 28). Later, he changes the *Pater Noster* into a death prayer and pictures a God Who is characterized by killing, not creating. "God who kills so often, . . . kill once more" (p. 363). When Foxy is having her abortion Piet keeps a vigil, by sitting on a park bench helplessly; he makes a contribution, by giving a "snuffly bum" twenty-five cents; and he fasts, by going without a doughnut and coffee for the first hour. The baby is being sacrificed for the good of the community, but unlike the God who stayed Abraham's hand at the last moment, Piet does not "smash the door down with a hammer" as Foxy cried that he would.

What has replaced belief in God is belief in each other. Like Buddy's worship of Conner in *The Poorhouse Fair* and Eccles' social-worker ministry in *Rabbit, Run*, the people in Tarbox have exchanged an upward orientation for a horizontal one. As Freddy says, "People are the only thing people have left since

God packed up" (p. 155). Angela explains Freddy's belief as early as the opening scene: "He thinks we're a circle. A magic circle of heads to keep the night out. . . . He thinks we've made a church of each other" (p. 12). Foxy, although she goes to church, appears to feel the same. She tells Piet that she sees "God" and "the world" as meaning the same thing (p. 215).

Replacing God, people also supply each other's moral incentives. The Applebys and little-Smiths, who spend their Sundays visiting each other, agree to discontinue their sexual arrangements; but when the rest of their friends leave town on a skiing weekend, they resume. "For much of what they took to be morality proved to be merely consciousness of the other couples watching them" (p. 168). The promise of immortality that Piet finds in church, Harold finds in bed with Janet: "as if a glowing tumor of eternal life were consuming the cells of his mortality" (p. 147). The "new stigmata," says Harold, is a cut thumb from opening poptop beer cans at parties.

To replace the liturgical cycle, Piet and Matt Gallagher have begun a "round of sports . . . a calendrical wheel of unions to anticipate and remember" (pp. 116-17). Freddy, high priest of the new church, presides over these rituals which conjure up silhouettes of ageless pagan and Christian religious forms. At the basketball game, Freddy, the priest-victim, is wounded by Piet and the rite begins:

> Hanema had kneeled to Thorne. The others made a hushed circle around them. . . . A snap softer than a twig breaking . . . shocked the silent circle. Freddy rose and held his hand, the little finger now aligned, before his chest as something tender and disgraced that must not be touched. . . . The other players had divided equally into two sympathizing rings. Freddy Thorne, holding his hand before him, led Angela and Constantine and the neighbor boy and Saltz into the house, in triumph. (pp. 74-75)

At a gathering after swimming (pp. 249-57) Freddy, feeling chilly, wraps an Afghan blanket around his shoulders "like a shawl." He and Piet are "alone with many women." Piet holy-rolls on the floor saying, "Say it, brother, say it" and Freddy speaks "solemnly." Carol pours the circle of glasses full of wine from an Almaden jug, "making of it a dancer's routine." Finally, each person in turn makes an intimate confession of what they think is the most wonderful thing in the world. Then Freddy gives a sermon and the gathering leaves. On the way home Piet catches a glimpse of his real church but it is "featureless"; he can see only "a stately hollow blur." The human church is replacing it. (Echoes of this seem to appear in the ritualized readings and debates of *Rabbit Redux*.)

The night after Kennedy's assassination, a party is held at Freddy's house. He is once again the priest and provides the traditional feast which sends the dead soul on its journey surrounded by plenty. Holding the ritual cooked pig, Freddy leads the procession, accompanied by the queen and priestess; Mass and Communion begin:

> Triumphantly upheld by Freddy flanked by Georgene and Angela, the ham, the warm and fat and glistening ham, scotched and festooned with cloves, was fetched from the kitchen. Bea Guerin . . . followed holding a salad bowl heaped full of oily lettuce, cucumber slices, avocados, tomatoes, parsley, chives, chicory, escarole. Their blessings were beyond counting. With a cruciform clashing of silver Freddy began to sharpen the carving knife. Out of the gathering audience Frank Appleby boomed, "Upon what meat does this our Caesar feed, that he is grown so great?" . . . Freddy's eyeglasses flickered blindly as he carved; he was expert. . . . "Take, eat," he intoned, laying each slice on a fresh plate a woman held out to him, "This is his body given for thee." (p. 334)

The wake-like party itself shows the reaction of the couples to Kennedy's assassination. They are tense and uneasy; Bea grieves that they "couldn't stay home and mourn decently," but, in fact, none of them knows how to mourn. They drift from cocktails to television set unable to find what seems a dignified and appropriate role, unable even to change significantly the nature of their gossip and flirtations.

With the demise of Christianity, Updike is suggesting,

people no longer understand guilt. Foxy earlier mourned the fact that Ken "shirked the guilt she obscurely felt belonged to life" (p. 45). Now his only way of reacting when a people kill their president is to wear onyx cuff links to the party. The afternoon of Kennedy's death, Foxy senses that the "town gripped guilt in its dirty white gables," but the people in the town do not see or experience the guilt. Piet is the only one who is able to feel and recognize guilt. He felt guilty about his parents' deaths and "in the same way he felt guilty about Kennedy's death" (p. 334). He displays the Puritan need to punish himself. "You're quite hard on yourself," Foxy observes to him on one occasion (p. 210). At the party he jumps from the Thorne's second-floor bathroom window. Afterwards, during dinner, he tastes the ashes of mortification and penance: "His mouth felt full of ashes that still burned. . . . His knee did hurt" (p. 335). Ben, salvaging fragments of his Jewish heritage, explains that these ashes give life significance: "What does matter is to taste your own ashes. Chew 'em up" (p. 440).

Scenes like the above illustrate Updike's principal technique for portraying the demise of Christianity: He envisions it as becoming gradually reabsorbed by the pagan religions which preceded and surrounded it. Stripped of the belief which preserved the distinct Christian ritual forms, the forms join the stock of our cultural heritage, the mythic patterns which Jung says shape our perceptions and behavior. Stylistically, therefore, *Couples* stands closer to *The Centaur* than do the other novels, since it incorporates highly allusive patterns of imagery. Descriptions invoke not just the Greek pantheon but echoes of vegetation-fertility rituals, land, sea and sky deities, and medieval romance traditions. The overall impression which is created seems to suggest that as Christianity becomes a less powerful influence, other elements of our mythic unconscious become more visible.

The novel's frequent use of sexual scenes may be due in part to the ritualistic appearance of sexual activity—human dramas so old that time seems nonexistent when we view them. Harold recalls sex as "conversations of tranced bodies" where there is "little distinct to recall, only the companionable slow ascent to moon-blanched plateaus where pantomimes of eating and killing and dying are enacted, both sides taking all parts" (p 129). In this sense the sexual scenes and the frequent dining scenes may be somewhat in parallel, since feasts are another primeval ritual.

2. The Vegetation-Fertility Rituals

To anyone familiar with James Frazer's *The Golden Bough,* or its most famous twentieth-century artistic incarnation in *The Waste Land,* the figures of Piet and Freddy in relation to their community are easily identifiable in terms of basic vegetation myths. The fact that the novel opens in spring shortly before Easter hints at the significance of the vegetation cycle.[4] Piet recalls Angela's parents as wanting "fertility at all costs." But, as in the Fisher King's country, the spring is sterile for Piet. Angela wants no more children and will not make love to him. And Ken provides a similarly sterile environment for Foxy, although she, like the spring, is pregnant with coming life. Piet notices the lilacs struggling to grow near Foxy's house, but as in Eliot's April, these seem to promise death in life—"a tangled hurrying toward death" (p. 85). The spring has "terror," as Eliot's April is "the cruelest month."

Piet, who represents the hero-quester-victim, is the one who senses that something is wrong in the community. He meditates in the opening scene on the fact that "the men had stopped having careers, and the women had stopped having babies. Liquor and love were left" (p. 17). He connects liquor with evil ("Liquor. Evil, dulling stuff") and sees their lives as barren: "They were growing old and awful in each other's homes" (p. 16). In a metaphor, which also recalls Hans who found the hole in the dike, Piet is given his role: "Piet felt, small brave Dutchboy, a danger hanging tidal above his friends" (p. 17). He is the savior.

In *The Waste Land* Eliot recasts vegetation-ritual materials from Frazer into an ironic form. The dryness and barrenness of the land and its people is observed sadly by the speaker, but the people do not want regeneration or new life; they prefer the easier existence of the living death to which their spiritual aridity has confined them. This is why April might be cruel and why Madame Sosostris warns that water is a threat. The same ironic use of the vegetation cycle appears in *Couples.*

Piet bears the ritualistic identity of both the scapegoat and the vegetation god whose death should guarantee new life. This is Christ's role in the Christian tradition. His "cruciform blazon of hair" and his symbolic identity as the last Christian further identify him with Christ. It is again early spring when, after the confrontation in the Whitman's living room, Angela and subsequently the community banish Piet from society. Frazer describes a ritual in which a human scapegoat is banished from the church at the beginning of Lent.[5] He walks around the city but may speak to no one. This is Piet's role when he lives in the hotel. His building firm has no work for him, no one invites him to dinner, and when Harold attempts a brief conversation, Piet appropriately maintains his alienation by becoming offensive.

However, the community is not restored by Piet's banishment. Ironically it may be his vitality and lingering moral energy which they want removed rather than any spiritual impediments to a new life. Georgene suggests this when she advises Piet and Foxy to leave town. "You're poisoning the air," she complains at first, but then admits, "Maybe the rest of us are poisoned and you two upset us with your innocence" (p. 403). At the end of *The Waste Land* thunder comes but no rain. At the end of *Couples* there is rain but it is not the life-giving rain of the vegetation rites; it is rain which conjures up the rain of fire on Sodom and Gomorrah. The sun is "swallowed" and the first drops reflect light in such a way that they become "spears of fire."

But as the rain is ironic in terms of the vegetation-rebirth tradition, it is also ironic in terms of the Judeo-Christian tradition: Instead of signalling—as did the rain of fire on Sodom— the triumph of God over paganism, it signals the end of God's power over paganism. The church burns down, the spiritual life it promised is promised no more, and Piet, the last surviving Christian, is permitted to accept mortality and a purely physical identity. Pedrick protests that the church still exists because it has nothing to do with the building but is "people, my friend, people. *Human beings*" (p. 466). But thus Pedrick himself unknowingly echoes Freddy's perception that it is an era in which people have made a church of each other. The supernatural, upward-oriented church of Hook, Rabbit, and Piet is no longer in evidence.

The echoes of *The Waste Land* in the novel are amplified by the character of Freddy. His role as a seer is suggested by his role as priest. But in addition he is given the special characteristics of Tiresias, the blind androgynous prophet of Greek classics and the principal narrator of Eliot's poem. The first description of Freddy is through Foxy's eyes. She sees him as having a mouth "neither male nor female," and his eyes are "lost behind concave spectacle lenses" (p. 31). When Freddy wears his skin-diving suit "his appearance in the tight shiny skin of black rubber was disturbingly androgynous; he was revealed to have hips soft as a woman's" (p. 238). Since his mask cannot accommodate his glasses, Freddy's eyes are "blind and furry." He has a "wise old woman's face" (p. 244).

As Tiresias was changed into a female and then back to a male again, Freddy displays changes of sexual identity, too. Playing the male role at a party he offers to have an affair with Janet; but he can quickly slip into a female role. "Have a little affair with me and that circus you're supporting will pack up and leave town. . . . Terrific dress you have on, by the way. Are you pregnant?" (p. 176). At the ski lodge Freddy espouses sex as the only thing people have left and tells Marcia she looks "terrific." He also flatters Janet but then confides: "You've lost some weight, that's a shrewd move. For a while there you had something bunchy happening under your chin. You know, honey, you're a fantastic piece—I say this as a disinterested party, girl to girl . . ." (p. 156). The speaker later explains that although Freddy "seemed aggressive toward women, he really sought to make alliance with them" (p. 180).

There is a certain sense, too, in which Freddy's cynical but concerned attitude is related to the speaker in several sections of *Couples* in a manner not unlike Tiresias' role in the narration of *The Waste Land*. The tone of the chapters describing the Applesmiths, for example, seems marked by his affectionate cynicism. As the counterpart of the unchanging seer whose life spans several generations, he alone has the overview which makes comedy possible. When she first admits her love to Frank, Marcia becomes a recognizable soap-opera heroine:

> "I'm fighting for my life. I know you don't love me and I don't think I love you but I *need* to talk. I need it so much" —and here, half artfully, she lowered her face to hide tears that were, after all, real—"I'm frightened."
> "Dear Marcia [says Frank]. Don't be." (p. 121)

Dialogue like this, along with the dead-pan chronicling of the slow but predictable path to adultery, reflects in its delicate satire, not Piet's superserious view of reality, but Freddy's circumspect wryness. It foreshadows *Bech's* comic realm.

3. Land, Sea, and Sky Gods

Superimposed on this interweave of Christian tradition and vegetation-fertility tradition is a third general mythic framework which sees the world shared by a sky god, a land god, and a sea god. Freddy's ambivalent sexual behavior at once suggests Poseidon; Angela, as an angel, is connected with the heavens, and Piet's physicalness makes him an earth god.

Angela's angelness—the spiritual, nonphysical quality which symbolizes life to Piet—is suggested by the imagery surrounding her, which sees her as a heavenly, noncorporeal being. But more than angelic, Angela is repeatedly described as a deity connected with the heavens or the sky. In the opening scene she is the source of lightning: As she undresses "lamplight struck zigzag fire from her slip." When Foxy talks to her during the basketball play, she must look upwards "toward a luxurious detached realm where observations and impressions drifted nodding by one another" (p. 66). At the ski lodge Angela's skin has "an unearthly glow" and Freddy describes her eyes as "full of sky." "I look at that ass," Freddy quips, "and I think Heaven" (p. 157). In an earlier scene Piet had sarcastically told her "But Angel, the rest of us think of you as never having left Heaven" (p. 86). During sex she "descends like a cloud," and when Piet makes love to her "her whole fair floating flesh dilated outward toward a deity" (p. 205). She is a "foul proud queen," and he tells her "your cunt is heavenly." Later he describes it as "hair and air," an "ambrosial chalice." Angela's eyes are "sky," her back contains a "constellation of scars" (p. 424), her buttocks are "moons heaved from an ancient earth" (p. 386), and she sleeps "in the cradle of the stars, her uncle's web" (p. 271).

The fish imagery surrounding Freddy seems less connected with other aspects of the symbology or theme than does Angela's divinity, which is necessary to Piet's story. Freddy's lack of hair —Updike's mark of unphysicalness or asexuality—might suggest a fish and his homosexual tendencies could recall Poseidon, but for the most part, the repeated images of shellfish and sea monsters are not utilized beyond establishing Freddy as a sea deity.

The first time Foxy sees Freddy she notices a "fishy inward motion of his lips" (p. 31) and later, when she sees him drive up to the basketball game his "pink head poked from the metal shell like the flesh of a mollusc" (p. 71). When he walks to his cabin from the ski lodge the "liquorish sweat of his chest froze into a carapace" (p. 158). The most extended image occurs at the Constantines' after Freddy has been skin-diving. He keeps his wetsuit on and "with the obscene delicacy of a hydra's predatory petals his long hands flitted bare from his sleeves' flexible carapace. This curvaceous rubber man had arisen from another element" (p. 239). In this scene Freddy becomes a monstrous sea king:

> Like a giant monocle his Cyclopean snorkeling mask jutted from his naked skull, and his spatulate foot flippers flopped grotesquely on the Constantines' threadbare Oriental rugs. When he sat in a doilied armchair and, twiddling a cigarette, jauntily crossed his legs, the effect was . . . monstrous and regal. . . . (p. 239)

Later Freddy stubs out his cigarette on his own forehead, on the mask. His body streams with water. "I'm a monster from the deep," he tells Piet. Piet's hatred of Freddy when arranging the abortion recreates this impression: "Freddy's hairless face

became very ugly, the underside of some soft eyeless sea creature whose mouth doubles as an anus" (p. 376).

Freddy's sea-god appearance is noticeable primarily in those
scenes which involve Angela as a sky goddess. The quote above
occurs after Freddy states that he wants to make love to Angela, and several lines later Foxy tells Piet, "She's your divine
wife, settle it between yourselves" (p. 377). In the scene describing Freddy's skin-diving suit, Angela says that walking
among the stars is the most wonderful thing she can think of;
and when Foxy sees Freddy drive up to the basketball game she
has just been looking up at Angela's "luxurious detached realm."
The night Freddy goes to bed with Angela he smiles at Piet
"fishily," and as they walk upstairs his mouth opens "as if to
form a bubble."

A small mythic narrative is hidden in the imagery of this
scene; in order to copulate with the sea god, Angela the sky
goddess must become a sea creature (pp. 384-89). "Her big
breasts swayed in the poppy glow like sluggish fish in an aquar-
ium of rosewater." She enters the bed as if diving into the
ocean: "She went to the window, glanced out quickly, peeled
off her nightgown, and jackknifed herself, breasts bobbing, into
the tightly made bed. 'Oh, it's icy,' she cried." To attract Freddy,
she then describes herself as a dolphin—Piet's word for her when
during sex she would lie stomach down. Yet, throughout, she
remains a sky goddess, her buttocks "moons," her breasts swimming "into star light," and her hair a "halo." After this brief
metamorphosis, however, Angela seems to retain traces of the
change. Weeks later in the Whitman's living room, her face is
willing "like a sea anemone, to be fed by whatever washed
over it" (p. 420), and she later goes home to the comfort of a
deep, sploshing bath.[6]

Piet's role as earth god is less directly portrayed and is
more complicated. Several sets of images contribute to it, and
it evokes traces of the dualistic attitudes which appear in several
of the novels. Piet's physical, sexual nature is a symptom of his
earthiness. In the opening scene Angela is described as filmy
and noncorporeal; whereas Piet, by contrast, has large feet,
hands, and genitals "as if his maker, seeing that the cooling body

had been left too small, had injected a final surge of plasma" (p. 14). In the next scene, his love of the land is mentioned: "Each pebble, tuft, heelmark, and erosion gully in the mud by the church porch had been assigned its precise noon shadow . . . he had grown to love this land" (p. 27). Later he tells Foxy "I like lots of land around me."

Piet's love of flowers also marks his connection with the earth. He dissociates them from Angela in a direct statement: "You can't take them with you, Angel. Flowers don't grow in Heaven, they only spring from dung" (p. 301).

Another series of images which associates Piet with the land are the references to his sense that he walks on the "skin" of the earth. The speaker notes that, since the death of his parents, "the world wore a slippery surface for Piet; he stood on the skin of things in the posture of a man testing newly formed ice" (p. 24). Piet's situation is described by the chapter title as "thin ice," and when catastrophe occurs it is a "breakthrough," symbolically immersing Piet in water—Freddy's domain, in which he is in Freddy's power. Narratively, he must submit to Freddy to procure the abortion. Angela tells Foxy in an early conversation that Piet "likes to skate but isn't much of a swimmer" (p. 69).

Appropriate to his identity as an earth god, Piet is uneasy when Georgene wants to make love outdoors under the sky— "sensing and fearing a witness, Piet looked upward" (p. 60). He is also jealous of Georgene's love of the sun. He considers the sunlight "solar jism" and her a "whore" for enjoying it. When they discuss the danger of being discovered, Piet hears "miniature thunder" as the wind ripples sheets of reflective aluminum foil.

Piet's most complicated connection with an earth god involves his identity as the "red haired Avenger" which is pointedly mentioned on two occasions. Tradition identifies this title with the devil, and medieval philosophers considered the devil to have been the original earth king—having lured heavenly spirits down to earth and into physical bodies. The body, in the Dualist tradition, remains foreign to us but imprisons the soul and subjects it to terrestrial appetites. Piet is clearly a representative of these appetites and thus becomes the demiurge earth king. He, like the other entrapped spirits, reaches up towards Angela—the spirit of light who remains in heaven—but eventually he reconciles himself to his earthly identity and becomes the archetype of the other humans who have learned to accept mortality. This medieval view of the devil is described in de Rougemont's *Love in the Western World* where Updike surely saw it.[7]

When Angela the sky goddess suffers her final humiliation and shock in the Whitman's living room the night of the confrontation, she is finally subjected to Piet's earthiness—his lusts and the social disruptions they have caused. Her cries in the car on the way home are "animal, less than animal," and she kneels on the car floor in symbolic subjugation. At home in the bath her back is described as "an animal brown." But her dismissal of Piet frees her again and at the end he kneels to her, wrapping his arms around her legs while she holds his head down with her hands. At the end she has returned to her father—"a well-tailored, wise smiling small man." He is a figure of some ancient god who must have provided, along with the uncle, her original cradle in the stars. Piet, who finally settles for his earthly domain, is happy with his Fox.

4. Tristram and Iseult: *Love in the Western World*

The central mythic framework of the novel is the one built around the medieval romance tradition which would see Piet as the courtly lover (Tristram), Angela as the beautiful but unattainable lady (Iseult), and man's love of beautiful women as a manifestation of his desire for heaven.[8] The most famous and expansive formulation of this tradition is, of course, de Rougemont's *Love in the Western World*, and we know from Updike's own comments that it is a book which has been frequently on his mind. As late as 1965 when he was writing the foreword to the collection *Assorted Prose*, he devoted nearly one-third of that introduction to his reactions to de Rougemont's theories. In 1963—when he must have been working intensively on *Couples*—Updike wrote a review of de Rougemont's *Love Declared*, an elaboration and clarification of the earlier book, *Love in the Western World*. The review itself deals at length with *Love in the Western World*, and thus not only indicates Updike's own understanding of the contents but also shows what aspects of the theory he found particularly interesting.

What the medieval romance tradition offers Updike is an explanation for the strange thirst—the inability to find emotional satiety—that has marked his protagonists. And it is an explanation which is as sexually oriented as the protagonists themselves. Of course, it is not impossible that elements of the romance tradition influenced Updike from the very beginning, but the whole structure of the tradition centers around the figure of the Lady and nothing prefiguring Angela appears in Updike's fiction except for the brief, second-hand glimpses of Joan in *Of the Farm*.[9]

The appearance of the romance Lady in Western culture is a phenomenon that has long been viewed with interest. Even before the publication in France of *Love in the Western World*, C. S. Lewis had written his famous *Allegory of Love* tracing a development of the female figure which is not unlike the process described by de Rougemont. Drawing from both descriptions, Lewis and de Rougemont, it appears that there was a gradual blending of a Virgin Mary worshipped more and more enthusiastically—a phenomenon sometimes called the "Cult of Mary"—and a divine Venus whose unattainability gradually earned her what Updike calls a "cult of chastity" (*AP*, p. 221). Drawing further from the medieval philosophers who saw the original earth king, the devil, as responsible for human physical beings, Updike sees a blending of this Venus-Virgin with *"sophia aeterna*, an Eternal Feminine that preexisted material creation" (*AP*, p. 221) and is the focal point of man's yearning to return to his spiritual, heavenly home.

Such a female figure becomes the archetype of the courtly lady, the heavenly Beatrice, the beloved of the sonnets, and the heroine of the romance narratives such as Tristram and Iseult. Like Venus she is utterly desirable and sexually arousing, but like Mary she is absolutely inviolable, and like both she is wholly unattainable in any sense. Yet, like *sophia aeterna*, she is the object of all man's desires, and separation from her is the mark of man's abject state of suffering and deprivation, which marks his identity as a human.

It seems clear that the character of Angela was formed from this mould. In the opening scene she is described as maternal and fertile. The first child was born "nine months after the wedding night" and the "forward cant of her belly remembered her pregnancies." She has large breasts and hips, a "polleny pallor," and "luxuriant pudenda." Yet she seems "maiden like" and is totally hostile to any sexual overture—"her skin breathed hate." On the morning of the infant Kennedy's death, Piet watches Angela set the breakfast table, aware of her nipples swaying against her nightie. Yet she is not real or concrete. "She seemed to Piet to be growing ever more beautiful, to be receding from him into abstract realms of beauty" (p. 227).

She becomes the Virgin Mary when she feels that Kennedy, after his death, is near to her; but in her bath she becomes Venus, perhaps even the giant Venus of Shakespeare's *Venus and Adonis.*

> Her breasts slopped and slid with the pearly dirty water; her hair was pinned up in a psyche knot, exposing tenderly the nape of her neck. . . . Angela rolled a quarter-turn. The water sloshed tidally. . . . Her buttocks were red islands. . . . A slim bit of water between. . . . [When] she stood in the tub, Angela was colossal: buckets of water fell from the troughs among her breasts and limbs and collapsed back into the tub. (pp. 423-25)

Piet becomes aroused at the sight of her but, appropriately, may not have her. Angela's "abstract" beauty, her frequent sexual refusals, and the infrequency of her orgasms combine to render her unattainable, as the myth decrees she is. It is interesting to note how Updike seems occasionally to borrow an exact word from the English edition of de Rougemont to fix his portrayal. De Rougemont explains the evanescent nature of the Lady:

> Eros has taken the guise of Woman and symbolizes both the other world and the nostalgia which makes us despise earthly joys. But the symbol is ambiguous since it tends to mingle sexual attraction with *eternal* desire. She [Iseult] stirred up a yearning for what lies beyond embodied forms. Al-

though she was beautiful and desirable for herself, it was her nature to *vanish*. (*LWW*, p. 66)

On Georgene's sunporch, Piet notes her solidness, in contrast to Angela. "Touch Georgene, she was there," Piet muses, "Touch Angela, she *vanished*" (p. 54, my italics).

From the Lady's identity as man's resident spirit in heaven and the Virgin Mary, it becomes a short step to seeing her as the guardian of man's soul, his spiritual protector, in fact, his church, "the way to salvation" (*LWW*, p. 123). Updike quotes de Rougemont: "Bernard Gui . . . shows that although the Cathars venerated the Blessed Virgin, she was not, in their belief, a woman of flesh and blood, the Mother of Jesus, *but their church*" (*AP*, p. 221, quoting from *LWW*).

Such an understanding of Angela gives another dimension to Marcia's warning to Piet, "Without Angela, you'd die." When Piet begs Angela not to divorce him he cries, "You're what guards my soul. I'll be damned eternally" (p. 425). De Rougemont develops this further: "Mystical union with this feminine divinity," he says, "is then tantamount to participation in the legitimate power of the luminous God, a 'divinization'" (*LWW*, p. 119). When Angela asks Piet if he enjoys being with her, he responds, "Oh, Jesus, yes. Being with you is Heaven" (p. 413). Shortly after Angela abandons Piet, the Congregational Church burns down, too. "The best part is over," Angela observes as Piet watches her walk away from the smoldering ruins.

All women, of course, partake to a degree in the qualities of the Ideal Lady. So, too, the various women in *Couples* whom Piet seeks out share attributes proper to Angela. Foxy has difficulty in reaching orgasm and thus retains an essential unpossessableness which would attract Piet. And Bea, like her Dantean namesake, seems "remote" and made of "ectoplasm."

On several occasions *sophia aeterna's* nature as a "female Form of Light" as Updike terms it, bathes Piet's lovers in light, like the Platonic light of the Ideal Beloved. Angela "shimmered like a chandelier" at Freddy's party. Our first view of Foxy ends in a moon-drenched house with her face rhythmically lighted by a beacon: "The tide was high; moonlight displayed a silver saturation overflowing the linear grid of ditches. . . . the lights of another town . . . spangled the horizon. A revolving search-light rhythmically stroked the plane of the ocean. Its beam struck her face at uneven intervals" (p. 51). When Foxy lies down to sleep, she is again wrapped in light: "The moon, so bright it had no face, was framed by the skylight and for an hour of insomnia burned in the center of her forehead like a jewel" (p. 52).

From Foxy's moonbath, we go to Georgene's sunbath. Her sunporch is blindingly bright, and Piet associates Georgene with early-in-the-season sunbaths. The speaker notes their excessive politeness: "Their politeness was real. Lacking marriage or any contract they had evolved between them a code of mutual consideration" (p. 57). This, of course, is reminiscent of the courtly tradition; and, as in the courtly tradition, it is the woman who requests or denies sexual attention.[10]

The pattern of light imagery is completed by references to things which seek light (as mortals would). This is made explicitly sexual when, being fellated by Foxy, Piet "would seek the light with one thrust" (p. 235). Ominously, this description follows the section on the death of the premature Kennedy infant in which Piet sees the world as filled with abortive things—"friendships, marriages, conversations, all aborted, all blasted by seeking the light too soon" (pp. 233-234). Our journey towards Heaven must be a gradual process.

The character of the romance lover—the counterpart of Tristram—takes its shape from the fact of the Lady's unattainability. Man becomes desirous, not of possession, but of passion itself—passion forever unsatisfied due to the definitional obstacle posed by the Lady's unpossessable nature. "Her essence is *passion itself*," Updike explains in his review, "her concern is not with the possession, through love, of another person but with the prolongation of the lover's state of mind" (*AP*, pp. 221-222). Thus Foxy, who is not an Iseult, gloats in feeling "taken"; but Angela, Piet says, seeks to "salvage" her "pure self" from men. De Rougemont's basic theme in *Love in the Western World* is that the nature of the Lady, as she came to be perceived, has created in Western culture a love of unsatisfied desire. Speaking of lovers like Tristram and Iseult, he explains: "what they need is not one another's presence but one another's absence. Thus the partings of lovers are dictated by their passion itself, and by the love they bestow on their passion rather than on its satisfaction or on its living object" (*LWW*, p. 43). When Piet lives his lonely life in the hotel, it is a "nostalgia for adultery itself" that he feels, "the tension of its hidden strings" (p. 450).

De Rougemont contends that, in the absence of any real obstacles to possession, lovers need to create them; Tristram, for instance, places a sword between himself and Iseult before they sleep. "The most serious obstruction is thus the one pre-ferred above all," de Rougemont continues; "it is the one most suited to intensifying passion" (*LWW*, p. 45). Piet's adultery poses natural obstacles (the danger of discovery), and seeks only unattainable women (those already married). But more impor-tant, de Rougemont's belief in the necessity of an obstacle helps explain Piet's refusal to let Angela have psychotherapy. She re-quests it in order to be a better wife—to be better sexually: "Oh Piet, I'll be a wonderful wife; I'll know everything" (p. 223). This threatens to remove the obstacle which her frigidity and aloofness create, the obstacle which makes her the ideal object of passion.

De Rougemont says that Don Juans—men with a compulsion for a succession of affairs—may be created by the lack of ob-stacles in a society: "he is the victim of a social organization in which the obstructions have been cheapened. They break down too soon" (*LWW*, p. 299). Georgene is "right there wait-ing," and Bea makes an offer early in the book. Foxy asks on one of Piet's early visits "Would you like to kiss me?" and it is well known that Carol is "not too fussy." Thus, although it seems that Angela's sexual reluctance drives Piet to other women, in another sense the reverse may be true. Their availability drives Piet to Angela.

The need for an obstacle leads to the love of peril for its own sake—de Rougemont calls this the "lovers' secret" (*LWW*, p. 45). He describes Tristram's leap from his own bed to the queen's—a leap which opens up his recent wound. The leap is necessary to avoid discovery since the floor between the beds has been spread with flour to guarantee the queen's chastity. De Rougemont, of course, feels that it is the leap itself Tristram wants more than the final embrace with Iseult. This is Foxy's reaction, too, when Piet makes his Tristram-like leap from the

Thornes' bathroom window. "I wanted to tell you not to be silly and kill yourself," Foxy says afterward, "but . . . you were clearly in love with the idea of jumping" (p. 332).

Thus the love of suffering is also a feature of the romantic lover. He desires the suffering created by obstacles and he desires the suffering of separation from the beloved. De Rougemont says, "To love love more than the object of love . . . has been to love to suffer" (*LWW*, p. 52). The popular success of the Tristram story, he suggests, shows that "we have a secret passion for what is unhappy." He calls this the "secret that Europe has never allowed to be given away."

Updike quotes this line in his review. In the novel, Piet's European heritage is stressed frequently; he is a "Dutchboy"—a European in whom the secret still resides. Piet believes in suffering and tells Angela that children are "supposed to suffer" (p. 13). In Ken's living room, after the ordeal of Foxy's abortion, Ken snaps at Piet, "You're enjoying this; you've *enjoyed* that girl's pain" (p. 421). Piet leaves the Whitman house "elated" even though they have all gone through an agonizing evening.

Love in the Western World and *Couples* both suggest a relationship between suffering and understanding. Sufferings, de Rougemont says, "are a privileged mode of understanding" (*LWW*, p. 54). Piet defends adultery to Foxy by saying that it's a way of "giving yourself adventures" and "seeking knowledge" (p. 359). This is, of course, simply another byproduct of the connection between the mystical passion and the erotic passion, the connection produced by the coalescing of *sophia aeterna* and Venus: To seek passion is to seek knowledge of the Ideal.

Both de Rougemont in his book and Updike in his review spend considerable effort explaining that the ultimate goal of passion is death—insofar as passion is what-is-suffered and death is its limit. (*Passion* must be understood in its metaphysical sense as the opposite of *action;* it is what is undergone). "Unawares and in spite of themselves," de Rougemont says, "the lovers never had but one desire—the desire for death!" (*LWW*, p. 47). Updike, in his review, puts it this way: "Passion secretly wills its own frustrations and irresistibly seeks the bodily death that forever removes it from the qualifications of life, the disappointments and diminishments of actual possession" (*AP*, p. 221).

Thus, although Piet consciously flees from death, he is unconsciously attracted to it and fits Freddy's description of our death wish.

The postponement of passion, consequently, is also related to flight from death since it symbolically rejects being subjected in any sense. Piet's fear of death and his attraction to Angela's sexual aloofness are roughly equivalent drives. Since Angela's frequent and expected sexual refusals postpone lust for Piet, she aids in the delay of passion which unconsciously means delay of death. This further explains why sex with other women does not seem to help Piet escape death (although sex for others like Harold is clearly such an escape): other women invite and encourage passion which is a symbolic invocation of death.

The fact that passionate love conceals a desire for death gives greater significance to the role of Freddy in the novel. His passion is, even on the conscious level, directed at death; and it is he who makes the description of death as the ultimate passion—"it's getting screwed by God." As Piet's alter-ego, he demonstrates overtly what Piet keeps repressed at the unconscious level: a lover's fascination with death.[11]

In this sense, the series of symbolic deaths Piet undergoes and his final acceptance of the fact of death may be symptoms of his ultimate choice of passion (Foxy), even though it is a choice of death. Being the demiurge earth king, passion and death are both proper to him. Unquestionably the character of Foxy is contrived to suggest the relationship between the two. But, in abandoning his attempt to escape them and reach towards the heavenly female spirit of light, Piet loses the hope that makes possible joy and disappointment. The romance tradition itself equates satisfaction with defeat. As Updike says of Piet, "he becomes a satisfied person, and in a sense dies. In other words, a person who has what he wants, a satisfied person, a content person ceases to be a person" (PR, p. 101). And so another connection between passion and death is revealed: Satisfied passion means the death of the human spirit.

The Tristram story offers one final comment on Piet's defeat: the death of God which makes Piet an anachronism seems ominously predicted there. At one point Iseult undergoes a divine judgment of her honesty and wins through a clever deception.

She claims that no man has ever held her in his arms except the king and a poor pilgrim who has just carried her ashore. She then grasps a red-hot poker and is not hurt. It was the literal truth—the pilgrim was Tristram in disguise. Thus it seems that either God Himself is powerless over such subterfuge or that He is not the just Calvinist God Piet believes in Who "Nails His joists of judgment down firm, and roofs the universe with order" (p. 418). He is a pagan God Who has His whims and allows adultery to thrive unpunished. The judgment scene in "Tristram" is paralleled in *Couples* when Piet, after his last visit to Foxy, catches sight of the weathercock and is "exhilarated once again at having not been caught" (p. 357).

De Rougemont's discussion of Iseult passing the ordeal may contain a clue to the origin of the church weathercock image itself. Gottfried of Strasbourg, a thirteenth-century clerk much interested in the Tristram legend, reacted bitterly to this portion of the story. De Rougemont quotes him as writing, "It was thus manifest and proved that the most virtuous Christ swings to every wind *like a weathercock.* . . . He lends Himself and can be adapted to anything" (*LWW*, p. 141, italics mine).

The loss of the God Whom men seek through love of the Lady renders the values of the Western romance mythology as ironic as the loss of that God renders the Christian rituals. The nihilism suggested by the annihilation of value systems in *Rabbit, Run* has borne fruit in the last novel which seems to demonstrate an undeniable basis for that annihilation. Piet may "cease to be a person," as Updike puts it, but it no longer matters. With the loss of Christian values, the loss of the status of *human person* ceases to be significant. We are left in a landscape in which tragedy is no longer possible. The only legitimate attitude appears to be Freddy's affectionate cynicism; the future appears to offer only comedy with the bathos of *Bech* as its deepest sentiment.

Rabbit Redux: The Search for Stature

1. America 1969

The central figures of each of Updike's first five novels have been characters who fill the role of life-givers to an increasingly sterile, arid society. In *The Poorhouse Fair* Hook's faith is contrasted with Conner's scientific coldness; in *Rabbit Run* Rabbit's beliefs are compared to the minister Eccles' lack of belief in anything; in *The Centaur* Caldwell's sense of an invisible world of values lends importance to people and events deemed trivial by others; in *Of the Farm* Joey returns to his mother's myth-making vision to re-establish his sense of identity; and in *Couples*, Piet's sexual vitality is a metaphor for his moral energies, unique in his Wasteland community of earthbound and dissipated suburbanites. Each of these life-giving protagonists possesses vision and a faith which lends importance to men and the things men do—a world in which tragedy is still possible.

However, Christianity, in one way or another, lies at the base of the systems of values of these central figures. In *Couples* Updike apparently abandons this base and burns down Piet's church once and for all. The next book, *Bech: A Book* is left— as one might predict—in the world of comedy where nothing matters very much because there is no certainty that men matter very much. *Rabbit Redux* might be described as tragi-comedy; Updike is searching for a non-Christian mythos which can provide stature for his humans.

To re-state—in order to write in a noncomic mode, one needs the same thing that the characters need to vitalize themselves: a mythos, a system of belief, a theology (though not necessarily *theistic*, if you will) to give things identity and importance. In the post-Christian era of his writing and, as he ap-

parently sees it, of his society, Updike is discovering whether the
society itself can provide the system of belief. Can belief in America elevate patriotism, citizenship, and a sense of national identity
into a humanistic religion which can invigorate his emotionally
and morally enervated characters? (Vague, generalized socialistic
goals were already shown to be unsatisfactory in *The Poorhouse
Fair.*) In *Couples* the suburbanites "made a church of each
other," as Freddy Thorne put it. Here that situation has been
extended to a larger but specified community, the country as a
whole. In *Rabbit Redux* Updike examines whether a society with
surprising social awareness can utilize this intellectual-emotional
energy to vitalize itself in the absence of any more transcendent
mythos—can his characters do so, and can he as a writer do so.
Rabbit, with his American flag decal on the car window, is the
central subject; black Skeeter, the anti-American American is his
antagonist.

Rabbit, indeed, is the dreamer of the American dream:
"American dream. When he first heard the phrase as a kid he
pictured God lying sleeping, the quilt-colored map of the U.S.
coming out of his head like a cloud" (p. 106). Skeeter is a self-
proclaimed Christ, whose dream is of America's destruction in
fiery revolution.

America in 1969 is represented by three central concerns:
space flights, the Vietnam War, and black militancy. These com-
pose the T.V. news broadcasts which punctuate the book like a
refrain, and conversations between characters constantly return
to these topics. Updike's characteristic metaphoric descriptions
are also woven about this three-point frame.

The book's imagery, for instance, frequently portrays the
characters in the vocabulary of these three social concerns. Constant use of the word "space" or synonyms like "empty" and
frequent use of military metaphors give his major characters the
appearance of microcosms of the United States as a whole. This
suggestion—that individuals are mirrors of the whole society—
is made overt when Jill accuses Rabbit: "If you loved your country, you'd want it better." Rabbit replies, "If it was better I'd
have to be better" (p. 153). (Updike has stated in the past that
he thinks the society even reflects each presidential administration. Recall that in *Couples,* he establishes a resemblance between

Piet and President Kennedy.) Thus, Rabbit frequently refers to his "inner space." His house is a "spacecraft . . . slowly spinning in the void"; his father is "a piece of grit on the launching pad"; and he and Jill are, in one scene, the earth and moon viewed by the "mother planet" of the television set.

More startling perhaps are the military metaphors. When he makes love to Jill, Rabbit imagines that the semen on her skin leaves invisible burns "like a napalmed child" (p. 142). Her eyes are like "tree leaves, a shuffling concealing multitude, a microscopic forest he wants to bomb" (p. 151). Making love to Janice, he sees her body as a "barren landscape lit by bombardment, silently exploding images . . ." (p. 68). He refers to his short haircut as "the enemy's uniform," and when Janice buys Nelson expensive clothes on Rabbit's charge accounts he exclaims, "So it's war!" He tells Stavros he won't bargain with him over Janice's future: "If you want to pull out, pull out. Don't try to commit me to one of your fucking coalition governments" (p. 161).

Either the moon landing or the Vietnam War *could* provide the belief and fervor to vitalize American life. Space flight recaptures our identity as explorers, voyagers, conquerors, adventurers—the American as pioneer. (There is at least one specific comparison with Columbus.) And being either hawk or dove on Vietnam should elicit a system of values and beliefs from any American which would closely relate to his understanding of America's identity and his own role within that identity.

However, the war and the excitement of the moon shot fail ultimately to revitalize the society. When Rabbit and his father watch the lift-off on a barroom television, the sound is turned off (a recurring Updike metaphor for separation) and the men in the bar only murmur restlessly—"They have not been lifted off," the speaker says, "they are left here." "Those pretty boys in the sky," Rabbit's father complains, "Nixon'll hog the credit" (p. 20). The extent of society's reaction to the event seems to be the "Lunar Special" that Rabbit orders at Burger Bliss—a double cheeseburger with an American flag stuck in it.

The Vietnam War is similarly devalued. The doves consider it an imperialistic-capitalistic reflex—"the pentagon playing cowboys and Indians all over the globe" Charlie Stavros calls it. Rabbit, as a hawk, tries to give it meaning: "We're trying to give ourselves away to make little yellow people happy" (p. 48). But his attempts disintegrate into empty romantic rhetoric: "America is beyond power," he thinks, "it acts as a face of God. . . . Beneath her patient bombers, paradise is possible" (p. 49). And finally he, too, reveals the threadbare state of his belief: "My opinion is, you have to fight a war now and then to show you're willing, and it doesn't much matter where it is" (p. 50).

In his first novel, *Rabbit Run*, Rabbit was a priestly figure, the only character with a sense of belief strong enough to vitalize others. In his second novel, Rabbit has become one of the burnt-out cynics—the washed-out, dissipated Americans in need of a priest and life-giver. The role of vitalizer is assumed in *Rabbit Redux*, by Skeeter, the angry young black whose hatreds and militancy have provided the necessary system of values and the emotional energy to invest in these values. His hostility lends importance and identity to the features of American society. Listening to Skeeter's bitter, foul-mouthed description of whites and race relations, Rabbit slowly realizes, "There seems to be not only a history but a theology behind his anger" (p. 112). Later during the long talks in Rabbit's living room, it becomes clear that history *is* Skeeter's theology. In extended monologs he recounts his view of American history, at times so emotionally involved that he is screaming or crying (or, at one point, masturbating). At the conclusion of one of these lectures recounting black humiliations and suffering Skeeter asks, "You believe any of this?" "I believe all of it," Rabbit calmly replies. "Do you believe, do you believe I'm so mad just telling this if I had a knife right now I'd poke it in your throat and watch that milk white blood come out and would love it, oh, would I love it" (p. 207). Saying this, Skeeter is weeping uncontrollably.

Skeeter has done through hatred what Updike has maintained throughout his writing is necessary both for himself as a writer and for his characters—he has used American history as myth. The irony is that it is a belief and a vision based on bitter condemnation. Nonetheless, only Hook, the old former history teacher of *The Poorhouse Fair*, was able to invest American history with such importance and to become so passionately involved in it. Skeeter calls himself Jesus—the real Jesus, the black Jesus. In the novel's terms, this is true. He is the only one with beliefs deep enough and a vision of America strong enough to be a priest and life-giver.

Updike's three point complex (space/blacks/Vietnam) thus assumes a specific shape. Space flight becomes the symbol of American technology and is associated with the sterile, mechanized white Americans. At the other pole are blacks, especially Skeeter. "We are what has been left out of the industrial revolution," says Skeeter, "we are the nature you put down in yourselves" (p. 208). It is significant that Skeeter never discusses the space flight. In the middle, acting as a kind of touchstone, is the Vietnam War. Discussed by the white characters in the book, it has no real significance; but discussed by Skeeter (who fought there) it is a monumental event—horrible, fascinating, and holy. It is "where God is pushing through"; it is quintessential Americana. A closer look at each of these three points of reference should explain Updike's logic.

2. The Sterility of White America

America's interest in space flight in 1969 is represented not only by the news of the moon shot but also by frequent reference to the movie 2001 which several of the major characters see early in the book. Charlie Stavros found the movie boring. "It wasn't sexy," he says, "I guess I don't find technology that sexy." A scene in the movie specifically mentioned is the moment when the ape-man throws a bone into the air which becomes, by slight of camera, a satellite. The scene, of course, symbolizes the industrial revolution in general, the rise of technology leading to space flight.

The characters in the movie live totally mechanized lives aboard a space ship to Jupiter. They eat chemically reconstituted food, have health-program jogging as their only recreation, and have emotional relationships with no one except the computer that they talk to. Updike sees contemporary American life as similar. Heating a T.V. dinner for himself, Rabbit reads the ingredients: ". . . maltodextrin, tomato paste, corn starch, Worchestershire sauce, hydrolyzed vegetable protein, monosodium glutamate, nonfat dry milk, dehydrated onions, flavoring, sugar, caramel color, spice, cysteine, and thiamine hydrochloride, gum arabic" (p. 28). Later that night he looks at his living room and "everywhere in his own house sees a slippery disposable gloss. It glints back at him from the synthetic fabric of the living room sofa . . . the synthetic artiness of a lamp . . . the steel sink" (p. 31). This room is later described as filled with "gadgets designed to repel repair, nothing straight from the human hand" (p. 69). At his linotype job, Rabbit sets an article describing how, in the course of bulldozing a new parking lot, workers are unearthing (and demolishing) old handmade artifacts—wall murals, sign boards shaped in the forms of cows, beehives, and plows, stone grinding wheels, and even arrowheads. The old America found behind the poorhouse walls of the first novel is surrendering to the artificial world of technology.

Even outside Rabbit sees all the lawn sprinklers twirling in unison and a "barren sky raked by slender aerials. A sky poisoned by radio waves" (p. 60). When he goes to buy Mom Angstrom a present, the sky is colorless (like space)—bright and barren— and the drugstore is full of "ingenious crap." Watching the moon walk on T.V. the Angstroms are described in mechanical terms, too. Mom's legs are "bulbs" and she is propped on pillows. Pop is "an old pump" that keeps going. Neil Armstrong says something from the moon but his voice is only a crackle and his leg "a snakey shape."

The imagery of coldness pervades the book, beginning in the opening scene in an overly air-conditioned bar. The moon, we are frequently reminded, is *cold*. Coldness is synonymous with a lack of life; in the novel it is also carried to the extreme of things being *frozen*. On the Jupiter ship in *2001* there are several frozen humans who will be revived when the ship lands. Although this is never directly mentioned in the novel, it is alluded to by Mom Angstrom's dream; she dreams she finds a man frozen in the icebox. This is related to several of her other dreams in which Rabbit and his sister Mim are dead and in coffins or in dreams in which humans have been reduced to puddles of slime connected by tubes to machines. In short she sees frozen, dead, dehumanized humans.

In the novel, Rabbit is repeatedly described as being

"frozen." Listening to Skeeter's history and worried about Nelson
seeing and hearing too much, Rabbit is "frozen" and can't think
of what to do. He acts out of instinct, Jill tells him, because his
"thought is frozen." Ice, of course, is white, not black; and Jill
at one point "freezes white" when embarrassed by Rabbit.

The white color of the Caucasian characters in the book is
stressed constantly. And it is nearly always coupled with a sense
of their dissipation and lack of vigor. The opening scene also
connects whiteness with coldness and ice. The first sentence sets
the motif: "Men emerge pale from the little printing plant at
four sharp, ghosts for an instant. . . ." The sky in that scene
is "blanched white" and "colorless"; the city looks like a "frozen
explosion." The father has "washed out eyes" and "no color hair";
his face is "washed empty" and the younger man, Rabbit, is
"pale and sour." They walk into a cold bar, two anonymous figures; Rabbit orders a frozen daquiri and watches a couple on
T.V. win a frozen food locker.

When Janice looks at Rabbit in a later scene she sees a "big
white body, his spreading slack gut, his uncircumcised member
hanging boneless . . . from its blond roots. . . . a large white
man a knife would slice like lard" (p. 39). When he enters the
all-black Jimbo's Lounge, Rabbit feels himself "a large soft white
man" and wants to apologize for his "bloated pallor." Jill's colors
are silver and white—that is, white and a dirty white. Her dress
and car are white, and she first appears to Nelson clad in a bed-
sheet. She and Rabbit are described as "two bleached creatures."
Jill represents an exaggerated state of loss: "rejecting instruction
and inventing her own way of moving through the world, she has
lost any vivid idea of what to be looking for" (p. 119).

Thus a pattern is established relating space, emptiness,
blankness, coldness, whiteness. Technology, the new mythos, is
sterile. It symbolizes dehumanization, mechanization, emptiness.
It is not, as Charlie says, *sexy*. After the moon landing we listen
to a long conversation between the astronauts and Houston:

> we have a P twenty-two update for you if you're ready to
> copy. . . . P one one zero four thirty two eighteen; P
> two one zero four thirty two eighteen; P two one zero four
> thirty-seven twenty-eight and that is four miles south. This is

based on a targeted landing site. . . . Our mission timer is now reading nine zero four thirty-four forty-seven and static. . . . (pp. 89-90)

This jargon, meaningless to the average American is the ritual of the new religion.

Having lost their older religions and their sense of a human America, these characters are incapable of finding anything of consequence in their world. There are no more heroes. Roosevelt, described by Janice's father, becomes a crazy old man who made a war to bail him out of the Depression. When Nelson mentions watching a movie glamorizing John Kennedy's war experiences, the grandfather spouts, "Pure propaganda. They made that movie because old Joe owned a lot of those studios." LBJ, the old man claims, went into Vietnam just to "get the coloreds up into the economy." He expresses disgust at the events of Chappaquidick, claiming that Kennedy got the girl pregnant and then killed her. America, he says, "is a police state run by the Kennedys. . . . That family has been out to buy the country since those Brahmins up in Boston snubbed old Joe." Not even Jackie Kennedy is salvaged—"Now they've got the young widow to marry a rich Greek in case they run out of money. Not that she's the goodie gumdrop the papers say . . ." (pp. 77-78). Rabbit's father calls Nixon "a poor devil" who's trying his best, but confides, "I don't have much use for Tricky Dicky and never have . . ." (p. 304).

Even Rabbit, with his American flag decal, says of Nixon: "Poor old Nixon, even his own commissions beat on him. . . . He's just a typical flatfooted Chamber of Commerce type who lucked his way into the hot seat and is so dumb he thinks it's good luck. Let the poor bastard alone" (p. 200). Mim, Rabbit's sister, is a symbol of the new white generation that "lives on pollution" and is "hard" as "cockroaches." She entertains the family by doing humorous take-offs on Disneyland mechanical dummies representing Lincoln and Washington.

In this kind of demoralized society, emptied of belief in anything, the characters are emotionally paralyzed—frozen. When his wife admits to having a lover, Rabbit says, "See him if you want to. Just as long as I don't have to see the bastard." And at that moment he catches sight of himself in the mirror—

"a big pink pale man going shapeless" (p. 75). Even Peggy is amazed at Rabbit's lack of feeling: "Ollie would have strangled me." And later Janice complains that Rabbit could have fought for her a little harder. Similarly, Rabbit is unable and unwilling to help Jill escape from Skeeter and even watches Skeeter sexually humiliate Jill. "I don't mind if she doesn't," he says, although Nelson protests that Jill *does* mind and begs his father to help her.

The ability to feel personal ties and personal responsibility is directly connected, in the novel, with faith in the culture's deeds and heroes: Janice explains Rabbit's heated defense of the war by telling Charlie that her husband came back after the baby's death (in the earlier novel) for "old-fashioned reasons" and therefore is forced to defend old-fashioned patriotic attitudes, too. But now the crackly voice "that used to sell them Shredded Ralston between episodes of Tom Mix" has become the voice from the astronauts spinning out technical data; and Janice views Charlie's and Rabbit's care about the war as eccentric, strange, and silly. "How silly. How silly it all is" she thinks, "it wouldn't have mattered if we hadn't bothered to be born at all" (p. 56).

Without myths, without heroes, without values and feelings, the people of white America have no goals, no upward direction. When Rabbit travels through Penn Park, the wealthiest of the nearby suburbs, he notices the houses with their two-car garages and curved driveways. "In Brewer County," he thinks, "there is nowhere higher to go than these houses" (p. 22). It is an ironic line containing in its deepest recesses a bitter truth. Nelson (who likes to watch space shots) tells this truth to Skeeter: "I don't want God to come. . . . I want to grow up like *him* [Rabbit] average and ordinary" (p. 230).

The mythless, heroless, dead society of white America is symbolically represented by the baseball game that Rabbit, his son, and his father-in-law go to watch. Baseball symbolizes America—it is "a game whose very taste, of spit and dust and grass and sweat and leather and sun, was America" (p. 79). Unaccountably, however, the game is boring, even to Rabbit who used to love sports. "The *spaced* dance of the men in *white* fails to enchant, the code beneath the staccato spurts of distant motion refuses to yield its meaning" (italics mine). The crowd boos coarsely; "the poetry of space and inaction is too fine, too slowly spun for them." There is only one thing at the game that excites the crowd enough to make them yell—the black player: "Ram it down his throat, Speedy." "Kill that black bastard!" Even ironically, blacks are the source of vitality.

3. Skeeter: The Lover as Militant Minority

Skeeter, who rages and weeps and calls upon God, is the antithesis of the morally, emotionally dried-up whites. Updike at one point suggests that deprivation has preserved the minority group's energies. Rabbit tells Jill that everything is "dead" for her because it was given to her. "Fear. That's what makes us poor bastards run," he says. "You don't know what fear is, do you, poor baby? That's why you're so dead" (p. 152). Even Janice seems to share something of the perception that minority groups retain their vitality. After listening to Charlie's animated criticisms of American war policy she thinks, "How strange of Charlie to care, *as if he's a minority*" (p. 56, italics mine). This is the same internal monolog in which she reveals her own feeling that nothing matters.

Blacks in the book have not been sterilized by the industrial revolution, as Skeeter points out. Sterile technology is a force in opposition to them. In the bar, Rabbit thinks of the home to which he must return as a "cast off space capsule," but he feels that blacks have a "dread of those clean, dry places where Harry must be." Several pages later he refers to their bodies as "liquid" —a repeating metaphor describing blacks throughout the book. They are not dried up.

One of the highly lyrical prose passages in the book describes Babe's piano playing. Babe is the black entertainer and sometime-prostitute in Jimbo's Lounge. She plays all the old tunes with deep, urgent feeling. She still knows, the speaker says, "the lyrics born in some distant smoke, decades when Americans moved within the American dream."

What does Babe play? All the good old ones. All show tunes. "Up a Lazy River," "You're the Top," "Thou Swell," "Sum-

mertime," you know. There are hundreds, thousands. Men
from Indiana wrote them in Manhattan. They flow into each
other without edges, flowing under black bridges of chords
thumped six, seven times, as if Babe is helping the piano to
remember a word it won't say. . . . Or saying, *Here I am
find me, find me.* (p. 114)

"Broadway forgot the tune," the speaker says, "but here it all
still was in the music Babe played." Like the old people in
The Poorhouse Fair, Babe preserves both handicraft and the
sense of an older, more invigorating America.

In the opening scene described earlier, Updike pictures a
white, washed-out, dry, cold setting. After leaving his father, Rabbit gets on a bus to go home; this scene is written in bold contrast to the previous one. The bus riders are primarily black.
They have bushy hair—"that's O.K.," thinks Rabbit, "it's more
nature, Nature is what we're running out of." He recalls the way
they laugh and notices their eyes—"brown, liquid in them about
to quiver out." (His father, remember, has "washed out" eyes.)
They are "noisy" (even when a moon rocket takes off, the whites
in the barroom earlier only murmured)—their noise "comes out
in big silvery hoops," like their gold hoop earrings. He compares
them to lions and then to tropical plants smuggled into a garden.
Later, when Rabbit goes into Jimbo's Lounge, it is a streaming pit
of life containing sports, sex, music, high emotions, and mystery.
The blacks refuse to give Rabbit his customary frozen daquiri;
instead he drinks a stinger.

This contrast with whites is underlined by the frequent
reference to whites as "ghosts." Men coming out of the printing
plant are "ghosts" in the opening line. Janice sees Rabbit as "a
pale tall man going fat . . . a ghost, white soft" (p. 57). Even
Rabbit's mother is a "shade" when she greets him on the day
of her birthday. Rabbit and Jill (first called "a smokey creature")
are said to "haunt" the house; and Jill, after her death, seems
to pay Rabbit a spiritual visit. Indeed she is pictured as a dis-
embodied spirit all along. The *physical* in these characters is
lacking.

In contrast to Jill's smokey white dress, Babe wears a red
dress "the blood color of a rooster's comb." (As pointed out in

the introduction, red is frequently Updike's color for sexuality (see page 9). Blacks in *Rabbit Redux* are always described very physically—hair, arms, legs, and so on. In the bar, he sees them as "panthers." Thus the two races are contrasted in terms similar to Eldridge Cleaver's "primeval mitosis" theory: Whites have become all sterile, bodiless intellect (technology), and blacks are the physical—fertile, sexual.[1]

Throughout his novels, Updike has always used sex as a metaphor for moral and emotional vitality. Here he repeatedly associates the blacks with sex. When a colored couple appears on the T.V. quiz show (where the whites have just won a freezer), Rabbit "wonders how that black bride would be" and indulges in a sex fantasy about blacks in general. ". . . the men are slow as Jesus, long as whips, takes everything to get them up, in there forever, that's why white women need them . . ." (p. 25). In a later scene Rabbit is interrupted during a sex fantasy by his father-in-law's complaint about race riots. Another stream of conversation moves in less than a page from a discussion of Nature to Rabbit's mother (life principle) to sex to blacks (p. 148). Towards the end of the book Rabbit must picture a black woman in order to masturbate. This motif culminates, of course, in the sexual attraction Rabbit feels towards Skeeter, which is vaguely reminiscent of Eccles' fascination with Rabbit in the earlier book.[2]

Rabbit's sexual attractiveness in the novel *Rabbit, Run* is correlative with his identity as a life-giver and a Christ figure. In that novel he is several times compared with Jesus (usually ironically) and once, when looking at a glass-covered painting of Christ, sees his own face reflected in the glass. In *Rabbit Redux*, Skeeter labels himself a Christ, and Updike's imagery reinforces this. Skeeter's glasses "toss haloes" of light; Jill warns that the police will "crucify" Skeeter if they catch him. When Skeeter undresses, Rabbit has never seen such a chest "except on a crucifix." And at the end Rabbit takes Skeeter to a place called Galilee where Skeeter spits in Rabbit's hand—an ironic blessing (or perhaps even a baptism)—an echo of the spit which signifies "America" in the baseball game.[3]

Admittedly use of imagery like this is ambiguous; it might mean that Skeeter is an antichrist and is being ironically compared with the original Jesus. However, Skeeter's behavior and his influence on other characters often reinforces his charismatic identity and argues for his similarity to the Rabbit of *Rabbit Run*. Skeeter is a believer in a world of nonbelievers. He not only believes in God (interestingly enough still a mark of Updike's life-givers) but in the importance of men. The history of black people in America and their present sufferings have convinced Skeeter that things *do* matter, that there is a cultural entity called "America" and that it is a force to be reckoned with, a force that has made an enormous mark on history. Of course, Skeeter's assessment is damnation of America; but his anger awards to its object the stature which is denied in the white world's sophisticated ennui. When Rabbit talks about "poor old Nixon" the hapless Chamber of Commerce type, Skeeter's response is a fiery denial: "That honky was put there by the cracker vote. . . . He is Herod, man, and all us black babies better believe it" (p. 200).

Given the motivation of bitterness, Skeeter has become an American-history buff. Like Babe, who remembers the old tunes and plays them with feeling, Skeeter revitalizes the old stories, sees them in a perspective meaningful to him and invests them with deep feeling and importance.

> Anyhoo, you had this war. You had these crazies up North like Garrison and Brown agitating and down South a bunch of supercrackers like Yancy and Rhett who thought they could fatten their own pie by splitting, funny thing is . . . they didn't, the Confederacy sent 'em away on a ship and elected all play-it-safes to office! Same up North with cats like Sumner. (p. 204)

> So then you had these four million freed slaves without property or jobs in this economy dead on its feet thinking the halleluiah days had come. . . . that was the most pathetic thing, the way those poor niggers jumped for the bait. They taught themselves to read, they broke their backs for chickenshit, they sent good men to the fuckhead Yoo Ess Senate, they set up legislatures giving Dixie the first public schools it ever had, how about that. . . . And all this here

while . . . the crackers down there were frothing at the mouth and calling our black heroes baboons. (p. 205)

It is not inaccurate, ultimately, to say that Skeeter functions· as a kind of redeemer figure. In contrast to the evenings in which Rabbit and Nelson wandered aimlessly around, eating T.V. dinners, they have begun evenings in which the group engages in debates and readings resembling the religious rituals forgotten by the age of technology. Nelson, who appears to dislike and fear Skeeter, is nonetheless markedly changed by Skeeter's presence. The boy begins to take an interest in the news and remember it. ("Hey Dad, Robert Williams is back in this country.") Earlier Rabbit had worried about the boy's lack of interest in sports; after Skeeter's arrival, Nelson begins to play soccer and joins Skeeter for basketball games in the backyard. He gets intensely emotional about Skeeter's behavior towards Jill and is able to argue with his father about moral responsibility and human alternatives. He realizes Jill is being drugged and needs help. "Stop him," he tells his father. "How can I?" Rabbit responds "You can kick him out." "We can't live Jill's life for her." "We *could* if you wanted to. If you cared at all" (pp. 255-256). Nelson has even had several street fights with neighborhood boys over the issue of Skeeter's presence in the house. He has come a long way from the kid who whimpered about the food in the Greek restaurant.

There is the suggestion that Rabbit, too, is changing. In the novel's terms, he is becoming black. Skeeter forces Rabbit to read from books of black oratory, and praises him telling him he makes "a good nigger." Immediately afterward they watch a *Laugh-In* skit in which, symbolically, Arte Johnson (white) and Sammy Davis (black) are dressed as mirror-image doubles. A few nights later Skeeter offers Rabbit his marijuana cigarette asking him if he wants to "know how a Negro feels"; Rabbit accepts. By the end of the book Rabbit feels that his ejaculations, which used to resemble "space flight" (white/technology) are now "shouts of anger" (black militancy?). Rabbit is acquiring, it is hinted, a new identity.

Rabbit's neighbors are also affected by Skeeter's presence. Previously they were uninvolved with their society and hardly knew each other. They come and go in vans, but are never seen, Rabbit notes early in the book. "They get together to sign futile petitions for better sewers . . . but otherwise they do not connect" (p. 73). Again in the realm of irony, Skeeter changes this. The neighbors organize to oppose Skeeter's presence, particularly his association with Jill. They meet with Rabbit, keep the house under close surveillance, and finally unite for their ultimate act of discipline and punishment.

Therefore, although his mode is ironic (as Rabbit's often was in the earlier novel), Skeeter in various ways energizes and vitalizes his surroundings. The first night of Skeeter's arrival, appropriately, laughter sounds like "cackling" and the house "is an egg cracking because they are all hatching together" (p. 190). Perhaps rebirth has begun.

4. Vietnam: The Touchstone

The most conspicuous mark of Skeeter's identity is his feeling about the war in Vietnam. The imagery of war and the Vietnam War in particular is ubiquitous in the novel. Not only are the people described with metaphors of war—as shown earlier—but the American scene as a whole is so pictured. As Skeeter says, Vietnam reveals the essential America: "Nam is the spot where our heavenly essence is pustulatin'. Man don't like Vietnam, he don't like America" (p. 232). When the whites firebomb Rabbit's house, Skeeter describes a "whoosh and soft woomp, reminded me of an APM hitting in the bush up the road." "The war," Skeeter recalls thinking, "is come home."

In the novel's terms, the war has been here all along. Death and killing seem to be a principal mark of the society. Janice is already a killer and Rabbit will "kill" Jill, as he later sees it. Just before Jill's death, Rabbit looks uneasily at Peggy's casserole and wonders "how many animals have died to keep his life going, how many more will die." "To be alive is to kill," he finally decides. Rabbit's father would agree. "Killing's not the worst thing around," he says watching some peace marchers; "rather shake the hand of a killer than a traitor" (p. 304). Killing is

American, is the implication—a contrast to being a traitor. Appropriately, Skeeter's American-history lectures are punctuated with references to the Civil War. Perhaps it is the death they carry within them that makes the members of the society kill. Rabbit now regrets that he was never sent to Korea. He thinks about himself: "He had never been a fighter but now there is enough death in him so that in a way he wants to kill" (p. 117).

The Vietnam War seems to represent the American Way, not only for Skeeter but for Rabbit's neighbors. One battle-scarred man tells Rabbit that he fought and got wounded so he could "have a decent life here" meaning he wants conventional segregation enforced in his neighborhood. In Vietnam he notes, blacks followed the American way; that is, they knew their place. "I fought beside them in Vietnam because we all knew the rules." Anyone who didn't, the neighbor brags, "got fragged" (pp. 252-254).

Rabbit, who considers himself a hawk, presumably supports the war and sees its importance. He explains to Charlie Stavros in the restaurant that the United States is doing it to make Vietnam happy—"make a happy, rich country full of highways and gas stations." The Vietnamese, he claims, want our help, as opposed to "a few madmen in black pajamas" who "would rather bury 'em alive." Hearing people oppose the war makes Rabbit "rigid." He feels "treachery and ingratitude befouling the flag, befouling him." Yet his vision quickly becomes hyperbolic and unreal. "Wherever America is, there is freedom, and wherever America is not, madness rules with chains, darkness strangles millions. Beneath her patient bombers paradise is possible" (p. 49). America is "something infinitely tender, the star lit with his birth."

Because Rabbit lacks Skeeter's solid value system, he must rely on romantic emotions and ultimately can only defend the war, in *practical* terms, by a weak *ad hominum* argument. "Better there than here. Better little wars than big ones," he tells Charlie. Later he says to Jill in the bar, "If you stayed out of every mess, you'd never get into anything." He admits that America only "halfway works" but halfway is "better than no way at all." Look at the Japanese, Rabbit points out to Charlie, "happy as clams and twice as sassy, screwing us right and left. We fight their wars for them while you peaceniks sell their tinny cars" (p. 51).

Statements like this put Rabbit, the hawk, relatively close to Charlie, the dove. Charlie sees the war as a mistake in the disreputable game of international politics. "We've been playing chess with the Russians so long we didn't know we were off the board. . . . Kennedy's advisors who thought they could run the world from the dean's office pushed the button and nothing happened. Then Oswald voted Johnson in who was such a bonehead he thought all it took was a bigger thumb on the button" (p. 48). Charlie feels, we later learn, that the war will be over just as soon as the big industrial interests see it is unprofitable.

Skeeter, on the other hand, sees the war as an existential moment of horror, a point of cosmic creation of the essence of America. His sense of its importance places him in thematic opposition to both Rabbit and Charlie. When Skeeter describes the war, the narrative switches to his point of view for the first time. He feels the need to "do it justice." Skeeter articulates the book's stylistic and thematic implications that the war is a definitionally American activity. Rabbit asks him, "Is our being in Vietnam wrong?" Skeeter answers:

> Wrong? Man how can it be wrong when that's the way it is? Those poor Benighted states just being themselves, right? Can't stop bein' yourself, somebody has to do it for you, right? Nobody that big around. Uncle Sam wakes up one morning, looks down at his belly, sees he's some cockroach, what can he do? Just keep bein' his cockroach self, is all. (p. 231)

The allusion to cockroaches from Kafka's *Metamorphosis* foreshadows Mim's description that the new generation is training themselves to "live in the desert" (the arid American society) by becoming cockroaches. "They're going to make themselves hard," she says, "like cockroaches."

Since the United States is capitalistic and on the international scale capitalism can promote imperialistic tendencies, our presence in Vietnam is seen by Skeeter as perfectly logical.

I'm not one of these white liberals like that cracker Fulldull
or Charlie McCarthy . . . think Vietnam some sort of mistake,
. . . it is *no* mistake, right, any President comes along falls
in love with it, it is liberalism's very wang, dingdong pussy,
and fruit. . . . What is liberalism? Bringin' joy to the world,
right? Puttin' enough sugar on dog-eat-dog so it tastes good
all over, right? Well now what could be nicer than Vietnam?
We is keepin' that coast open. (pp. 231-232)

According to Skeeter Vietnam is the acme of all our past wars
since it is most unequivocally a product of our capitalistic, imperialistic, racist tendencies: "Nam is an act of love, right? Compared to Nam, beatin' Japan was flat out ugly. We was ugly
fuckers then and now we is truly a civilized spot. . . . we is
what the world is begging *for*."

Beyond its historical political content, moreover, Skeeter
treats the war as an existential experience. It is so horrible and
horrifying that it infinitely expands outward the normal boundaries of human perception and sensation, the boundaries of the
bearable: "And, you know, you could do it," Skeeter muses
wonderingly. "You didn't die of it. That was interesting." He
recounts some of the horrors and adds, "It does blow your
mind."

Vietnam is a situation which dramatizes the primeval confrontation with death: "And the dead, the dead are so weird,
they are so—dead. . . . I mean they are so out of it, so peaceful,
there is no word for it . . ." (p. 228). He recalls a young soldier
who the night before had been describing love-making with his
girl friend—"the VC trip a Claymore and his legs go this way
and he goes the other. It was bad." Skeeter remembers stepping
on a wounded man's insides and hearing him scream out and die;
he tells of a man cut in two by bullets, still firing away. "It was
bad," he repeats, "I wouldn't have believed you could see such
bad things and keep your eyeballs." Nelson doesn't want to hear
about it, but Rabbit makes the proper existential response, "It
happened so we got to take it in. We got to deal with it somehow" (pp. 228-229).

Skeeter's sense of the significance of Vietnam gives it the
appearance of something cosmic and holy. He is frustrated and

dissatisfied with his own descriptions, which he considers inadequate. "I'm not doing it, I'm not doing it justice, I'm selling it short. The holy quality is hardest to get," he thinks at one point. His memories are colored by this sense of holiness; he remembers "Tao crosses, Christian crosses, the cross-shaped bombs the Phantoms dropped. . . ." He tries to explain that Vietnam is, ironically, a place of creation—that the destruction, death, heroism, energies, and Americansim of the war make it a special point in time and space. He explains one scientific theory of the structure of the universe to convey this notion: "there is a steady state, and though it is true everything is expanding outwards, it does not thin out to next to nothingness on account of the reason that through strange holes in this nothingness new somethingness comes pouring in from exactly nowhere." [4] Vietnam, he explains, "is the local hole. It is where the world is redoing itself. . . . It is where God is pushing through" (p. 230). Later he calls peace demonstrators antichrists. "They perceive God's face in Vietnam," he says, "and spit upon it" (p. 242).

Though moved by Skeeter's presentation, Rabbit is still the dried up American, a counterpoint to Skeeter's energies. "Shit," he replies to all this, "it's just a dirty little war that has to be fought."

5. The Reawakened Sense of Causality

The white middle American has lost his Christian faith and his faith in his country. His religions, his myths, have dried up. In a certain sense, the central symbol of the novel's theme is Rabbit's mother, his life source. Throughout the story she is dying —her life artificially prolonged by drugs, by technology. Rabbit dreads visiting home, the speaker says, because he hates to see his mother "the source of his life, staring wasted" (p. 20). This is a symbolic description of his environment as a whole.

Human relationships between the white characters fail to improve their plight. Stripped of the energies for involvement, Rabbit does not want to get close to anyone. "The trouble with caring about anybody," he thinks, "you begin to feel overprotective. Then you begin to feel crowded" (p. 26). (It is signifi-

cant that Skeeter's personality is geared to avoid this reaction.)
Janice explains her interest in Charlie by claiming that he has
"a gift, Charlie does, of making everything exciting—the way
food tastes, the way the sky looks, the customers that come in.
. . . He loves life" (pp. 70-71). Yet, on a deeper level, Charlie, the
cynical American liberal, cannot provide the vitality Janice and
the other characters need. She considers marrying him but feels
that the possibility "opens an abyss." "A gate she had always
assumed gave onto a garden gave onto emptiness" (p. 65).
Charlie, too, lacks the ability to respond to people as significant
individuals. Describing Janice he says crudely, "She wants what
every normal chick wants. To be Helen of Troy" (p. 161). And
within the next few lines he refers to Jill, variously, as "hippie,"
"flower baby," "nympho," and so on.

One of the few moments of deep pleasure for Rabbit is the
scene where he accuses Janice of having an affair and she denies
it, causing him to hit her. For a moment the old values are
revitalized. She denies adultery; he is jealous and angry; she is
punished. "Harry feels a flash of pleasure: sunlight in a tunnel."
But almost immediately, Janice proudly admits to her relationship with Charlie and Rabbit's excitement fades. "Keep him, if
he makes you happy," he finally offers; and both return to the
newer world of moral ennui.

Several characters during the course of the novel articulate
this new amoral morality. Peggy has a simple philosophy, "Living
is a compromise between doing what you want and doing what
other people want." Surrounding this line she is portrayed as a
crude seductress. Buchanan states Rabbit's philosophy of noninvolvement by way of sympathetic agreement: "I am . . . a man
trying to get . . . from the cradle to the grave hurting the fewest
people I can. Just like Harry here" (p. 120). The old man in
charge of guarding Rabbit's gutted house explains the logic of
noninvolvement. He will turn the other way and pretend not to
see Rabbit illegally enter the house. "See no evil is the way I do
it." And he warns Rabbit, "Any damage you do yourself, you're
the party responsible" (p. 288). The message? Don't get involved
so that you won't be responsible for any damage.

Throughout most of the book Rabbit has followed this
philosophy. He refuses to encourage or force Janice to return.

He is unwilling to respond to his father's urgent requests to pay frequent visits home. He tells Nelson that he can't help Jill because they can't lead her life for her. He makes a similar statement to Jill. "Suit yourself," he snaps when he learns she is still in contact with Skeeter's drug culture at Jimbo's Lounge, "It's your life to fuck up" (p. 170).

Yet, it is important to note that the imagery of rebirth is scattered throughout the novel. His mother asks him to pray for it, "Pray for rebirth. Pray for your own rebirth." Rabbit rejects this with the realization that "freedom means murder. Rebirth means death" (p. 175). However, the novel offers us the required death. Does Rabbit gain the rebirth? The first step would have to be a sense of significant involvement with his surroundings, a sense of true causality. This, basically, would mean the move from the realm of comedy to the realm of tragedy.[5]

As in *Rabbit Run*, Updike's final situation is ambiguous. The book is set in autumn, the time of death, not rebirth. Yet at several points Rabbit is grappling with the realm of moral responsibility. Early in the book he reconsiders his desertion of Ruth, an event of the earlier novel. He had felt at the time that he shouldn't try to get in touch with her but now realizes, "that the rules were complicated, that there were some rules by which he should have" (p. 66). After Jill's death all the people Rabbit meets tell him he's only responsible for himself. His boss, upon firing him, advises him to leave his family, even Nelson, "You're number one, not the kid" (p. 298). And Skeeter maintains his role of ironic redeemer to the last; his rejection of guilt may in the long run elicit it from Rabbit. "How could you let her die?" Rabbit asks Skeeter. "Man, you want to talk guilt, we got to go back hundreds of years," Skeeter replies. "Everybody stuck inside his own skin, might as well make himself at home there, right?" (p. 291). Rabbit seems unsure and, ten pages later, is on the edge of the basic tragic vision of Oedipus; he looks at the world of "blameless activity" and feels that "he would never be allowed to crawl back into that world."

Yet simultaneous with his dawning sense of causality, of involvement, is a new awareness of his ordinariness, his unimportance. His street, for instance, seems "an ordinary street anywhere. Millions of such American streets hold millions of lives and let them sift through, and neither notice nor mourn, and fall into decay, and do not even mourn their own passing." He recalls nostalgically a lost time when this street "excited Rabbit with the magic of his own existence . . . here the universe had centered" (p. 324). When, in the closing scene, Janice asks, "Who do you think you are?" He responds "Nobody."

This, basically, is the comic vision which is forced on Piet at the end of *Couples* when he and Foxy must settle for being just "another couple." What Updike seems to be testing here is whether this sensibility can co-exist with the more tragic sensibility of causality and significance. Rabbit and Janice at the end do go, symbolically, to a place of safety and escape—the *Safe Haven* motel. Yet Rabbit persists, "I feel so guilty." "About what?" Janice asks. "About everything." "Relax," she coaxes, "Not everything is your fault." "I can't accept that" is the last line he speaks in the book.

He is, it turns out, still looking for the "something else" (p. 344) that makes things run and when he prepares, at the end, to go to meet Janice, he wears, ritualistically, his old high-school athletic jacket. "Harry prepares for a journey," the speaker solemnly declares. His old clothes burned by the fire, he finds older clothes which, although they "bind across his chest and belly," still strike him as the right choice. As the speaker says, "he begins that way."

Bech's Comic Realm: The Other Side of the Coin

1. The Nature of the Comic

This study of Updike's novels has not so far dealt with *Bech: A Book* partly because the structure of this sixth book leaves its classification as a "novel" somewhat open to question. Updike himself chooses to call it "a book." However, the primary reason for considering it apart from the main body of the study is that, of the longer works, it is Updike's only truly comic book and as such must be approached with an entirely different set of categories and values. Although there are many somewhat comic scenes in the other novels and many truly funny moments (recall that Updike calls *The Centaur* his "gayest" book and says he laughs when he reads it), it is clear that, in their basic view of the human world, the other six novels are *serious* whereas *Bech* is unquestionably *comic*.[1]

It has long been recognized that criticism or analysis of comedy is extremely difficult. As everyone knows, whenever one tries to explain how or why something is comical, the comical aspect itself disappears. The reason for this also explains why this study has been so far forced to neglect the comic aspects of Updike's writing: Criticism in itself is essentially serious—it awards to its object the very dignity and importance which comedy subtly denies. Thus, although the bathroom scene in *Couples* which ends with Piet's two story jump through the window is in one sense broad comedy,[2] it is impossible simultaneously to interpret its significance and point out its comic aspects, since these tend to demean and tease both doer and event and shrug off any significance.

Thus this final chapter on *Bech* provides an opportunity to examine the other side of the coin. The comic and the serious often seem to coexist, dialectically, in Updike's work; the major characters often struggle against insignificance, against perhaps the acceptance of a comic rather than a serious world. In *Bech* Updike has relinquished his vision wholly to the comic world; thus it provides a reference point against which to define the nature of the serious in 'Updike's other work, the nature of the comic in *Bech* itself, and the dialectic between the two, especially in such books as *Couples* and *Rabbit Redux*.

In the centuries-long discussion about what constitutes the nature of the comic, critics and writers at least agree on this much: there is almost no material which is definitionally comic or serious in essence. Comedy is the product of a viewpoint, an approach, a vision which encourages certain reactions in the beholder and discourages others. It is a view which suggests that what is occurring is not serious or important in any far-reaching sense. The events of comedy are not threatening to us in any way because they do not suggest a cosmos in which the characters can cause or come to any real harm. The characters are, in a sense, bouncing off of rubber scenery which is more or less impervious to their movements.[3] Comedy also suggests a certain distance between the characters and ourselves (if we take ourselves seriously) and a difference between us; this insulates and protects us from their situation and gives us room to laugh with safety.[4]

It is safe to say that this viewpoint must be established nearly at once in a literary work. The audience must know from the beginning what set of responses are appropriate; until they do, they will be cautious and confused. (An author might want to prolong this state for reasons of his own, of course, as in Albee's *Who's Afraid of Virginia Woolf*.) In *Bech* we have not only the "introductory letter" from Bech himself which is whimsical and demeaning but also an opening which teases the readers ("Students [not unlike yourselves] compelled to buy paperback copies of his novels . . .") and establishes a frame in which a narrator (presumably the "John" Updike addressed in Bech's letter) is describing these incidents as a series of pictures or "slides"—a discontinuous autobiography of events that are already completed and nearly forgotten. Bech, we already know, has survived them all without any visible damage and so we are shown at the beginning their ultimate unimportance.

Contrastingly, in his other novels, Updike has twice used the present tense to intensify the sense of an immediate event and, even in *The Centaur* where a narrator reveals that the events happened years before, this narrator—Peter—is not introduced until the book is well underway (page 40 in the Fawcett Crest edition), and he immediately establishes the fact that the remembered events had significant effects upon him (and others) in later years. In *Of the Farm*, the narrator is Joey, one of the central characters; and his role as narrator helps demonstrate the intensity of his relationship with his mother and the threat her approaching death poses. The other third-person novels use the conventional past tense which is intended to be interpreted as present and both books (*The Poorhouse Fair* and *Couples*) open with lines of dialog—"What's this?" "What did you make of the new couple?" In all these cases a sense of immediacy is the result, and the distance between the reader and the world of the novel is intended to be small.

2. The Landscape of Inaction

Perhaps the major difference between what I shall call *comedy* and more serious works lies in the fact that in comedy, the major characters are placed in a cosmos in which their actions do not matter—they either cannot or will not perform significant actions, or their attempted actions produce little or no permanent effect. That is to say, in comedy the characters are not causal agents to any significant degree either through choice or because their environment is seen as basically unchangeable.[5] In *King Lear*, for instance, Lear's misassessment of the universe causes not only death and suffering but carries implications whose shock waves rebound through time and space, and matter in some important way to all of us (thus Aristotle's "fear"). But the miscalculations of the characters in *The Alchemist* carry little further than Lovewit's house and indeed make very little difference even there; the cosmos implied there is basically impervious to any actions those humans can perform.

A similar comparison can be drawn between *Bech* and Updike's other novels. The basic action line and the endings of the other novels place the protagonists in situations where actions are called for and in which they struggle to perform these actions with varying degrees of success. Hook, in *The Poorhouse Fair*, is one of the last of a dying generation who still have a system of belief and values necessary to human dignity; as Hook approaches death, the novel creates an urgency that Hook impart his vision to the surviving generation, especially to Conner. By the end of the story the message still has not been formed, and if it never is formed, a tragic loss is imminent. Hook must act and intends to try.

Rabbit, in *Rabbit, Run,* is similarly a quasi-mystic who has something to offer those around him. His misdirected attempts to do so cause suffering and death, and pose a significant dilemma —how can such a life-giver operate both outside and inside society's norms? His run at the end suggests the desperate extent of his action-oriented drive and the importance of finding a workable direction for it.

Caldwell's continuous action of sacrificial life-in-death in *The Centaur* gives life and the promise of a future to the others in his world. His action is as necessary and significant as is the existence of a cell in the volvox—it insures survival for its community which goes on long after its own death.

By the time we get to Piet of *Couples*, however, a gradual movement has begun out of this realm of true causality. Piet struggles to hold off mortality and insignificance; he fights death. Yet he is repeatedly subjected to symbolic deaths until, by the end of the book, he is forced to abandon his struggles as not only ineffective but ludicrous—there is no higher plane to hope for; the church has burned down and Angela is gone. No actions of significance are possible any longer. Updike has removed the status of protagonist—there are no more struggles that matter.

Although *Bech* must be dealt with separately, its place in the chronological sequence of Updike's major writing is wholly consistent. The chapter on *Couples* in this study traces the gradual movement from Piet's original Christian cosmos to a cosmos offering no basis for upward struggles from mortality, no place for redeemer-lovers, and no specialness for Piet or anyone else—he and Foxy must become just "another couple." This loss of stature sets the stage for the comic. Updike then creates Bech whose major characteristic is his ordinariness and his vivid sense of that ordinariness (along with his acceptance of it). Appropriate to this comic mode, Bech attempts few actions at all and certainly no actions of any importance (such as a proposal of marriage). The next novel, *Rabbit Redux,* places its major character in such a setting at the beginning. Rabbit emerges from his printing plant at five o'clock, just another blue collar, middle-class white. He rejects any hint of his own abilities to act well, or even to act at all. He does not see himself as a causal agent of any importance—Janice, his parents, Jill, and Nelson will do what they will do—he feels he cannot influence their lives in any significant degree. By the end of the novel, he has begun the painful move back to a sense of power and responsibility, back to a sense of significant human causality and ultimately the status that accompanies it. Thus the two surrounding novels can be seen to move towards the comic realm of *Bech* and then away from it.

Bech is both unable and unwilling to act and, in fact, sees no arena in which actions are called for. He is supposed to be a writer but by the time we see him in the book, he cannot write and has written essentially nothing for years. He doesn't even answer letters; he has designed a set of rubber stamps which all impart basically the same message: Bech cannot do what the writer requested.

HENRY BECH REGRETS THAT HE
DOES NOT SPEAK IN PUBLIC.

SORRY, PETITIONS
AREN'T MY METIER.

HENRY BECH IS TOO OLD AND ILL
AND DOUBTFUL TO SUBMIT TO
QUESTIONNAIRES AND INTERVIEWS.

IT'S YOUR PH.D. THESIS:
PLEASE WRITE IT YOURSELF.

Even Bech's interviews are pointless and repetitive—"the same questions more or less predictable, and his own answers, terribly familiar to him by now, mechanical, stale, irrelevant, untrue, claustrophobic" (p. 72). They accomplish nothing. His sex life, too, accomplishes nothing. It never leads to deeper involvements and never even seems to make much of an impression on the women involved. Bea can turn motheringly to her son only moments after sex with Bech, and Merissa in London is never moved enough to reveal to Bech anything of her personal life or even to call him again to wish him good-bye. In one case—the Southern college English teacher—Bech chooses to have no sexual relationship at all (a choice most of the previous protagonists would have found astonishing!).

Whenever anyone tells Bech that his Iron Curtain country tour has accomplished much good for the cause of international relations, he dismisses this with a bit of cynicism meant to make the compliment seem romantic and foolish. "You spent the evening with *him?*" the embassy man crows in Rumania; "That's fabulous. He's the top of the list, man. We've never laid a finger on him before; he's been inaccessible. . . . you really went underground." "I think of myself," Bech responds, "as a sort of low-flying U-2" (p. 61).

From this viewpoint it becomes obvious that Updike's previous protagonists were constantly involved in activity, usually of an obvious and measurable type. Rabbit in *Rabbit, Run* plants flowers (and revels in his causality when they grow), gets a woman pregnant, and indirectly causes a death. The mother in *Of the Farm* is seen as supporting her son's life and, by analogy, the farm's life—"throughout the farm, a thousand such details of nurture [were] about to sink into the earth with her. Death seemed . . . a defect she had overlooked in purchasing these acres . . . (*OF*, p. 122). Piet builds houses, makes love to several women, gets Foxy pregnant, arranges an abortion, and so forth. Even the notion of handicraft which has played such an important role in Updike's writing has, as its principal value, its sense of a permanent mark made by a human—as suggested in the short story "Packed Dirt." Towards the end of *Couples*, however, Piet stops building, stops seeing women, and his family, business, and community no longer need him. The couples and Angela form new lives without him; his realm of action disappears.

Bech has almost no realm for action at all. In the Iron Curtain countries he is led around by guides and interpreters and has his agenda entirely planned for him by the embassy officials. In "Bech Takes Pot Luck," Wendell forces his company on the group, initiates games for the children, brings the marijuana, and talks Norma out of taking acid. In "Bech Panics" Bech's one free hour on his lecture trip to Virginia is appropriated for judging a poetry contest. Even in his relationships with Norma and Bea, he is described as entirely passive—a victim: "As to love, he had been recently processed by a pair of sisters, first the one, and then the other" (p. 151).

Additionally, even the unique short-story structure of *Bech* implies the very limited extent to which Bech should be seen as a causal agent. Each story has a different set of characters which, with almost no exception, we never see again. The effect of Bech upon their lives is never shown; no long-range influences or results play a role in the book. Whatever Bech does, the consequences are viewed only for the period of a few days, after which they are forgotten. What becomes of Kate? Of Norma? Of Bea? Of Wendell? Or Merissa? Are any of them affected or harmed by Bech? Such questions—the questions of serious vision, not comic—are definitionally excluded from the book by its discontinuous structure. Continuity is correlative to human causality, not to comic inefficacy.

In *Rabbit Redux* which follows *Bech*, the question of whether or not there exists an arena for significant human action is confronted directly. It is, in fact, the central thematic line of the novel. At the outset Rabbit does not act, feels he cannot act in any meaningful way, and consequently accepts no responsibility for anything that happens. He feels that the universe moves totally apart from his agency. Thus he will not try to get Janice back, although she complains that he should. He will not stop

Skeeter's abuse of Jill, although Nelson begs him to. And when Jill dies, he rejects Nelson's condemnation, asking if it couldn't simply be "bad luck." Janice also makes her "nothing matters" monolog in the early part of the novel.

Skeeter, however, does not see this comic world of human impotence but a serious, even tragic world of human power and sometimes malice. America—capitalistic, imperialistic, militaristic, and racist—has been created so by white Americans: their deeds and collective power have shaped history. He also feels that blacks have it in their power to shape the future. Skeeter has been to Vietnam, a stunning testament to human causality, and returns with his revolutionary message of the power of people.

By the end of *Rabbit Redux*, Mim as well as Skeeter has demonstrated to Rabbit that people can act. Mim steps into the Janice-Charlie relationship and helps send Janice back to Rabbit. Janice, too, has had her moment of truth. She feels that by sheer power of love and being she has rescued Charles from the brink of death. And Rabbit begins to see his role in Jill's death and knows he will never again feel that he exists in a world of "blameless activity." The basically comic view is losing its grip. Bech alone remains from beginning to end in the Prufrock land-scape of inaction. In a line which recalls the "coffee spoons" pas-sage of Eliot's poem, Bech thinks, "He thought back through his life, so many dreams and wakings, so many faces encountered and stoplights obeyed and streets crossed, and there was nothing solid; he had rushed through his life as through a badly chewed meal, leaving an ache of indigestion" (p. 176).

In the comedy of *Bech* not only are we presented with an environment in which humans perform no actions of significance, but the events also demonstrate the inefficacy of the small actions which they do attempt. The first story, "Bech in Russia," offers an example of the classic comic reverse. Usually one has many things to buy and not enough money. In Russia, Bech has too much money and not enough things to buy. Finding his Russian expense and lecture fees embarrassingly generous, Bech decides to alleviate his guilt by spending all of that money in Russia— ". . . we must spend it! Spend, spend. . . . We'll make Mother Russia a consumer society." Kate, his interpreter, warns, "It's not so simple." Sure enough, try as he might, Bech cannot spend the money. He shops every spare moment but even with his departure imminent, he has over 1200 rubles left. At the last minute he finds that furs are expensive enough to use up his money but, appropriately, these fall out of his suitcase on the way to the airplane.

In Rumania Bech meets a man who epitomizes comic man. Even the tiniest actions, the tiniest assaults upon his life space are impossible for him: Petrescu cannot get a clean shave. When he keeps Bech waiting for him in a bar, Bech asks,

> "Where have you been? I've had four martinis and been swindled in your absence."
> Petrescu was embarrassed. "I've been shaving."
> "Shaving!"
> "Yes, it is humiliating. I must spend each day one hour shaving and even yet it does not look as if I have shaved, my beard is so obdurate."
> "Are you putting blades in the razor?"
> "Oh, yes, I buy the best and use two upon each occasion." (p. 47)

Bech concludes solemnly, "This is the saddest story I've ever heard."

However, all of the stories in *Bech* are similar sad stories. After the first story in which he couldn't spend money, Bech meets a driver in Rumania who will not stop blowing his horn and drives, heedless of their protests, like a maniac. Bech later remembers, furthermore, that he forgot to give him the customary tip. In Bulgaria Bech wants only to see the attractive poetess with whom he feels he has fallen in love. Yet embassy business and his full agenda keep them apart until he only has time to scrawl a drunken sentence to her on a copy of one of his novels. In "Bech Takes Pot Luck" he tries to get high on marijuana but only succeeds in getting sick. And in London he seeks adventure and romance and ends up as a five-sentence item in a trite gossip column—"Swinging L. was a shade more swingy this week when the darling American author Henry . . . Bech dropped in at Revolution and other In spots" (p. 185).

In the most serious of the pieces, "Bech Panics," Bech uncharacteristically accepts a speaking engagement requested via telephone by a passionately enthusiastic undergraduate Southern belle—"Ouah English instructah . . . *sayd* you were immensely hard to gait, but you have *so* many fayuns among the girls heah, we're all just hopin' against hope" (p. 120). He goes, suffers agonies of aging when surrounded by such a concentration of youth, delivers talks which simultaneously bore and upset him, and on the way back to the plane discovers that the worshipful girl on the telephone spent the whole time attending a wedding —"Ah had to attend mah sisteh's weddin' . . . and jes got back this mawnin! Believe me, suh, Ah am *moh*tifahd!" (p. 147).

3. The Safety of the Comic World

Bech is not deeply injured by the co-ed's blithe excuses; in fact, he is not hurt at all. "Never you mind," he says comfortingly—"and touched his inside breast pocket to make sure his check was in it." This is in keeping with another aspect of the comic realm: the central characters are safe from serious harm. In the previous story, "Bech Takes Pot Luck," Bech is exposed to the acerbic and bitchy Norma. Bored and frustrated by Bech's conservative life style she wants to experiment with drugs and assaults him castratingly: "After keeping you company for three years I've forgotten what goes on in any normal man's mind." Such insults would have unsettled Rabbit or Piet. Bech is relatively unruffled. Norma pushes harder: "I want to have an experience. I've never had a *ba*by, the only wedding ring I've ever worn is the one you loan me when we go to St. Croix in the winter. I've never been to Pakistan, I'm *never* going to get to Antarctica" (p. 100). Bech survives this with equanimity. "I'll buy you a freezer," he volunteers.

In a later story, Bea is similarly destructive: ". . . you'll fly a thousand miles to some third-rate finishing school on the remote chance you can sack out with Scarlett O'Hara. You are sick, Henry. You are weak, and sick" (p. 121). But Bech is indestructible. "Actually," he offers, "I'll be there two nights. So I can sack out with Melanie, too." Bea begins to cry at this, but even her tears produce no effect nor does Bech feel he can comfort her.

"He tried to fetch up some words of comfort but he knew that none would be comfort enough but the words, 'Marry me.'"

Since he forms no deep attachments, Bech is relatively safe from human attacks. This is in sharp contrast to Updike's other protagonists whose vulnerability is one of their chief characteristics. Hook is near death and under the power of Conner and the other administrators; his vision, too, is under constant attack from younger, more vigorous men. Rabbit's sense of frustration and defeat by his environment in *Rabbit, Run* is so great that at times suicide seems not an impossible option for him. By the end he has been reduced to helpless flight. Caldwell's life is being eroded by poison and ever-present death. Desperate for appreciation, he is faced with thoughtless student malice and administrative disapproval. Joey's life is still tragically dependent upon his dying mother. And Piet struggles for survival in a landscape that threatens to extinguish his hopes for specialness. In each case the struggles for survival are real and the outcome uncertain.

By the end of *Couples*, however, Piet has survived his threats and seems to have become invulnerable. He has lost his Angela, his building trade, his church, and his lovers and is thus safe from further harm. He has, in a sense, entered the realm of comedy which Bech will inhabit in the following book. In *Rabbit Redux*, appropriately, the problem is whether Rabbit can re-enter the serious realm where he can respond to other humans, where he *can* be hurt. At the beginning of the novel, he still exhibits Bech's emotional isolation. When Janice admits that she sleeps with Charlie, Rabbit responds, "Ah shit; of course you do. . . . Good." and only worries that she will become "another cripple he must take care of." He is willing to let her continue her affair and seems to suffer only slight dislocation when she moves out. He can remain calm in the face of Skeeter's threats and tantrums and shows little emotion when Jill's burned body is removed from the house. Grief begins to dawn only gradually in the closing section of the novel, and he finally dreams of Jill with an intense sensation of longing for her. He begins to feel he wants Janice back and in the last few pages makes the effort of trying to salvage something of the marriage.

In Bech's safe world the most serious moments occur in

the story "Bech Panics" in which he undergoes what he grudg-
ingly calls "a religious crisis" during his visit to the Southern girls
school. Surrounded on all sides by young women, a generation
younger than himself, he is startled into an awareness of the
generations upon generations of life in which he is only a tiny
moment:

> Their massed fertility was overwhelming; their bodies were
> being broadened and readied to generate from their own
> cells a new body to be pushed from the old, and in time
> to push bodies from itself, and so on into eternity, an ocean
> of doubling and redoubling cells within which his own con-
> scious moment was soon to wink out. (p. 127)

Later he goes into the surrounding woods and falls to his knees
to beg "Someone, Something" for mercy. While kneeling there
he becomes aware of the abundance of tiny life processes around
him. He gains a realization that "the earth is populated infinitely,
that a slithering slug was slowly causing a dead oak leaf to lift
and a research team of red ants were industriously testing a
sudden morsel, Bech's thumb . . ." (p. 141).
    This closely resembles the religious experience of David
in "Pigeon Feathers" when he discovers the infinite tiny beauties
of a pigeon's colored feathers. However the reactions of Bech
and David are subtly different and illustrate the contrasting
comic and serious worlds of their stories. David becomes convinced that a God who would lavish such attention on tiny things
would not render those things pointless by failing to make
humans special and ultimately immortal. Bech, however, is en-
abled to see himself as *one* of these tiny things which are promised life and shouldn't worry. He then goes back to the mundane
and demeaning tasks of his visit (such as judging a contest of
sophomoric poetry), rejects the possible adventure of a quick
affair with Miss Eisenbraun, and smiles quietly at the co-ed's
melodramatic apologies for missing his visit. In David's case
humans are proven important; in Bech's they shrink to secure
miniaturization.

4. Comic Miniaturization

This shrinking of characters is, of course, another of comedy's trademarks. In tragedy, it is sometimes said, characters are made larger than life; in comedy they become smaller. Bech, with his self-conscious comic vision, uses this demeaning treatment as the basis of his continuous stream of jokes and wisecracks. When Kate, his Russian interpreter, seeks to describe the mysteries that humans sense when they behold the heavens, he deftly applies his deflating wit. Kate says, "In a way it is terrible, to look up at the sky, on one of our clear nights of burning cold, at the sky of stars, and think of creatures alive in it." Bech replies, "Like termites in the ceiling" (pp. 30-31). Like the characters in *Rabbit Redux* who belittle political leaders, Bech also demeans historical giants. Tuttle, interviewing him in London, says, "Maoism does seem to be the coming mood." Bech quips, "The mood of t'mao" (p. 159).

Bech considers himself second rate, "flirting with the senility that comes early to American authors" (p. 94), and without much to say. When being "lionized" or paraded around as an American author, he sees himself as perpetrating a fraud, as pretending importance when he has none. He sees himself as *posturing*, a word which he himself uses on occasion. In the story "Bech Swings?" this view of role-playing becomes the central metaphor. When he looks at himself in the mirror he sees a "congressman from Queens hoping to be taken for a Southern senator." He envisions his conversations as dialog out of one of his own novels. When Merissa asks why he's impotent, he answers "Old age?" and hears a voice inside him say *"Old age? he tentatively said."* Without a quick reply at one point he thinks, "A gap in the dialog. Fill in later." His urgent question to Merissa—"How can I find you again?"—elicits an inner warning "Victorian novel? Rewrite." When at the end of his visit he discovers his exhausting interviews with Tuttle turned into a coy and snide profile and his fairly romantic few days with Merissa nothing more than material for her gossip column, he decides he has been reduced to "a character by Henry Bech" and shrugs it away with a chuckle.

His good-natured demythologizing extends to others as well.

He is fascinated and touched by the fact that Kate, his Russian interpreter, is probably a Party spy. He wonders "what in him would be worth spying out" and sadly notes that for all of us the shame is "that the secrets to be discovered are so paltry and few." When Kate cries one day at his politically indiscrete response to the man who attempted to buy his overcoat, he feels guilty but maintains his cynicism: "Bech had never seen her cry in day-light—only in the dark of projection rooms" (p. 26). When Kate kisses him good-bye he is momentarily unsettled by the realization that he had been expected to sleep with her, yet he deromanticizes at once by recalling that her kiss had been "color-less but moist and good, like a boiled potato." In "Bech Takes Pot Luck" he listens with dead-pan patience to Wendell's solemn warnings about the adventures and danger of LSD—Wendell: "You must understand, Norma, it's a not a playful experience. It takes everything you have." But his reductive reflex wins: "It'll even take," Bech offers, "your Saks charge-a-plate" (p. 96).

This comic response of making human things small, unim-portant, insignificant, unglamorous, unromantic, and ordinary is brought to a climax during Bech's religious crises in "Bech Panics." Eating dinner with a table full of female under-gradu-ates, he suddenly sees the smallness of all human existence, and in a passage that recalls Piet's similar moment of truth under the stars one summer night, Bech creates a long and lyrical litany to human insignificance:

> He looked around the ring of munching females and saw their bodies as a Martian or a mollusc might see them, as pulpy stalks of bundled nerves oddly pinched to a bud of concentration in the head, a hairy bone knob holding some pounds of jelly in which a trillion circuits, mostly dead, kept records, coded motor operations, and generated an excess of electricity. . . . And to think that all the efforts of his life —his preening, his lovemaking, his typing—boiled down to the attempt to displace a few sparks, to bias a few circuits within some random other scoops of jelly that would, in less time than it takes the Andreas Fault to shrug or the tail-tip star of Scorpio to crawl an inch across the map of Heaven, be utterly dissolved. The widest fame and most enduring

> excellence shrank to nothing in this perspective. . . . he saw
> that the void should have been left unvexed, should have
> been spared this trouble of matter, of life, and worst, of con-
> sciousness. (p. 131)

This is Bech's crisis. This is the ultimate belittlement which has
been implied all along in his jokes, his self-effacement, his reluctance to act, and his cynicism. After a short period of nervous
unhappiness, he accepts the implications of his vision since, in
one sense, it is a truth he has always known. It is interesting to
note that Piet's reaction in the previous novel to his own hum-
bling moment beneath the eternity of the stars is similar. He
decides that his troubles with Foxy are less serious than they
seem and that henceforth he will love her less—a truly Bech-like
decision.

5. The Comic and the Serious in the Other Novels

Seen through the rose-colored glasses of comedy, Updike's
other novels appear filled with whimsical and humorous scenes.
In *The Poorhouse Fair* Greg's vitriolic insults, usually disasters of
illogic, are often grotesquely funny. When he discovers that
Conner has tagged the chairs with inmates' names, he snaps,
"The f.ing bastard I have half a mind to snip every one of these
rotten tags off and throw them in his birdbrain face" (*TPF*, p. 8).
It is also amusing to contemplate the delivery boy's amazement
and confusion when he arrives to deliver some soda and en-
counters a maniacal old man at the front gate; Greg has planned
a daring escape: "Slam her through, dump the p., and I'll get in
the seat beside you and crouch down. Then step on it. Don't
look back. Do you have a gun, kid?" (*TPF*, p. 43). Conner, the
superscientific and efficient prefect of the poorhouse is seen in
leisure moments, lulled by music, to have Walter Mitty daydreams as romantic as any teenager's. He pictures himself a
handsome Greek Adonis playing with a maiden on a sun-
drenched beach. In a later dream he is the discoverer of a cure
for cancer and delivers a triumphant announcement to a room
of prestigious-appearing men. (See p. 26 of this study.)

In *Rabbit, Run*, Rabbit, after leaving Janice, seeks the advice of his old coach, Tothero, who is at first full of solemn moralizing about repairing Rabbit's marriage. But a few hours later, lubricated with drink and the expectation of a date, Tothero is a raving devil-may-care. "You'll like my lady, I know you will, a city flower" (*RR*, p. 45). When Rabbit tries to press him for his promised advice about Janice, Tothero erupts, "Janice! Let's not talk about little mutts like Janice Springer, Harry boy. This is the night. . . . The real women are dropping down out of the trees. Plippity, plippity." Many of the larger events of the novel, viewed from a distance are outrageous. A rather ordinary middle-class Magi-peeler salesman, thinking he's the Dali Lama, or some other mystic, picks up a stout, plain-looking prostitute and in true Don Quixote fashion treats her like a mystical female of raving beauty. A local Protestant minister who pictures himself as a cross between Scout leader and psychotherapist uses a golf course to hold lessons in social responsibility. And when Rabbit, after months away from his family with no explanation, finally returns to visit Janice in the hospital, he is outraged to discover that she didn't keep up all the rent payments in his absence: "The trouble with you," he complains, "is that you just don't give a damn."

Updike himself calls *The Centaur* a funny book. Caldwell's self-deprecating remarks are very like Bech's but more intense. And his bullish manner along with his appearance—the kid's knitted cap and pocket full of old pencils and combs—presents quite a picture. Though the thematic impact of the scene with the drunk on the street is serious and effective (see p. 74 of this study) it is still outrageously funny to see Caldwell's desperate sincerity counterpointed by the drunk's depravity and lechery. "What sort of old lech do you call yourself," the drunk says to Caldwell whom he assumes has sexually propositioned Peter. "How much is it worth to you not to have me call the cops and have you picked up with this flower?" But Caldwell, oblivious to it all, thinks he has been in a philosophical discussion about death. "I've enjoyed talking to you," he tells the drunk warmly, "and I'd like to shake your hand. You've clarified my thinking" (*TC*, p. 122).

The mother's wry wit in *Of the Farm* often resembles both Caldwell and Bech. When they tease her about not working on

Sunday she counters, "That's right, poke fun of an old woman's superstitions." Additionally, there are several fairly funny scenes. Peggy, picking berries in her bathing suit, has hidden from some men in a poison ivy patch and rushes off to scrub with yellow soap. And Joey sits atop the tractor, mowing, in his father's baggy pants and a woman's beribboned straw hat to ward off sunstroke.

Couples, on one level is almost constant comedy, beginning with an early party scene of bald, repulsive Freddy secretly rubbing the thigh of the pregnant Foxy who is nauseous and wants only to go home. As the novel progresses, the comedy never disappears for long. We get the dead-pan chronicling of Frank and Marcia's absolutely trite discovery of adultery, beginning with Marcia's predictable promise that their first lunch together is innocent—"This is just talk"—and proceeding through Janet's tackle of Harold atop the dirty clothes in the basement laundry room:

> "No," she said. "We can't. Not here."
> "One more kiss," he begged. (*C,* p. 144)

We see Freddy, slippery and rubbery in his skin-diving suit, wrestled to the floor by Carol and Angela as they search for his pornographic play; in the tussle Carol's nipple flips into view—it is dyed orange to match her dyed orange hair. An abortion is arranged in a dentist's office; a tuxedoed man jumps two stories from a bathroom window and finishes with a backwards somersalt into an adultrous couple necking; and the night Freddy gets Angela as payment for the abortion and revenge on Piet, Freddy is impotent while Piet again enjoys Georgene.

The comedy of *Rabbit Redux* also borders on the grotesque. The manner in which Charlie Stavros accidentally reveals his affair with Janice during the course of a restaurant conversation is as intricately set up and timed by Updike as a night-club comic's routine. Later, after going to live with Charlie, Janice displays indignant moral disgust when she learns that Rabbit has a girl living with him. "I don't want Nelson exposed to this sort of thing," she preaches. "What sort of thing?" Rabbit asks, "you mean the you and Stavros sort of thing?" (*RRx,* p. 140). Skeeter takes himself too seriously and, contrasted with Rabbit who takes very little seriously, can emerge as a somewhat comic figure, too. His sermons, temper tantrums, and masturbation while listening to readings from Frederick Douglass make him a hyperbolized caricature of the black militant. Even the closing section of the book has its lighter side. Mim, now a professional call girl on the West Coast, decides she can help restore Rabbit's marriage. To accomplish this, she hustles Charlie Stavros, sleeps with him three times, and confuses Charlie and Janice enough to bring on a heart seizure in Charlie and send Janice doggedly back to Rabbit. The modern marriage counsellor at work.

In addition to being humorous, there is another sense in which Updike's novels could be considered somewhat comic: They frequently rely heavily on the customs and manners of a particular social milieu. The category "Comedy of Manners" is given to comedies which focus most intensely on such material, but, in fact, it is often noted that comedy in general tends to deal with a specific sociocultural environment, often contemporary and by implication also *tem*porary. James Feibleman in his *Aesthetics* articulates this very adroitly:

> It is a notorious historical observation that customs and institutions rarely enjoy more than a comparatively brief life; and yet while they are the accepted fashion they come to be regarded as brute givens, as irreducible facts, which may be depended upon with perfect security. . . . It is the task of comedy to make this plain.[6]

The suburban swapsies of *Couples* and the pot-smoking of *Rabbit Redux* are two obvious examples. However, most of Updike's novels have a specific social setting and incorporate a certain amount of corresponding detail. (He himself has noted that he pictures a certain presidential administration for each setting, which colors the behavior patterns of the respective societies.) In fact Updike's canon has clearly moved in the direction of an increasing use of such fashion with each book. *The Poorhouse Fair* is projected into the future and thus has the most neutral setting. *Rabbit, Run* includes radio and television programs, commercials, contemporary Protestant religious manners and other such details which place its characters in a specific era and location. Caldwell's high-school students are concerned with sex and cigarettes, distinct from the automobile-and-athletics era which preceded or the drug fascination which followed. *Of the Farm* introduces us to the adultery and divorce fashion which become the trademark of the sixties and which *Couples* focuses upon more intensely. And *Rabbit Redux* uses U.S.A. 1968 not only as a setting but also as a central thematic force.

Given the often amusing situations and the attention to manners, then, how does Updike succeed in creating, ultimately, the serious vision and not the comic in these novels? How does he manage to give contemporary things size and stature and the appearance of more than temporary importance? Partly, as this chapter demonstrates, it is by placing his characters in a causal realm where they want to and can perform effective actions and where they are not invulnerable to harm from each other or from some outside agency. The threats to each of the central characters are made visible and serious. But more than that, Updike—in order to portray the serious quality of his cosmos in each novel—has relied on perhaps the oldest and most categorical differentiation between the comic and the serious: the fact of death—the absence of which marks the comic and the presence of which calls forth the serious.

Updike's pervasive use of death in his novels has been one of the central concerns of this study. In the light of *Bech's* comedy (which appropriately has no taint of death other than Bech's brief "panic") another aspect of the focus on death becomes clear: It places the novels solidly in the realm of the serious and allows Updike to deal with manners and other potentially comic material without seriously compromising the significance of the struggles and the resulting stature of the central characters. Updike can demonstrate the maturity of his speakers in each novel (as well as his own maturity) by hinting at their ability to see the comic aspects of their world, yet he can force them and the reader to maintain a basically serious view, a dignifying view, by insisting upon the life-and-death nature of human struggles.

We can laugh at Gregg's outrageous insults but only in the light of his legitimate frustration, his subtly dehumanizing treatment, and his rapidly approaching death. Rabbit's accusation to

Janice that she was irresponsible in neglecting to worry about the rent may be funny, but it is in a context in which his next absence will cause the baby's death. Caldwell's desperate search for appreciation and sincerity makes us laugh but not so much that we forget that his failure to find these is killing him. The acid wit of Joey's mother is correlative to her approaching death, which she uses to help set the stage for her studied grumpiness but which Joey is not yet prepared to face.

Only in *Couples* does this seriousness begin, at the end, to be compromised. Here the frequency of death seems to push the world of the novel beyond tragedy into the realm of the absurd. In his book *Comedy*, Wylie Sypher feels that this intellectual twilight zone is a twentieth-century product. He says, "we have lived among the 'dust and crashes' of the twentieth century and have learned how the direst calamities that befall man seem to prove that human life at its depths is inherently absurd." [7] Death, that is to say, is a two-edged sword in the realm of art. It can demonstrate the essentially serious nature of our struggles, but when it begins to seem ubiquitous and its inevitability is repeatedly stressed, it hints at the futility and unimportance of these struggles.

In *Rabbit Redux*, Updike is confronting this ambiguity. We have only one death—Jill's—and by considering the waste of her life and his role in her death, Rabbit is trying to use the fact of death to rediscover that humans can create their own significance, can become important. The previous serious protagonists felt that they were important and searched feverishly for a way to demonstrate their specialness. Rabbit in *Rabbit Redux*, having journeyed through the limbo of Bech's comic vision, must reconstruct the basis for human significance. It is interesting to note that Skeeter's vision of human importance is also shown to be coexistent with his vision of death—the threatened deaths of revolution and his experiences in Vietnam.

Unlike each of Updike's other novels, there is no physical death in *Bech* and no immediately threatening one. A sense of death intrudes itself only once, in the story "Bech Panics," and here it is caused by Bech's close contact with a group of people who do take themselves seriously, who do feel significant—the coeds at the Southern girls school. As he talks to a gathering of them, he becomes aware of an internal swelling of "dread" and a "recognition of horror."

> The presences at his feet—those seriously sparkling eyes, those earnestly flushed cheeks, those demurely displayed calves and knees—appalled him with the abyss of their innocence. He felt dizzy, stunned. . . . Death hung behind everything, a real skeleton about to leap through a door in these false walls of books. (p. 125)

Bech has so far eluded death's dread by seeing the very thing which the other protagonists resisted: his own insignificance. These young girls, however, do take themselves seriously and therefore seem to Bech unaware of the fact of death and thus vulnerable to it. Worse yet, they expect him to take *himself* seriously and to behave as a famous, talented American author. In this way they inadvertently erode the armor which protects Bech from fear and depression—his refusal to entertain any notion of his own stature which might subject him to disillusionment, disappointment, or dread.

> He felt what was expected of him, and felt himself performing it, and felt the fakery of the performance, and knew these levels of perception as the shifting sands of absurdity, nullity, death. His death gnawed inside him like a foul parasite while he talked to these charming daughters of fertile Virginia. (p. 126)

In addition to protecting him from death's menace, Bech's comic vision shields him from all serious harm. As has been pointed out earlier, he is not easily hurt by others; moreover his own failings do not deeply upset him. He is annoyed and frustrated that his artistic energies seem to be running out but he can survive it. When he realizes that he had been expected to sleep with Kate, his Russian interpreter, his response is little more than an implied shrug. Even when he finds himself sexually impotent one night with Bea, he seems undaunted and the third-person speaker (not really "John" at this point, but clearly Bech himself) can joke about it drily: "Though his suburban mistress . . . tried to bring his weakling member to strength by wrapping it in the velvet bandages of her lips, Bech couldn't achieve more than a two-thirds hard-on, which diminished to an even less usable fraction whenever the starchy fare within their stomachs rumbled. . . ." They eventually give up and return home from their date "as stiff with dried sweat as a pair of squash players" (p. 117). Needless to say either one of these events would have psychologically demolished Rabbit of *Rabbit, Run* or Piet of *Couples.*

Ultimately, Bech has little expectation of greatness, little sense of specialness, and thus no fear of smallness. He can surrender wholly to a comic vision because he has discovered that in total victimhood lies invulnerability, in self-effacement lies invincibility.

The dialectic between the comic and the serious in Updike's serious novels provides the landscape in which his redeemer figures are appropriate. In order for us to take these priest-lovers seriously, the novels must be essentially serious—there could be no such figure in the world of *Bech.* The priest figure must be correct in his sense of people's value. The threatened lapse into a sense of insignificance is precisely the force against which the redeemers like Hook or Rabbit (of *Rabbit, Run*) struggle. In these novels Updike sees a society of people who dislike a sense of their own insignificance but seem unable to resist it unaided— who need, in fact, a lover to reassure them of their own worth.

Bech, in contrast, has learned to live with this sense of insignificance, has learned to use it for protection. He is in a world in which redemption is not called for. In fact, in contrast to Rabbit's vision of his own face in the picture of Jesus, or Caldwell's belief that each cell in the volvox is a kind of self-immolating savior, Bech uses names of "world saviors" to put himself to sleep—"He went through the alphabet with world saviors: Attila, Buddha, Christ, Danton . . . Woodrow Wilson, Xerxes the Great, Brigham Young, Zoroaster" (p. 132). The denigrating effect of this list (as well as its comic effect) is accentuated by Bech's general assessment of such men: "There was some slight comfort," Bech concludes sleepily, "in the realization that the world had survived all its saviors. . . ."

Although it is a comic book, *Bech* is not a very hopeful

book. Serious or tragic literature is invariably more hopeful than comic. It is partly Updike's wry estimate of himself and as such may contain a subtle defense of the persistently serious mode of most of his work. Bech is safe, but he is also unproductive artistically; his comic vision may be unable to coexist with the structured, representative, symbolic, coherent, and sincere vision necessary to produce a work of art. During the romance of his brief affair with Merissa in London, Bech gets an inspiration for a novel: "The title of his new novel abruptly came to him: Think Big. . . . It held in the girders of its consonants, braced by those two stark 'i's, America's promise, pathos, crassness, grandeur" (p. 172). He plans the plot and his heart "trembled in excitement." But after another demeaning interview with Tuttle, Bech again sees the absurdity of it all, and Think Big dies and becomes "a ghost of a book, an empty space between the four faded spines . . ." (p. 175). Without the upward momentum denied by comic vision, without human stature and the hope of success, both art and the artist become inappropriate—contradictions within a system which offers them no materials and no motivation. Ultimately it is impossible for Bech to think big; he can only think small. It is to the compromised world of Couples and Rabbit Redux that Updike must return, for it is only within their complicated dialectic of serious and comic that his life-givers have a meaningful role and a plausible identity; and it is only within their intricate logic that his artistic impulse can be both circumspect and viable.

Notes

Chapter 1

1. Roughly: "Imagine a number of men in chains, all condemned to death, one of whom is executed each day in the sight of the others; those who remain see their own condition in that of their fellows and all of them look on with sorrow and without hope, waiting their turn. It is an image of the condition of man."
2. The best treatment so far of this aspect of Updike's work is: Michael Novak, "Updike's Quest for Liturgy," *Commonweal*, 57 (May 10, 1963), 192-195.
3. In the short story "Snowing in Greenwich Village" Richard notices that his wife Rebecca attempts similar story-telling feats and wonders how that evening itself might appear in one of her accounts (*SD*, p. 62).
4. Charles Samuels conducted an interview with John Updike, which was taped and then rewritten by Updike himself. It is the longest commentary on his own works that Updike has so far contributed. Although it is his works themselves and not the artist that provide the most reliable information on their contents, Mr. Updike's remarks are cogent and well thought out; I make frequent use of them in this essay. The interview appears in *Paris Review*, 45 (Winter 1965), 85-117.

Chapter 2

1. J. A. Ward has written a fine brief study of *The Poorhouse Fair* and *Rabbit, Run:* "John Updike's Fiction," *Critique*, 5 (Spring-Summer 1962), 27-41. I have been strongly tempted to adopt his vocabulary terming Conner (and therefore Eccles) as "humanists." Ward describes the first novel in this way: ". . . the schematic opposition of the ancient and the modern, of the

191

human and the humanist" (p. 32). He uses "humanist" to mean a person self-consciously dedicated to studying and serving man but in an atheistic frame of reference which loses sight of what is essentially human—to see oneself as special and valuable in the universe. The use of the term was also adopted by Dean Doner in "Rabbit Angstrom's Unseen World," *New World Writing*, No. 19 (1961), pp. 58-75. Updike himself uses the term in a review. However, in view of the somewhat technical meanings of "humanist" and its historical connotations, I have substituted "humanitarian." This, however, tends to paint Conner or Eccles as charity-workers, which is not quite my intent. They are, basically, atheistic humanists whose atheism has stripped them of the ability to enrich or comfort those whom they would serve.

2. This is a sign of Janet's lack of sexual vitality. Abundant hair, such as Ruth has, is a repeating image of sexual richness in Updike's novels. Peter of *The Centaur* eagerly awaits the growth of his own adult hair. Piet in *Couples,* appropriately, is covered with kinky red hair; but Freddy Thorne, his asexual neighbor, is bald.

3. Alice and Kenneth Hamilton, *The Elements of John Updike* (Grand Rapids, 1970).

4. The life-as-a-game metaphor is, of course, a traditional one in American culture—for example, the "game of life" or "the insurance game," and so forth. Sex is also saturated with game imagery—"to score," for instance. Updike has given these metaphors a more vivid spatial sense, increased comprehensiveness, and considerable thematic burden.

5. This combined identity of life and death sources is examined in each of Updike's novels. Caldwell's students and the Robinson farm both have this ambivalent effect on the protagonists. It culminates in *Couples* where the symbols of a greenhouse (flowers planted for funerals) and a dead mother form the imagistic basis of the final examination. Literature has long contained evidence of a basic womb-tomb motif; Updike sees it as a central perceptual experience.

6. Published by University of Texas Press, Austin, 1966. I realize that the term "Existentialist novel" is looked upon with suspicion by many critics. Although the large group of philosophers and writers who are often collected in the category *Existentialist* are admittedly a heterogeneous gathering, the attack on conventional value systems spearheaded by Camus and Sartre still

provides a useful ideational category, I believe. It still includes only a minority of the novels written in the twentieth century.

7. See, for instance, Paul Doyle, "Updike's Fiction: Motifs and Techniques," *Catholic World*, 199 (September, 1964), 356-362.

Chapter 3

1. The designing of allusive details into obvious mythic parallels also provides a playful overtone which may contribute to internal "tension"—the book's test of itself, as Ransom described it. Updike himself candidly admits that books should have "secrets" as a "bonus for the sensitive reader," and any reader aware of the mythic allusions becomes amused at their intricacy and persistence. Updike recalls *The Centaur* as "my gayest and truest book; I pick it up and read a few pages in which Caldwell is insisting on flattering a moth-eaten bum who is really the God Dionysius, and I begin laughing" (*PR*, p. 103).

2. David Galloway, p. 46.

3. In addition to offering certain values, the adoption of a mythic framework also provides an artist with narrative and descriptive details with which to flesh out his theme. Like memory, it is a storehouse of materials, often complete with affective connotations. Vera, for instance, will have red hair (as does Botticelli's Venus) and be sometimes attractive, sometimes whorish. Reverend March will be an ex-military hero, too efficient and strong to be very likable; Al Hummel will have a crippled foot and do metal work; details of the hitchhiker's clothes must resemble the winged shoes and other garments of Mercury; a purple cape is suggested for the drunk, and so forth. The artist's preliminary work of forming a mental picture of his characters is somewhat simplified.

4. Perhaps the line that best characterizes the father is found in Updike's recollection of his father's reaction to the novel *The Centaur*: ". . . once, returning to Plowville after *The Centaur* came out, I was upbraided by a Sunday school pupil of my father's for my outrageous portrait, and my father, with typical sanctity interceded, saying, "No, it's the truth. The kid got me right" (*PR*, p. 91).

5. The arrow may represent not hate, but, as Cassie says, disguised love. However, for the cells of a volvox, love is what kills.

6. George's symbolic death when he enters school each morning

is depicted earlier on page 130. Peter watches in terror as Caldwell, approaching the school door, appears to grow smaller and smaller until he becomes "a moth impaled on the light he pressed against. The door yielded; he disappeared." The image of a soul in the form of a moth escaping the dying body appears frequently in art. On a deathbed a moth is sometimes pictured hovering above the nose and lips; and in *The Devil and Daniel Webster* the devil carries around souls in the form of bees and moths, tied in his handkerchief.

7. This vision of a larger cosmos may be related to the vision of "an unseen audience" which Peter feels his father performs for (see pages 53 and 56 in *The Centaur*).

8. Cecrops and Inachus were the first kings, respectively, of Athens and Argos. Cecrops made a decision against Poseidon, at one point, and Inachus was the son of Oceanus; so both are connected with water deities.

Chapter 4

1. Although we do not get extensive mother portraits for most of Updike's other protagonists, these men exhibit character traits strongly resembling Joey's. Rabbit's ambiguous and contradictory relationships to women, for example, are not unlike Joey's and the mother-influenced relationships of Piet in *Couples* are clearly of the same stock.

2. Compare this with Peter's love of myth discussed on page 64 of this study.

3. Joey's inability to deal with sex as an adult is also suggested by his reaction when he learns of Peggy's sex with McCabe after her divorce. "It could only mean," he decides, "that she had wanted him back and in the end he had not come" (p. 63). This simplified and peevish reaction judges Joey harshly as does his jealousy over the other lovers Peggy had before she met him. It resembles Rabbit's immature response to Ruth's past sex with Harrison.

Chapter 5

1. For example, H. Petter, "John Updike's Metaphoric Novels," *English Studies*, 50 (1969), 197-206.
2. It may be for this reason that Updike chose to place his next protagonist, Bech, into the landscape of pure comedy where only situational dilemmas threaten and death is never a factor.
3. This echoes Peter's question about whether people can steer by Venus because the North Star is too small and hard to find (*TC*, p. 212).
4. Symbolic rebirth settings in Updike novels include *Rabbit, Run* which begins on Palm Sunday and continues to summer solstice, and *The Centaur* which covers a three-day confinement like Jonah's ("We're in Old Man Winter's belly," says Caldwell) or Christ's.
5. In Theodor Gaster's abridgment of Frazer, *The New Golden Bough* (New York: New American Library, 1964) the ritual is described thus: "In this church every year they chose a man, who was believed to be stained with heinous sins. On the first day of Lent he was brought to the church, dressed in mourning garb. . . . At the close of the service he was turned out of the church. During the forty days of Lent he perambulated the city barefoot, neither entering the churches nor speaking to anyone. The canons took it in turn to feed him. After midnight he was allowed to sleep in the streets. . . ." (p. 616).
6. Similarly, when Piet makes love to Angela on page 205, he must become a sky creature and ejaculates "like a comet's dribble."
7. Denis de Rougemont, *Love in the Western World*, trans. Montgomery Belgion, revised and augmented ed. (New York: Fawcett, 1966). (This is referred to hereafter as *LWW*.) "In effect, God is Love but the world is evil. Hence God cannot be the creator of the world. . . . It was completed and also perverted in the material order by the Rebel Angel, the Great Arrogant, the Demiurge—that is to say, by Lucifer or Satan. The latter tempted the Souls or Angels, saying 'It is better to be down below, where you will be able to do both good and evil. . . .' The better to seduce Souls, Lucifer showed them 'a woman of dazzling beauty, who inflamed them with desire.' . . . The Angel-Souls, having followed Satan and the woman of dazzling beauty, were ensnared in material bodies even though these were and remained foreign to them. . . . A soul is then parted from its

spirit, which remains in heaven. . . . a soul actually becomes the prisoner of a body with terrestrial appetites and subject to the laws of procreation and death" (p. 83).

8. Some critics and Updike himself take it for granted that Foxy is Iseult since Piet is married to Angela. The analysis in this chapter constitutes my case against this assumption. Although she is Piet's wife, Angela is nevertheless essentially unattainable.

9. Several scenes which show the light imagery associated with the Lady do appear earlier, such as the scene of Lucy Eccles in church in *Rabbit, Run*.

10. Another aspect of the imagery in this scene takes its form from *Love in the Western World*. Piet and Georgene are repeatedly referred to as "Twins" or "Hansel and Gretel." Georgene's presence seems "Sisterly." Reviewing de Rougemont, Updike describes this impression: "A man in love, confronting his beloved, seems to be in the presence of his own spirit, his self translated into another mode of being" (*AP*, p. 222).

11. One might speculate that Freddy understands other aspects of the romance tradition as well. He only wants Angela once; he prefers attaining her by means of overcoming an obstacle, instead of simply asking (as she points out); and once she is within his reach, he creates his own hindrance by failing to get an erection. Thus she is not defiled and can remain in the proper mythic position for him.

Chapter 6

1. Cleaver's description in *Soul on Ice* of the categories of racial self image and interracial sexual attraction has become something of a classic. He sees an alienation between the function of mind and body. The white male becomes an "Omnipotent Administrator"—all mind, no body—who "is launched on a perpetual search for his alienated body"; he becomes, Cleaver continues, a worshiper of physical prowess (like Rabbit?). To be a sufficient contrast to his already effeminate image, the white female must be "Ultrafeminine"—a nearly spiritual, highly worshipped and inviolate creature. The black man, forced into physical labor, represents body, and becomes the "Supermasculine Menial." To fulfill the physical role neglected by the white "Ultrafeminine," and also by virtue of her physical tasks, the black woman becomes the "Amazon," fitting mate for the

"brute power" of the black man. Updike's portrayal of females like Angela of *Couples* and Jill of *Rabbit Redux* coordinates with Cleaver's theory. Rabbit's flaccid, unsexual body in his second novel depicts the vision even more clearly. Since each race is seen as having what the other lacks, interracial sexual attractions result. At the end of the novel, for instance, Rabbit must picture a "muscular and masculine" Negress to masturbate, whereas Skeeter enjoys violating the sacrosanct white Ultrafeminine.

2. The sexual attraction here is made much more overt than it was in the earlier novel. Eccles' attraction for Rabbit was cast largely into his unaccountably intense desire to spend time with Rabbit and his enthusiasm and general vivacity in Rabbit's presence (see page 48 of this study). Here Rabbit is shown to be continuously aware of Skeeter's body and to find it attractive—lean and muscular—in contrast, for example, to Peggy's fat softness. Peggy has a "pasty helpless look of white meat," "shiny skin stuffed to the point of shapelessness" and breasts like "spilling guts." In fact the sexual imagery of the book as a whole is homosexual (for example, women are physically unattractive) to increase the sense of the Rabbit-Skeeter attraction which culminates when, in bed with Jill, Rabbit prefers to feel himself united with Skeeter who is masturbating on the couch downstairs (*RRx*, p. 283).

3. Just as Skeeter is made more exaggeratedly a Christ figure than the other Updike "Lover" figures, he also hyperbolizes some of their other characteristics, too—in the enthusiasm of his sense of God, his selfishness (like Peter of *The Centaur* and the earlier Rabbit he is "stuck inside his own skin"), and his myth-making vision.

4. Skeeter is here describing what is called the steady-state theory of the universe. Proposed in 1948 by H. Bondi, T. Gold, and F. Hoyle at Cambridge, it opposes the "Big Bang" theory and describes the universe as expanding but remaining essentially the same with no beginning and no end. New matter, in the form of hydrogen atoms, is constantly being created at various points near the center; while old material at the edges dissipates. Skeeter's description, a testament to Updike's verbal skills, delightfully casts the theory into his own language patterns while sacrificing little, in my opinion, from the original scientific proposal.

5. This is explained in more detail in Chapter 7 of this study. In comedy characters have little true causality, and Bech, for in-

stance, is aware of this and accepts it wryly. It frees him, in a sense, from moral responsibility because it argues against his status as an *actor* generally. Characters in tragedy (or serious, noncomic works) are seen, and see themselves, as responsible agents whose mistakes and failures can create suffering and bring disaster.

Chapter 7

1. It is obvious, I hope, that the term "comic" is used here not in the simple sense of "funny" but refers to a viewpoint, loosely opposed to "serious," in which humans are diminished in stature. Serious artistic viewpoints suggest a significance and importance for the major characters which is correlative with a sense of human importance in general; comic viewpoints imply a universe in which humans are neither dangerous or endangered because they matter less in general. Laughter is the response appropriate to this vision; thus comedy's ability to be "funny."

2. This was pointed out by *Time's* reviewer who was clearly struggling with the problem in the 1968 cover story. He notes that American literature has turned to comedy (Nabokov, Barth, Bellow, Roth, and others) but feels that Updike is separate from this group: "It would be hard to exaggerate how far removed Updike is from this view of the world as lunatic comedy. . . . Scenes that other writers would play as burlesque, Updike plays straight no matter how absurd they are." He then recounts the Foxy-Piet bathroom scene, climaxing with Piet's two-story jump at the end. "The author," he notes with some puzzlement, "never even winks" (*Time*, April 26, 1968, p. 73.) This chapter of my study explains how such potentially comic material is kept essentially serious.

3. Updike's own view of comedy appears to be quite similar. "Don Quixote," he says, "is rubbery; he bounces back and suffers no scars. Contrast the brittle stony characters of Greek tragedy who, under the unforgiving pressure of fate's engines, irrevocably shatter." "Laughter," Updike goes on to explain, "can be construed as a signal of danger past or dismissed. It occurs within an arena . . . where the customary threats of life have been suspended. Dreams, jokes, play, and aesthetic pleasure alike mark a truce with the destructive forces of life."

4. It may be a quality of Theatre of the Absurd that it removes

this distance and forces us to recognize our share in the insignificance of the characters, making the laughs still real but strangely painful.

5. There is certainly the matter of degrees here. Characters in comedy do perform some actions and produce some effects. Face and Subtle in *The Alchemist* perform successful swindles; Jack and Algernon in *The Importance of Being Earnest* create fictional relatives and engage in romantic intrigues. Yet the major assumption upon which both comedies depend is that none of these characters can do much harm.

6. As reprinted in *Theories of Comedy*, Paul Lauter, ed. (Garden City: Anchor-Doubleday, 1964), p. 461.

7. From the chapter "The Meanings of Comedy" (Garden City: Doubleday and Co., 1956), p. 193. This chapter is reprinted in Robert Corregan's collection *Comedy: Meaning and Form* (Scranton: Chandler, 1965).

A Bibliography of Books and
Critical Essays on John Updike

Aldridge, John W., "The Private Vice of John Updike," *Time to Murder and Create: The Contemporary Novel in Crises.* New York: McKay, 1966.

Brenner, Gerry. *"Rabbit, Run:* John Updike's Criticism of the 'Return to Nature,'" *Twentieth Century Literature,* 12 (April, 1966), 3-14.

Brewer, Joseph E. "The Anti-Hero in Contemporary Literature," *Iowa English Yearbook,* 12 (Fall, 1967), 55-60.

Burchard, Rachael. *John Updike: Yea Sayings.* Carbondale: Southern Illinois University Press, 1971.

Burgess, Anthony. "Language, Myth, and Mr. Updike," *Commonweal,* 83 (February 11, 1966), 557-559.

De Bellis, Jack. "The Group and John Updike," *Sewanee Review,* 72 (Summer, 1964), 531-536.

Detweiler, Robert. "John Updike and the Indictment of Culture-Protestants," *Four Spiritual Crises in Mid-Century Fiction.* Gainesville: University of Florida Press, 1963.

Doner, Dean. "Rabbit Angstrom's Unseen World," *New World Writing,* No. 19 (1961), pp. 58-75.

Doyle, Paul. "Updike's Fiction: Motifs and Techniques," *Catholic World,* 199 (September, 1964), 356-362.

Duncan, Graham. "The Thing Itself in *Rabbit, Run,*" *English Record,* 13 (April, 1963), 36-37.

Enright, D. J. "Updike's Ups and Downs," *Holiday,* 38 (November, 1965), 162-166.

Finkelstein, Sidney. "Alienated Expression and Existentialist Answers," *Existentialism and Alienation in American Literature.* New York: International, 1965.

Fisher, Richard E. "John Updike: Theme and Form in the Garden of Epiphanies," *Moderna Sprak,* 56 (Fall, 1962), 255-260.

Flint, Joyce. "John Updike and *Couples:* The WASP's Dilemma," *Research Studies,* 36 (1968), 340-347.

Galloway, David D. "The Absurd Man as Saint," *The Absurd Hero in American Fiction.* Austin: University of Texas Press, 1966.

Geismar, Maxwell. "The American Short Story Today," *Studies on the Left,* 4 (Spring, 1964), 21-27.

Geller, Evelyn. "WLB Biography," *Wilson Library Bulletin,* 36 (September, 1961), 67.

Guyol, Hazel Sample. "The Lord Loves a Cheerful Corpse," *English Journal,* 55 (1966), 863-866.

Hamilton, Alice. "Between Innocence and Experience: From Joyce to Updike," *Dalhousie Review,* 49 (1969), 102-109.

————, and Kenneth Hamilton. *The Elements of John Updike.* Grand Rapids: Eerdmans, 1970.

Hamilton, Kenneth. "John Updike: Chronicler of the Time of the 'Death of God,'" *Christian Century,* 84 (June 7, 1967), 745-748.

Hicks, Granville. "Generation of the 50's: Malamud, Gold, Updike," *The Creative Present,* ed. N. Balakian. Garden City: Doubleday, 1963.

Hill, John S. "Quest for Belief: Theme in the Novels of John Updike," *Southern Humanities Review,* 3 (1969), 166-175.

Hyman, Stanley Edgar. "The Artist as a Young Man," *The New Leader,* 45 (March 19, 1962), 22-23.

Kauffman, Stanley. "Onward With Updike," *New Republic,* 155 (September 24, 1966), 15-17.

Klausler, A. P. "Steel Wilderness," *Christian Century,* 78 (February 22, 1961), 245-246.

La Course, Guerin. "The Innocence of John Updike," *Commonweal,* 77 (December 7, 1962), 512-514.

Mailer, Norman. "Norman Mailer vs. Nine Writers," *Esquire,* 60 (July 1963), 63-69, 105.

Matson, Elizabeth. "A Chinese Paradox but Not Much of a One," *The Minnesota Review,* 7 (1967), 157-167.

Mizener, Arthur. "The American Hero as High School Boy," *The Sense of Life in the Modern Novel.* Boston: Houghton Mifflin, 1964.

Muradian, Thaddeus. "The World of John Updike," *English Journal,* 54 (October, 1965), 577-584.

Novak, Michael. "Updike's Quest for Liturgy," *Commonweal,* 78 (May 10, 1963), 192-195.

O'Connor, William Van. "John Updike and William Styron," *Con-*

temporary American Novelists, ed. Harry Moore. Carbondale: Southern Illinois University Press, 1964.

Petter, H. "John Updike's Metaphoric Novels," *English Studies,* 50 (1969), 197-206.

Podhoretz, Norman. "A Dissent on Updike," *Doings and Undoings.* New York: Noonday, 1964.

Rupp, Richard. "John Updike: Style in Search of a Center," *Sewanee Review,* 75 (1967), 693-709.

Samuels, Charlies T. "The Art of Fiction XLIII: John Updike," *Paris Review,* No. 45 (Winter, 1968), pp. 85-117.

———. "John Updike," *Univ. of Minn. Pamphlets on Amer. Writers,* No. 79.

Schwartz, Jonathan. "Updike of Ipswich," *Boston* (August, 1965), p. 35.

Standley, Fred. "*Rabbit, Run,* an Image of Life," *Midwest Quarterly,* 8 (1967), 371-386.

Stern, Richard. "The Myth in Action," *Spectator,* No. 7057 (September 27, 1963), p. 389.

Stubbs, John C. "The Search for Perfection in *Rabbit, Run,*" *Critique: Studies in Modern Fiction,* 10, ii (1968), 94-101.

Suderman, Elmer F. "The Right Way and the Good Way in *Rabbit, Run,*" *University Review,* 36 (1969), 13-21.

Sullivan, Walter. "Updike, Spark, and Others." *Sewanee Review,* 74 (Summer, 1966), 709-716.

Sypher, Wylie. *Comedy.* New York: Doubleday, 1956.

Tate, Sister M. Judith. "Of Rabbits and Centaurs," *Critic,* 22 (February-March, 1964), 44-47, 49-50.

Taylor, C. Clarke. *John Updike, A Bibliography.* Kent, Ohio: Kent State University, 1968.

Taylor, Larry. *Pastoral and Anti-Pastoral Patterns in John Updike's Fiction.* Carbondale: Southern Illinois University Press, 1971.

Theories of Comedy. Paul Lauter, ed. New York: Anchor-Doubleday, 1964.

Time Magazine: "View from the Catacombs" (April 26, 1968), 66-75.

Waldmeir, Joseph. "Accommodations in the New Novel," *University College Quarterly,* 11 (November, 1965), 26-32.

Ward, John A. "John Updike's Fiction," *Critique: Studies in Modern Fiction,* 5 (Spring-Summer, 1962), 27-41.

Wyatt, Bryant. "John Updike: The Psychological Novel in Search of Structure," *Twentieth Century Literature,* 13 (1967), 89-96.

Yates, Norris. "The Doubt and Faith of John Updike," *College English,* 26 (March, 1965), 469-474.

Index

Works by Updike

Subentries refer to material not more fully developed in the chapter devoted to the novel

"Ace in the Hole," 108

"Alligators," 79

Bech: A Book, 1, 2, 4, 5, 7, 62, 109, 125, 133, 145, 146, 168-90

The Centaur, 2, 3-4, 13, 14, 16, 24, 61-83, 101, 102, 106, 110-11, 116, 118, 129, 146, 187; theory of art, 10, 11, 91; character of mother, 84; comic aspects, 168, 183, 186; first person narrator, 170; realm of action, 171; rebirth setting, 195; establishment of value system, 7

Couples, 1, 2, 4, 8, 11, 12, 13, 14, 16, 24, 26, 28, 35, 36, 56, 61, 63, 100-101, 102, 104-105, 106-145, 146, 147-48, 167, 187, 190; color scheme, 9; comic aspects, 168, 184, 185, 198; mother as life/death image, 99, 192; Oedipal complex, 97; nature of opening, 170; point of view, 10-11; realm of action, 171-72, 173-74; establishment of value system, 6, 7

"The Dogwood Tree: A Boyhood," 31, 32, 58

"The Family Meadow," 91

"Fanning Island," 14, 114

"Flight," 70, 84, 85, 93, 100

"Home," 17, 71

"The Kid's Whistling," 29

"More Love in the Western World" (review), 137-144 passim

"The Music School," 106

Of The Farm, 2, 4, 13, 16, 24, 61, 63, 67, 84-105, 111, 113, 116, 117, 146; theory of art, 10, 11; comic aspects, 183-84, 186; first person narrator, 170; realm of action, 173; establishment of value system, 7

"Packed Dirt," 30, 58, 174

"Pigeon Feathers," 70, 84-85, 92-93, 99, 101, 102, 111, 179

The Poorhouse Fair, 1, 2-3, 7, 9, 13-36, 37, 43, 47, 59, 60, 73, 108-109, 126, 146, 147, 149, 151, 156, 185, 186; comic aspects, 182; myth, 63; nature of opening, 170; point of view, 10; realm of action, 171; utopian novel, 61; establishment of value system, 5, 7

Rabbit Redux, 1, 2, 5, 8, 9, 14, 16, 24, 49, 61, 99, 109, 110, 128, 146-67, 180, 187, 190; comic aspects, 184-85, 186; use of present tense, 170; realm of action, 172, 174-75, 178; sex/death, 117; establishment of value system, 6-7

Rabbit, Run, 2, 3, 8, 9, 15, 23, 26, 37-60, 61, 78, 79, 106, 109-110, 126, 145, 146, 149, 157, 166, 195; theory of art, 11; color scheme, 9; comic aspects; 182-83, 185; presence of death, 13, 110-11, 186-87; character of mother, 86; mother as life/death image, 99; movie format, 61; myth, 63, 67; Oedipal complex, 97; Peter (*The Centaur*) similar to Rabbit, 81-82; use of present tense, 170; realm of action, 171, 173; sex/death, 102; establishment of value system, 5-6, 7

"Snowing in Greenwich Village," 191

"A Traded Car," 64, 71, 85-86, 89

Characters

Angela. *See* Hanema

Angstrom, Earl (father), *Rabbit Redux*, 151, 152, 153, 160, 165, 172; *Rabbit, Run*, 41

Angstrom, Harry "Rabbit," *Rabbit Redux*, 2, 5, 6, 7, 8, 9, 16, 49, 82, 117, 146-67, 172, 174, 178, 185, 187; *Rabbit, Run*, passim (esp.) 37-60

Angstrom, Janice (Springer), *Rabbit Redux*, 153, 154, 156, 160, 165, 167, 172, 174, 178, 184-85; *Rabbit, Run*, 37-56 passim

Angstrom, Margaret "Mim" (sister), 151, 153, 162, 175, 185

Angstrom, Mary (mother), *Rabbit Redux*, 14, 19, 84, 151, 156, 157, 164, 166, 172; *Rabbit, Run*, 41, 51, 86

Angstrom, Nelson, *Rabbit Redux*, 7, 24, 146-67 passim, 172, 174 *Rabbit Run*, 6, 42, 45, 57

Appleby, Frank, 10, 118, 127, 133, 184

Appleby, Janet, 101, 116, 127, 184

Appleton, Hester, 69

Babe, 155, 158

Bea (*Bech: A Book*), 173, 174, 177, 188

Bea (*Couples*). *See* Guerin

Bech, Henry, 4, 62, 125, 168-190

Buddy, 5, 16, 18, 20, 22, 33, 59, 126

Caldwell, Cassie (wife), 70, 79, 84-85

Caldwell, George, 3, 6, 13, 14, 16, 17, 24, 27, 36, 61-83, 84, 87, 88, 100, 101, 106, 110, 113, 118, 146, 171, 178, 183, 187, 189, 192

Caldwell, Peter, 4, 6, 10, 24, 31, 61-83, passim, 86, 88, 91, 101, 102-103, 111, 116, 183, 192, 194, 195, 197

Conner, 2-3, 5, 7-8, 9, 13-36 passim, 37-38, 41, 62, 67, 73, 88, 89, 98, 108, 126, 146, 171, 178, 182

Cook, Bea. *See* Bea

Diefendorf, 65, 69, 76, 80

Eccles, Jack, 3, 5, 7, 9, 16, 23, 26, 37-60 passim, 86, 98, 109, 126, 146, 157, 197

Eccles, Lucy, 16, 44, 46, 48, 51, 54, 59, 109, 196

Fogleman, Penny. *See* Penny

Fosnacht, Peggy (Gring), 154, 165, 197

Foxy. *See* Whitman

Franklin, Tommy, 19, 28-29

Gallagher, Matt, 112, 127

George. *See* Caldwell

Gregg, 17, 34, 47, 182, 186

Guerin, Bea (*Couples*), 112, 116, 118, 140, 142

Hanema, Angela, 4, 7, 9, 62, 101, 104, 106-145 passim, 171, 174, 178, 184, 195, 197

Hanema, Nancy, 6-7, 107, 115

Hanema, Piet, passim (esp. 106-145)

Hanema, Ruth, 6-7

Harrison, Bonnie, 47, 194
Harry. *See* Angstrom
Heller, 73
Hester. *See* Appleton
Hook, John, 2, 3, 4, 5, 13-36, 37-38, 41, 47, 48, 55, 67, 77, 87, 88, 106, 107, 113, 132, 146, 149, 171, 178, 189
Hummel, Al, 24, 78, 193
Hummel, Vera, 68, 69, 78, 81, 193
Janet. *See* Appleby
Janice. *See* Angstrom
Jill, 5, 7, 9, 14, 117, 146-67 passim, 172, 174-75, 187
Joey. *See* Robinson
Kate, 174, 175, 180, 181, 188
Kosko. *See* Margaret
Ken. *See* Whitman
Kruppenbach, Reverend, 40, 41, 51, 78
Latchett, Norma. *See* Norma
Leonard, Ruth. *See* Ruth
Lucas, George (*The Poorhouse Fair*), 17, 18, 47
McCabe, Mr., 7, 16, 95, 98
McCabe, Richard. *See* Richard
March, Reverend, 193
Margaret (*Rabbit, Run*), 48
Merissa, 173, 174, 176, 180, 190
"Mim." *See* Angstrom, Margaret
Morrison. *See* Wendell
Mortis, Amy, 10, 15, 17, 19, 20, 25, 37, 47
Nelson. *See* Angstrom
Norma, 174, 177
Ong, John, 13
Pedrick, 125, 131
Peggy (*Rabbit Redux*). *See* Fosnacht
Peggy (*Of The Farm*). *See* Robinson, Peggy
Pendleton. *See* Jill
Penny, 81, 92, 101
Peter. *See* Caldwell

Petrescu, 176
Piet. *See* Hanema
Richard, 6, 7, 63, 84-105 pasim
Rabbit. *See* Angstrom
Robinson, Joan (first wife), 89, 113, 138
Robinson, Joey, 2, 4, 6, 7, 10, 13, 16, 31, 54, 84-105, 106, 111, 112, 113, 114, 117, 146, 178, 184, 192
Robinson, Peggy, 4, 7, 63, 84-105 passim, 113, 184
Ruth (*Rabbit, Run*), 9, 13, 37-60 passim, 79, 81, 110, 166, 194
Saltz, Ben, 127
Skeeter, 5, 6, 7, 16, 24, 31, 48, 49, 82, 87, 88, 110, 146-67 passim, 174, 178, 184-85, 187
Smith ("little-Smith"), Harold, 11, 101, 116, 127, 129, 131, 184
Smith ("little-Smith"), Marcia, 118, 120, 123, 127, 133, 184
Smith, Mrs. (*Rabbit, Run*), 16, 48, 50, 88
Springer, Mr. (father-in-law), *Rabbit Redux*, 153, 154, 157; *Rabbit, Run*, 51
Springer, Mrs. (mother-in-law), 16, 40, 57
Stavros, Charlie, 154, 155, 161, 162, 165, 178, 184
Thorne, Freddy, 4, 6, 62, 100, 106-145 passim, 147, 184, 192
Thorne, Georgene, 109, 110, 112, 141, 142, 184
Tothero, 42, 44, 45, 47, 50, 51, 183
Wendell, 174, 181
Whitman, Foxy, 4, 7, 9, 17, 23, 24, 104, 106-145 passim, 167, 172, 173, 182, 184
Whitman, Ken, 6, 16, 22, 89, 98, 106-145 passim
Zimmerman, 24, 64, 65, 67, 68, 76, 78